Automobile Heritage and Tourism

T0270833

Automobile heritage encompasses a complex range of artefacts and activities. Beyond just historic vehicles which are the primary artefacts of this niche, it also includes communities of collectors and enthusiasts, private owners and public institutions, as well as historic motoring environments, literally thousands of museums, exhibitions and car shows throughout the world, and a range of paraphernalia that includes both original and replicated promotional materials, equipment and parts, and guide books.

Although automobile heritage has been the subject of some limited research, *Automobile Heritage and Tourism* is unique in examining its scope and role within tourism. The book looks at a vast array of topics, from the experience of using and collecting old cars, related destination development, automobile heritage and museums, to events such as vintage automobile racing, promotion and social change. It thereby provides a thorough review of the impacts of automobile heritage on tourism. A number of theories provide a framework and are analysed throughout, including those related to the collection, display, exhibition and use of historic automobiles. The title takes a global and interdisciplinary view of the subject with international contributions from both established and emerging scholars in the field.

This book adds to the industrial heritage tourism literature and will appeal to a diverse audience, in particular those in the fields of cultural heritage and industrial heritage tourism, but also practitioners involved with the planning, restoration, exhibition and management of automobile heritage attractions and events.

Michael V. Conlin is Professor of Management in the Okanagan School of Business at Okanagan College, Kelowna, British Columbia, Canada.

Lee Jolliffe is Professor of Hospitality and Tourism at the University of New Brunswick, Saint John, New Brunswick, Canada.

Routledge Advances in Tourism

Edited by Stephen Page
School for Tourism, Bournemouth University

Automobile Heritage and Tourism

Edited by Michael V. Conlin and Lee Jolliffe

Routledge
Taylor & Francis Group

LONDON AND NEW YORK

First published 2017 by Routledge

2 Park Square, Milton Park, Abingdon, Oxon OX14 4RN
605 Third Avenue, New York, NY 10017

Routledge is an imprint of the Taylor & Francis Group, an informa business

First issued in paperback 2022

Publisher's Note

The publisher has gone to great lengths to ensure the quality of this reprint but
points out that some imperfections in the original copies may be apparent.

British Library Cataloguing in Publication Data
A catalogue record for this book is available from the British
Library

Library of Congress Cataloging in Publication Data
A catalog record for this book has been requested

ISBN: 978-1-138-21910-6 (hbk)
ISBN: 978-1-03-233976-4 (pbk)
DOI: 10.4324/9781315436210

Typeset in Times New Roman
by Deanta Global Publishing Services, Chennai, India

Contents

Figures

Tables

Contributors

M. S. M. Aslam is a Senior Lecturer in the Department of Tourism Management at Sabaragamuwa University of Sri Lanka and Chairman, Board of Postgraduate Studies at Faculty of Management Studies. He has a B.Sc. Business Studies (Specialization in Tourism Management) from Sabaragamuwa University of Sri Lanka, an M.Sc. in Management from the University of Sri Jayawardenapura in Sri Lanka and a Ph.D. from Universiti Putra Malaysia. His research has focused on the role of inbound travel agencies, sustainable tourism development, tea tourism, sustainable rural tourism development, spice and herbs tourism, historic lodging, tourism planning and development, heritage motoring tourism and enterprising rural tourism. He has published individually and jointly in international journals, such as *Journal of Heritage Tourism, Journal of Tourism Policy* and the *International Journal of Economic and Financial Issues*. He serves as a resource person/advisor/consultant for national, provincial, local and community level tourism planning and development in Sri Lanka.

Gary P. Best is an Honorary Associate of La Trobe Business School, La Trobe University, Australia, and an independent consultant and author whose writing focuses on cultural tourism, gastronomy, and festival and event management. His research interests are diverse, but tend to focus on tourism and the media, automotive history, heritage and culture, travel writing, distinctive cultural interactions in touristic contexts, and the means by which all of the above operate in popular culture.

Ilenia Bregoli is a Senior Lecturer in Marketing at the Lincoln Business School, UK. She joined the University of Lincoln in January 2013, after having worked at the University of Northampton and at the University of Milan–Bicocca, Italy. She was awarded her PhD in 2011 from the Catholic University of Milan, Italy. Her research interests are related to destination management and marketing, destination branding from the supply perspective and experiential marketing. She has presented the results of her research at several international conferences and has published in the *Journal of Travel Research, Tourism Analysis* and the *International Journal of Tourism Research*.

Antonella Capriello is Assistant Professor at the Universita' degli Studi del Piemonte Orientale, Italy, a Member of Tourism Group for the EuroMed Research Business Institute (EMRBI) and a Member of Research Group in Sustainable Tourism organized by the Italian Academy of Management (AIDEA). She is a Research Advisor for the Business Incubator (Università del Piemonte Orientale), receiving the Award 'START CUP – Regione PIEMONTE – Premio speciale Turismo e Innovazione' for the project 'Innoviaggiando' in 2007 and for the project 'GEO4MAP' (in co-operation with De Agostini Group) in 2009. Her research activities focus on tourism marketing, public utilities and the governance of territorial systems involving colleagues in the UK, US, Canada, Taiwan, Libya and Turkey. She has published over 50 research contributions, including articles published in *Journal of Business Research, Tourism Management, Tourism Review* and *Journal of Hospitality Marketing and Management.*

Michael V. Conlin is Professor of Management in the Okanagan School of Business at Okanagan College, Kelowna, British Columbia, Canada. He is also an Adjunct Professor in the School of Hospitality and Tourism Management at the University of Guelph and the Faculty of Tourism and Hotel Management at Royal Roads University. He is the co-editor of three books: *Island Tourism: Management Principles and Practice* (1995) with Tom Baum; *Mining Heritage and Tourism: A global synthesis* (2011) with Lee Jolliffe; and *Railway Heritage and Tourism: Global Perspectives* (2014) with Geoffrey Bird.

Jerry L. Epperly II is a car enthusiast who has worked in the auto industry with different roles for over 20 years and has attended many car shows, races and other events over the years. Visiting places and attending events related to auto industry has always been a father–son bonding tool in his family. He currently works at Audi, South Orlando, Orlando, Florida, USA.

Paul Frost is a co-founder and chairman of the Historic Vehicle Research Institute (HVRI). Dr Frost has been active in researching and delivering education, training and development for over 30 years. First appointed as a Head of School with the University of Brighton in 1992, his roles have included Head of the Centre for Management Development, Head of the School of Service Management and his current position as Director of the University of Brighton in Hastings, UK. Before joining the university, Dr Frost worked for a number of international organisations, both in Europe and the USA. He was also co-founder and director of motor-base.com, an organisation dedicated to the sharing of information to unite the historic vehicle community.

Rafa Haddad is Assistant Professor of Tourism Management, Department of Tourism and Hotel Management, Philadelphia University, Amman, Jordan. She received her PhD from Bournemouth University, UK, in 2014 for her thesis entitled 'A critical analysis of the experiences of female business owners in the development and management of tourism-related micro and small handicraft businesses in an Islamic society: The Hashemite Kingdom of Jordan'. In addition, Rafa holds an MA in Tourism Management from Yarmouk University, Jordan, in 2007 and MA in Destination Development from Dalarna University, Sweden, in 2012. Research interests include women and entrepreneurship, gender and tourism, tourist behaviour and experience, tourism and local community, Halal tourism, museum studies and tour guiding. She has published articles in international journals, as well as book chapters, book reviews and book cases, and has presented papers at international conferences in Jordan and abroad.

Salem Harahsheh is Assistant Professor of Tourism Marketing and Head of the Department of Travel and Tourism, College of Tourism and Hotel Management, Yarmouk University, Irbid, Jordan. He received his PhD in 2010 from Bournemouth University, UK, with the thesis 'An evaluation of the image of Jordan in the British and Swedish markets and the implication for marketing the country as a tourism destination'. He also has an MA in European Tourism Management (Bournemouth University, UK, 2002) and an MSc in Science Communication (Dalarna University, Sweden, 2008). His research interest includes destination marketing and image, social media marketing, tourism and the media, tourist behaviour and experience, health tourism, tourism and local community, Halal tourism, museum studies and volunteerism. Salem reviews for journals including the *Journal of Destination Marketing* and *Management and Tourism Analysis*. He has published journal articles, book chapters, book reviews and cases, and has presented papers at international conferences in Jordan and abroad.

Matt Harvey is a Senior Lecturer in Law at Victoria University, Melbourne, Australia. He fell in love with historic racing at the 1978 meeting to commemorate the 50th anniversary of the first Australian Grand Prix and has also taken a keen interest in motor sport for many years while researching European Union law, constitutional law and wine law. Now concentrating on sports law, he has recently acquired a 1990 BMW convertible and has realised he needs more practical mechanical skills.

Bradford T. Hudson is Associate Professor of the Practice of Marketing in the Carroll School of Management at Boston College, Massachusetts, USA. He holds a Ph.D. in Business History from Boston University, a master's degree in services marketing from Cornell University, and a certificate in strategy from Harvard Business School. He is a former consultant in strategy and marketing to senior executives at numerous multinational corporations. His clients with historic brands included AT&T, Cadbury Schweppes, Cunard, Harley-Davidson, and Nestlé.

Lee Jolliffe is Professor of Hospitality and Tourism at the University of New Brunswick, Saint John, New Brunswick, Canada. She combines an academic background in sociology and museum studies with practical experience in hospitality to study the intersection between culture and heritage related to tourism. Publications include the edited volumes: *Spices and Tourism, Destinations,*

Attractions and Cuisines (2014) and *Sugar Heritage and Tourism in Transition* (2013), and the co-authored book with Hilary du Cros, *The Arts and Events* (2014). She sits on the editorial boards of a number of international hospitality and tourism journals and is the Resource Editor (Museums) for *Annals of Tourism Research*.

Cristina Jönsson is a Lecturer in Tourism and Hospitality Management at Department of Management Studies, The University of the West Indies, Barbados. She has published tourism related research extensively in peer-reviewed journals and books. Cristina has knowledge and experience from planning, development and management in the international tourism sector and has worked with both private and public sector organisations in various countries. While working as a regional tourism manager in Sweden she prepared and executed a tourism master plan for a municipal government, working in collaboration with government and other stakeholder groups. Cristina also worked in the tourism sector in Brazil as a regional tourism development planner. Additionally, she has worked on the development of a sport tourism strategy for Barbados in collaboration with the Ministry of Tourism of Barbados and various local stakeholder groups.

Jaime Kaminski is a Senior Lecturer and Research Fellow at the University of Brighton Business School, UK, where he specialises in the study and assessment of socio-economic impact and business issues associated with cultural heritage, especially vehicular heritage. He has conducted numerous economic impact analyses of UK heritage vehicle events. Jaime has a first class BA Hons and a PhD in Archaeology from the University of Reading, UK. He is also a Fellow of the Royal Geographical Society (FRGS), the Society of Antiquaries of London (FSA) and the Higher Education Academy (FHEA). Jaime is also a Director of the Historic Vehicle Research Institute, an educational charity devoted to historic vehicle research.

Irene Mastretta is based in Turin and specializes in communication and dissemination of cultural information. She experienced the world of fashion, working as a contributing editor for several magazines and later joined the automotive industry working as a training consultant for FCA – Fiat Chrysler Automobiles. She is currently working as a teacher of Italian Literature and History as well as Art History in Italian secondary schools. She co-operates in tourism and cultural research projects with the Department of Economic and Business Studies at the Università degli Studi del Piemonte Orientale, Italy.

Gordon Ramsey is an anthropologist and ethnomusicologist whose work has focused primarily on musical traditions in Ulster, Northern Ireland. His work has focused on the province's broad and diverse marching band culture, and on the Ulster-Scots folk-musical revival, paying particular attention to the relationships between these musical worlds and other traditions, especially Irish traditional music. He has published widely on these topics, and his book, *Music, Emotion and*

Identity in Ulster Marching Bands: Flutes, Drums & Loyal Sons was published in 2011. He is currently teaching anthropology at Queen's University Belfast, UK, and is an active community musician, playing in Ulster-Scots folk ensembles, Irish traditional sessions and marching bands.

Gregory Ramshaw is an Associate Professor in the Department of Parks, Recreation and Tourism Management at Clemson University, South Carolina, USA. His research explores the social construction and cultural production of heritage, with a particular interest in sport-based heritage. His research has been published in numerous academic texts and journals, including the *International Journal of Heritage Studies*, *Tourism Geographies*, *Current Issues in Tourism*, and *Tourism Review International*, among many others. He is the editor of *Sport Heritage* (2015) and the co-editor of *Heritage, Sport and Tourism* (2007) and *Heritage and the Olympics* (2014). He also serves on the editorial boards of the *Journal of Heritage Tourism*, the *Journal of Sport & Tourism*, and *Event Management*. He blogs at www.sportheritagereview.com and Tweets at @sportheritage1.

Geoffrey Smith is a co-founder and Director of the Historic Vehicle Research Institute (HVRI). He has been Vice President of the Federation of British Historic Vehicle Clubs (FBHVC) 2002-2013, prior to which he was Chairman 1998–2002. He has also been Vice President of FIVA (Federation Internationale Vehicules Anviens) 1999–2006 and President of the FIVA legislation commission 2004–2006. He comes from a career in the machine tool and motor industry (including manufacturing, engineering, training and human resources) and is a Member of the Chartered Institute of Personnel and Development (MCIPD).

Asli D. A. Tasci is an Assistant Professor of Tourism and Hospitality Marketing in the Department of Tourism, Events & Attractions in the Rosen College of Hospitality Management at the University of Central Florida, USA. Her research interests include tourism and hospitality marketing, particularly consumer behaviour. She completed a number of studies measuring destination image and branding with a cross-cultural perspective.

Leanne White is a Senior Lecturer in the College of Business at Victoria University, Melbourne, Australia. Her research interests include: national identity, commercial nationalism, popular culture, advertising, destination marketing and cultural tourism. She is the author of more than 50 book chapters and refereed journal articles. Leanne is the editor of *Commercial Nationalism and Tourism: Selling the National Story* (2017), and co-editor of *The Palgrave Handbook of Dark Tourism Studies* (2017), *Advertising and Public Memory: Social, Cultural and Historical Perspectives on Ghost Signs* (2017), *Wine and Identity: Branding, Heritage, Terroir* (2014), *Dark Tourism and Place Identity: Managing and Interpreting Dark Places* (2013) and *Tourism and National Identities: An International Perspective* (2011).

Acknowledgements

The motivation to produce this book can be traced back to two distinct but intersecting areas of interest, namely automobiles and particularly vintage vehicles and the study of cultural industrial heritage tourism with its links to museums, exhibitions, and their relevance to social development. One of your editors has been obsessed by automobiles from a very young age and the other editor is a recognized expert in the field of heritage tourism. And together, we both have a passion for the study of industrial heritage tourism. This book flows naturally from earlier collaborations focusing on mining heritage and then railway heritage. However, none of this would have been possible without the enthusiastic and expert input of 18 academics and practitioners from around the world who share our passion for this area. The diversity, richness, and rigorous inputs from our colleagues are what gives this book its real value and for that, we thank them.

We also owe a huge debt of gratitude to the two academic institutions who employ us and who have supported us throughout this project. Your first editor has received substantial financial and intellectual support from his colleagues at the Okanagan School of Business and in particular, Dr Heather Banham who is Dean of the School, throughout the course of developing this book. Your second editor received support and encouragement from the University of New Brunswick.

Finally, we would like to thank our families for being patient, attentive, and exhibiting real interest in this project. In particular, we would like to especially thank Roxi Alix, your first editor's spouse. As she has done with previous publications, Roxi has functioned on occasion as our manuscript manager, quietly and effectively keeping us on track with all the seemingly mundane but nonetheless very important aspects of editing and record keeping that accompanies a fairly complex project like this. Without her contribution, this project would have been a lot more difficult to bring to completion, so Roxi, many thanks.

Very importantly, we want to recognize the support and guidance of our colleagues at Routledge. We have both had successful collaborations with Emma Travis, Senior Editor for Tourism, in the past and Emma's professionalism is ultimately what made this publication possible. We also want to recognize the substantial contribution made by Pippa Mullins, the Senior Editorial Assistant whose support and co-operation has led to a very speedy completion of this project as it went to press. And finally, we thank Dr Stephen Page, the series editor, for his confidence in our book and his blessing, as well as his suggestions for strengthening the book, all of which we have thankfully embraced.

Part I
Introduction

1 Automobile heritage and tourism

A framework for study

Michael V. Conlin and Lee Jolliffe

Introduction

Cars are always something I've loved.

Ralph Lauren (*Autoweek*, March 9, 2008)

It would be hard to imagine growing up in the twentieth century without developing at least a passing interest in automobiles. For the past one hundred years, they have been a ubiquitous part of all developed and developing economies around the world (Eckermann, 2001). Since World War Two, with the growth of transportation infrastructure and the growth of the developed economies' middle class, they have become even more a part of our societies. Their pervasiveness and relevance to life in developed and developing countries have achieved virtual iconic status. They are an integral part of our lives and notwithstanding predictions of the decline of the automobile, their role in the development of our economic, social and cultural milieu cannot be denied (Sachs, 1992).

For the generations beginning with the so-called 'baby boomers' or those people born immediately after World War Two, memories of childhood have inevitably been inter-twined with aspirations about automobile ownership, and the subsequent experience of owning a car, driving it, caring for it, possibly modifying it, maybe racing it, and then selling it for a model even more desirable. Generations of families have developed affiliations with particular automobile manufacturers and more specifically, certain brands. The so-called battle between Chevrolet and Ford, symbolized most clearly in the virtual devotion by many 'boomers' and later generations in North America to either the Camaro or the Mustang 'muscle cars', is a well understood phenomena (Berger, 2001) The same situation can be seen in Australia where generations of automobile aficionados have sworn their devotion to either Holden or Ford models, and notably to Holden's Torano and the Ford Falcon GT in the 1970's and the 1980's (Conlon and Perkins, 2001). Even in war-ravaged Europe, the rivalry between Germany's iconic brands, Mercedes and BMW, and the almost slavish devotion of fans to one brand or the other, have fuelled the rise of motor sports and the growing importance of car collecting on that continent (Eckermann, 2001).

This interest in motoring heritage is not confined to the post-World War Two era. The establishment in 1950 of the Pebble Beach Concours d'Elegance in the

United States mirrored the earlier admiration of automobiles which events such as the Concorso d'Eleganza Villa d'Este, founded in 1928 in Italy, were based on. However, the practice of rebuilding automobiles and displaying them has now grown from a narrowly defined interest of the wealthy prior to World War Two to what is now a broad-based movement that encompasses concours events, auctions of heritage automobiles, and racing of vintage racing cars (Martin and Clark, 2013).

It is this fascination with automobiles that drives the growing interest in motoring heritage. For many of us, cars are symbols of what we were, what we are, and still for the majority of us, what we want to be seen as in the future. So it seems only natural that our fascination with cars going back to their invention in 1886 by Karl Benz and continuing on through to the present manifests itself in a desire to see, hear, smell, drive, and collect cars (Eckermann, 2001). It is this fascination that is the foundation of motoring heritage.

This volume seeks to explore this interest in motoring heritage, the various activities and behaviours that characterize it, and to analyse their impact on tourism. The sheer scale of these events alone underscores their impact on tourism. Two examples illustrate this scale. The Barrett-Jackson classic car auction held each year since 1972 in Scottsdale, Arizona in 2015 generated revenues of US$130 million in classic car sales and US$6.55 in related automobile memorabilia (Fox Sports, 2015). Although definitive attendance records are not made public, anecdotal estimates suggest that approximately one quarter of a million people visit this one auction alone over the week in which it runs each January. Similarly, the Goodwood Festival of Speed in England also takes place annually. However, unlike the Barrett-Jackson auction, it is a more broad celebration of automobiles and builds upon a rich heritage of automobile racing in the region that first began just before the outbreak of World War Two. From its inaugural narrowly designed format in 1993, the event has become a premier attraction in motoring heritage encompassing vintage racing, concours events, and a range of other activities which celebrate the automobile. It now regularly attracts upwards of 150,000 enthusiasts on each of the three days it runs.

While the Barrett-Jackson auction is possibly the largest of its kind in the world and the Goodwood meeting each year is one of the better known motoring heritage events, car shows, classic car auctions, and historic racing events can be found all around the world, as the chapters in this book illustrate. The pervasiveness of this interest in motoring heritage and the scale of it around the world make it an important aspect of consequential tourism that should be understood and capitalized upon by destinations. It is this phenomenon that this volume will analyse and discuss.

The growth of motoring heritage

The past decade has seen a significant growth in interest by tourism researchers (among others) in the area of heritage tourism (Timothy and Boyd, 2006).

This interest has been driven in part by the growing level of importance for tourism by a segment of the tourist population interested in culture, history, and people: in other words, heritage and all it entails. As this desire by a growing number of tourists to have as part of their travelling and leisure experience, an element of learning and enlightenment, destinations have increasingly looked to heritage attractions and events as key elements in sustaining both the social and the financial viability of their offering to the tourism industry.

Consequently, this growth in interest by researchers in heritage as an important element of tourism has spurred, logically, the increasing compartmentalization of the niche including what is known as industrial heritage tourism. This segment of the heritage niche focuses on artefacts, activities, and people involved in the evolution of societies and economies as a direct result of the development of activities and technologies that drove industrial growth since the mid-eighteenth century. Examples of these include activities such as mineral extraction and application to production of products, namely mines, mining support infrastructure, and industrial sites, as well as technologies related to transportation, most notably railways and water transport and latterly, wheeled motorized transportation and aviation.

Several of these industrial heritage areas have become the focus of research by tourism academics and others, most notably mines and mining as well as railways (Conlin and Jolliffe, 2011; Conlin and Bird, 2014). These books and other articles, for example Hospers (2002) and Firth (2011) now form the basis for increasing investigation into the scope of industrial heritage and its role in the growth and sustainability of tourism destinations. This chapter posits that an increased area of attention by researchers will be the wheeled motorized transport area, namely motoring heritage. This area includes examination of automobiles and other forms of wheeled motorized transportation such as motorcycles, buses, trucks and lorries, specialized equipment such as jeeps (Xie, 2006), military wheeled motorized vehicles, and truly specialized vehicles such as the NASA Crawler-Transporter used at Cape Kennedy to move Saturn rockets to their launching pads.

In addition to an examination of wheeled motorized vehicles, research of this area will also include the investigation of the role of infrastructure that supported the growth in use of this form of transportation, including road networks with historical significance, buildings that reflected both the needs of the technology but also the evolving architectural styles of those societies in which the development took place, and the inevitable involvement of people and organizations who took particular pleasure in being associated with this type of technology, namely the motoring enthusiast.

The fascination of motoring heritage

As Ralph Lauren has said about his car collection, 'Cars were always something I loved' (Autoweek, 2010). He is not alone in describing the role of cars in our societies and the emotional connection humans have formed for this type of technology. This sense of being with and part of cars is common to many people, particularly in the developed and developing world. One would have had to be born before 1879 to have known a world without cars. In the span of just 145 years, the car has become a truly ubiquitous part of life, especially in industrialized and developed societies. The car and its consequential other forms of motorized wheeled transport – buses, lorries, motorcycles, industrial equipment – have played a continually growing role in all our lives. This centrality may help to explain the fascination many of us have with cars, a captivation that manifests itself in many ways.

It should not be surprising, then, that research into the impact of this fascination with cars and their like should become an important subject for tourism researchers. By their very nature, cars have represented access to mobility (Doolittle, 1916) and enhanced opportunity for travel for an increasing segment of any societies' population. Inevitably, cars and tourism become linked, both in terms of rationale logistical symmetry but also in terms of individuals' emotion and fascination. As the subject of this chapter, this fascination increasingly manifests itself with cars from days gone by: in other words, heritage motoring and cars.

This attraction, however, is likely to be much more complex than simply the ubiquitous nature of cars. In themselves, cars and particularly vintage cars, may conjure images and emotions from another period of time, and another way of life. The noise they make, the smells they produce, and the thrill they provide when driven all combine to capture our imaginations and our sense of nostalgia. As this chapter will describe, this desire to be associated with heritage motoring, its artefacts, events, landmarks, and history has created an economic sector within the wider niche of industrial cultural heritage that allows for the participation of almost anyone, rich or poor, educated or self-taught, young and old, and increasingly both men and women.

A key differentiation of motoring heritage and other forms of industrial heritage is the relative ease with which individuals can participate in this area. Mines and their accompanying paraphernalia usually involve static collections of heavy, expensive, and potentially dangerous equipment that is not intrinsically suited to individual ownership, collection, and experience. The same constraints restrict the participation of individuals with railway heritage. As a result, the touristic aspect of these forms of industrial heritage invariably involve the visitation by people to sites where organizations, governments, and in some cases, commercial operators provide tours, viewing, and rides of and on these sites and equipment. This activity does generate economic activity for destination where these sites are located and operated and they also appeal to the emotional attachment many of us have for these technologies.

Motoring heritage offers tourists all of the experiences described above. However, it also offers in a significant way, an expanded opportunity for people to involve themselves in this area, namely through the active ownership, operation, and use of these industrial artefacts. This ability by individuals to own and operate these artefacts has spawned a greatly expanded range of activities having touristic significance for destinations. Car shows, auctions, historic races, and activities and destinations which use the cultural milieu generated by wheeled motorized transport over the past one and a half centuries all contribute to a significant tourism niche which is as up until now, relatively devoid of research.

Motoring heritage and relevance to tourism

As the Introduction has demonstrated, motoring heritage is very diverse. Beyond just historic vehicles which are the primary artefacts of this niche, motoring heritage also encompasses communities of collectors and enthusiasts, private owners and public institutions and historic motoring environments that include both the static and the moving environments for the automobiles of the past.

In terms of static environments, there are literally thousands of museums, exhibitions, and car shows throughout the world. The moving environments include classic car races, vintage car parades, motoring on heritage roads, as well as the ubiquitous informal periodic gatherings of enthusiasts and their heritage vehicles throughout the world. As for material culture, there is a range of paraphernalia associated with motoring heritage that includes both original and replicated promotional materials, equipment and parts, and guide books. The various components that make up motoring heritage are illustrated in Table 1.1.

Motoring heritage has much relevance to tourism, both directly and as a consequential contributor. Many of the places and products listed in Table 1.1 are both heritage motoring events as well as touristic destinations. Major car museums such as the National Automobile Museum in Reno, Nevada are considered part of the tourism offering of that city. The huge Barrett-Jackson auction held each

Table 1.1 Components of automobile heritage

Components	Description	Examples
People	Collectors/enthusiasts	Nick Mason, Ralph Lauren
	Curators/events managers	William Harrah, Robert Peterson
	Designers/builders	Moal Coachbuilders, Chip Foose BMW, Mercedes, Porsche,
	Brand managers/dealers	Wayne Carini
Places	Event environments	Pebble Beach, California, USA
	Attraction locales	The Henry Ford Village, USA
	Heritage highways/roads	Lincoln Highway, USA
	Regions/destinations	Lincoln Heritage Trail, USA
Products	Motor museums & attractions	National Automobile Museum, Reno, Nevada, USA
	Motor events	Concorso d'Eleganza Villa d'Este, Lake Como, Italy
	Classic car auctions	Barret-Jackson & Gooding & Co. Auctions, Scottsdale, Arizona, USA
	Historical/classic racing	Goodwood Festival of Speed, UK
	Souvenirs, collectibles	Bricklinalia

January in Scottsdale, Arizona is a major tourism attraction that draws upwards of 200,000 visitors, both enthusiasts and the simply curious, to the region each year. The Henry Ford Village in Detroit, Michigan attracts upwards of one and a half million visitors annually (Henry Ford Museum, 2000). In addition to iconic places and products, motoring heritage is also relevant to tourism due to its consequential impact on tourism. Many motoring heritage events are not planned or heavily promoted and are local in their appeal. Nonetheless, they can draw many thousands of visitors to towns and cities around the world, many of which have an economic impact on the destination.

In the search for a personal connection with the past (through one's automobile experiences) and an appetite for nostalgia both local residents and visitors are drawn to the experiences related to historic vehicles. Destinations with a strong motoring heritage demonstrate the extend of such heritage and the relevance to tourism, such as Detroit with its designated MotorCities National Heritage Area, an affiliate of the US National Parks System dedicated to preserving, interpreting and promoting the automotive and labour history of the State of Michigan.

There have been few comprehensive studies of motoring heritage in relation to tourism; those that do exist focus on components of motoring heritage tourism, for example, presentations and experiences in motor museums (Jeremiah, 1995; Clark, 2010; Clark, 2013). Consequently, the extent of motoring heritage tourism, that is tourism directly related to motor and motoring heritage is not known. However, the following facts are only some indicators of the motoring heritage that might be available for the development of related tourism products and experiences:

- Establishment of the World Forum for Motor Museums in 1998. The organization holds a bi-annual meeting for motor museum professionals, principals, owners and collectors (World Forum For Motor Museums, n.d.).
- The Classic Car Data Base lists over 150 automotive museums in the USA and Canada (Classic Car Database, n.d.).
- The members of the Vintage Automobile Club of Canada share a desire to preserve, restore and race historically significant cars: (Vintage Automobile Club of Canada, n.d.).
- Vintage Motorsport, The Journal of Motor Racing History, the official magazine of the Sportscar Vintage Racing Association lists not only events but also auctions (Vintage Racing Association, n.d.).
- The Hagerty Company offers valuation tools to anyone in the heritage motoring field with respect to classic and collector automobiles (The Haggerty Company, n.d.).
- According to the Coventry Telegraph, 25,000 people attended the Coventry Festival of Motoring in Coventry, UK in 2013 (Coventry Telegraph, 2013).

Clearly, motoring heritage is extensive and accordingly, is of relevance to tourism. The primary methods for collecting information for this chapter therefore were a literature review on motoring heritage and related forms of tourism as well as analysis of secondary information from the motoring heritage community (that includes classic car clubs, motor museums, motoring events etc.).

Views from the literature

Motoring heritage can be situated within the broad context of industrialization and globalization. Merriman (2009) notes the automobile or the car has had a profound influence on global mobility, settlement patterns, the global economy and the environment. Sociologists such as Urry (2004) have studied the concept of 'automobility' as the complex and extensive mobility system afforded by the use of the personal automobile. This notion could be used to examine the appreciation of past mobilities inherent in the collection and use of antique, classic and vintage automobiles. Jeremiah (1995) identifies three thematic themes through which the history of the motor-car and motoring heritage can be accessed as heritage as: motoring landscape, pursuit of performance and cult of ownership.

This 'automobility' system (Urry, 2004) or 'motoring landscape' (Jeremiah, 1995) includes not only the automobile but also the road system and supporting infrastructure such as motels, motor courts, diners, cafes, food stands and roadside attractions (Clark, 2008). In the heritage context there is considerable appetite for experiencing classic motoring recalling driving in the past (Jakle and Sculle, 2008) that includes experiencing historic roads, such as Route 66 in the United States. The route is celebrated by a roadside museum in Oklahoma and a state park in Missouri (Jakle and Sculle, 2006). In Canada, the transcontinental Trans-Canada Highway opened in 1962 and was completed in 1971, has similar historical significance but has not been specifically developed for tourism in the same way as Route 66.

However, in comparison to the experience of motoring and the sense of mobility afforded by the use and operation of classic automobiles, most motor museums, as Clark (2012) notes, exhibit automobiles in static situations, treating automobiles for the most part as objects of art and industrialization, rarely acknowledging the impact of these vehicles. (Jeremiah, 1995) also reflects on the static display of the automobile in the museum environment in contradiction to the actual motoring experience, which involves mobility. Few museums try to present the motor vehicle in a social history context; this would include the full range of human interaction with the automobile including road trauma. The dark history of the automobile is rarely told as Clark (2010) indicates 'motor museums seem comparatively slow to cultivate a genuinely broad-based and multi-voiced telling of motor history' p. 219. This may be a reflection of the fact that transport museums are noted to be an underdeveloped segment of the museum sector (Divall and Scott, 2003). In 'Tackling Transport' (Mom *et al.*, 2003) Divall provides an overview of transport museums in Western Europe, operated by private industry, government and private enthusiasts. Divall notes that the latter group of collectors and enthusiasts is the determining factor in much of the transport museum field, with many museums being under their entire control. Many of these are car or automobile museums, and this ownership theme addresses what Jeremiah (1995) refers to the cult of ownership. In contrast, Oddy (2005) in his review of 'Tackling Transport' indicates that in reviewing issues of transport museums the voices of academics and museologists are heard but not of the collectors and enthusiasts who dominate other areas of transport history.

The material culture of motoring heritage goes beyond the motor-car itself, providing a context for interpretation but also being collectable by individuals. Putting the automobile in context in motoring-related museums therefore requires the collection of what Clark (2010) refers to as 'motoring paraphernalia' that includes for example clothing, goggles and headgear; maps and guide books; tools, equipment and parts. These objects allow the motor museums collecting them to augment the stories presented by the static cars on exhibition, in the context of the material culture associated with them.

In contrast to the lack of mobility inherent in the static display of cars in motoring-related museums, classic car events afford the opportunity to view cars in an outdoor setting in a full range of mobile situations, from vintage car parades as part of local festivals to classic car rallies and races. This falls into the pursuit of performance theme of the study of motoring tourism noted by Jeremiah (1995). For the visitor, this provides an opportunity to view and experience the car and its relationship to mobility, to hear and smell the car. Kaminski and Smith (2013) refer to this as 'mobile heritage' identifying 'motor vehicle event tourism' as a sub-set of motoring tourism, noting the paucity of research in this area.

Automobile manufacturers, recognizing the significance of museums in brand engagement with their customers have contributed to the creation of a new generation of car museums that are more up to date in terms of museological practice and more interactive. Clark (2010) recognizes this evolution in motoring museums citing the new Mercedes-Benz Museum in Stuttgart that opened in 2006.

Motoring tourism thus offers a variety of experiences for collectors of vintage vehicles but also the visitors to museums and the spectators at classic car events. Jeremiah (1995) observes that motoring heritage is complex in terms of its multidisciplinary nature with ephemeral products and experiences appealing to multiple audiences. Considerable attention has been paid in the academic literature to the state of exhibition approaches in motor museums (Jeremiah, 2003; Jeremiah, 1995; Clark, 2010; Clark, 2013). A gap in research of motor vehicle event tourism has been identified by Kaminski and Smith (2013). However, there has not to date been a comprehensive and integrative assessment of motoring heritage in relation to tourism, a gap addressed by this chapter. The complex contradictions between ownership, presentation, interpretation and experiences related to historic motoring are a common thread through the existing literature that is worthy of further investigation.

Theoretical perspectives of motoring heritage tourism

Using the three themes within the components of motoring heritage, people, places and destinations, this part of the chapter reviews some of the theoretical perspectives in these categories with relevance to tourism.

People

First, in terms of people, the individual relationships to motoring heritage and tourism will depend on the roles of the individuals and their level of interest or enthusiasm regarding such heritage, as well as their personal or professional affiliations to motoring history. In particular, in terms of the ownership of classic and vintage automobiles that are the face of motoring heritage, there appears to be a continuum of involvement from the solely private sector (individual ownership) to the private/public sector (joint ownership/operation) to the public sector (ownership by government and/or on a not for profit basis (Table 1.2).

The urge to collect is an important motivator in terms of participation in the heritage motoring sector. The phenomenon of private collecting (Muensterberger, 1994), once the preserve of the rich and the famous has in the twentieth and twenty first century now become more accessible to all, at least in the developed world. The passion for collecting classic and vintage automobiles has led directly to the establishment of both private and public museum collections and indeed free standing museums devoted to these auto collections. Collecting is also part of our contemporary consumer society, being related to social identities and consumption (Belk, 1995). The collecting of classic cars also has a gender aspect, as it tends to be dominated by males. For the study of motoring heritage, collecting and the theories related to it are therefore relevant in particular in terms of the extent of and access to the collecting activity, which is more broad based than for example, in the art world, as well as the continued involvement of private individuals in holding and caring for vehicle collections, rather than turning them over to public entities, which is more predominant in the art world.

The motivation for involvement in the sector on a broad basis, from the collector, to the spectator is based on the desire to experience the heritage of motoring, that using McKercher and du Cros's (2002) cultural tourism typology the experience sought by these persons may range from deep to shallow, and the importance of cultural tourism (in this case related to motoring heritage) in their desire to visit a destination may range from low to high (Table 1.3).

Table 1.2 Continuum of collection involvement in automobile heritage tourism

Individual Collector or Exhibitor → Public/Private Collaboration → Public Institution

Table 1.3 Types of automotive heritage tourist experiences

Deep	*Serendipitous*	*Purposeful*	
to			
Shallow	*Incidental*	*Casual*	*Sightseeing*
Experience Sought	Low to High		

Source: Adapted from McKercher and du Cros, 2002.

However, what may differ motoring heritage from other aspects of heritage is the high level of private ownership that Jeremiah (1995) refers to as the cult of ownership. The private ownership ranges from the ownership of individual motor cars, to series of vehicles to whole collections that may or may not be open to the public. This latter characteristic is one of the defining aspects of the motoring heritage field and one that may pose a difficulty for researchers.

Places

Second, in terms of places, most locations in the developed world, and now in the developing world have some level of motoring history and heritage; in some cases, where the location is part of the history of motoring, this may provide a compelling reason for both the motoring heritage enthusiasts we discussed earlier as well as for the general cultural tourist to visit (also see Table 1.3).

Another practical tool from cultural tourism theory that may be applied to motoring heritage locations in terms of their potential for related tourism and ability to attract tourists is the market appeal-robusticity matrix of tourism potential (McKercher *et al.*, 2002). In this assessment, robusticity, or ability to withstand visitation co-related with market appeal allow for an attraction's market appeal and robusticity to be assessed as either: low, moderate or high. In the case of motoring heritage, some places will have a broad market appeal as mentioned above, for example Detroit with its deep automotive history will have more of an appeal than a small town car show, for example in Chatham, Ontario, Canada, a town that actually includes reference to classic cars in its place branding as well as indicating that it has Canada's best automotive festivals (Chatham Kent Tourism, n.d.) However, Chatham as a small town with a few festivals is less robust to withstanding the visitation of large numbers of tourists interested in motoring heritage than would Detroit, a large city with many sites related to such heritage that visitors can access.

Looking at places with motoring history; they can also be classified as types of motoring heritage destinations in relation to their size, appeal, and locale (see Table 1.4). However, even small destinations without a depth of motoring heritage per se can have a strong market appeal, as is evidenced by the classic car shows and events at small towns across North America. An example in the interior of British Columbia, Canada is the Okanagan Valley where the annual car show held in Peachland, where for the past 16 years, upwards of 500 owners of

Table 1.4 Typology of automotive heritage destinations with examples

Local	Regional	National	International
World of Wheels, Peachland, British Columbia, Canada	Classic Car Capital of Canada (Retrofest), Chatham, Ontario, Canada	Coventry Festival of Motoring, Coventry, UK	Ameila Island Concurs d'Excellence, Florida, USA

heritage vehicles meet for one day on the village's main street at the start of the North American summer season (Peachland World of Wheels, 2013). This event is organized by 'a small group of five dedicated local directors who arrange all aspects of the incredible day' (Peachland, n.d.).

Products

Third, in terms of products a predominant type of offering is of that of the myriad motor museums around the world, from private to public, from large to small and employing a variety of approaches to the display of historic vehicles. Our analysis of types of motor museums and motoring heritage collections (Table 1.5) employs Divall and Scott's (2001) theory about the differing methods of display of such collections and also adds the component of ownership.

Motoring heritage products can also be conceptualized on a continuum of motion (Figure 1.1) as being either static (as in the motor museum or the car show) (Clark, 2012) or moving (as in car parades and classic car racing) in what Kaminski and Smith (2013) referred to as 'mobile heritage'. This environment in motion ties in with Urry's (2004) theory of automobility as including not only the vehicles but also the operational environments. The movement involved with the product at the top end of the range reflects the pursuit of performance (Jeremiah, 1995).

Table 1.5 Analysis of types of automobile/automotive heritage collections

	Ownership	Focus	Exhibit Method
Musee Nationale de l'Automobile, Mulhouse, France – Cite de l'Atomobile	Public/ Private Partnership	Classic Autos/ Samples	Mass
Ulster Transport Museum, Cultra, Northern Ireland	Public Not for Profit	Automobile History/ Examples	Thematic
London Motor Museum, London, UK	Private	Classic Autos/Samples	Mass
Mercedes-Benz Museum, Stuttgart, Germany	Public Corporation	Technical/Examples Classic Autos & Examples	Labelled

Source: Divall and Scott (2001) with additions from other sources.

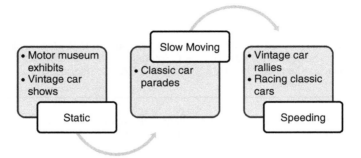

Figure 1.1 Range of motion in automotive heritage products.

People, place and product

Jeremiah (1995) notes the complexity of motoring heritage products as well as the interdisciplinarity of the field that leads to ephemeral products. What is clear from this brief theoretical analysis is that motoring heritage tourism needs to be analysed within the context of both industrialization and globalization, of which it is a product (Merriman, 2009) from an interdisciplinary perspectives, drawing from the fields of sociology, geography, destination studies, museology and cultural tourism. A number of theoretical perspectives have thus been explored, which may be of use in the study of tourism related to motoring heritage (theories about the types of motoring heritage tourists for example) while others have been proposed (such as the Continuum of Collection Involvement in Motoring Heritage Tourism and the Range of Motion in Motoring Heritage Products).

Conclusion

As the preceding discussion has shown, motoring heritage is relevant to tourism, both in terms of being a component of a tourism offering – a destination or region or festival or event – or in terms of being the attraction itself. In its myriad forms, it draws both enthusiasts as well as the simply curious. The sheer diversity of motoring heritage products and places attests to the range of experiences that people have as a result of visiting motoring museums, car shows, auctions, and vintage car races. Indeed, nothing attests to this diversity as much as what could be considered speciality products such as the 2011 display of some of Ralph Lauren's heritage cars at the Musée des Arts Decoratifs in Paris. The focus of this display was that of cars as 'moving art' and surely attracted a new audience to motoring heritage even if consequentially (Ralph Lauren Car Collection, 2011).

The review of existing literature examining motoring heritage demonstrates a number of issues facing tourism researchers. First, given the size of the motoring heritage niche, relatively little has been done to gain a full and comprehensive understanding of the financial, social, and emotional drivers of this niche. Second, little is known about the financial impact of motoring heritage on destinations.

Challenges in measuring this impact abound, particularly with the many ungated events, which comprise large parts of motoring heritage. Third, the dichotomy between enthusiasts and consequential tourists who include a motoring heritage experience as part of a larger tourism experience is not well developed. Motoring heritage event planners, sponsors, and curators will continue to be challenged in trying to identify key success variables in this niche.

What is clear, however, is that interest in motoring heritage is growing and its financial impact is increasing. Attendance at mega-events like the Barrett-Jackson auction is increasing and spawning a range of imitators and copies in other cities. The prices paid for collector cars are rising, in some cases, to virtually astronomical levels as evidenced by the recent sale of a 1967 Ferrari 275 GTB Spider for US$27.5 million (1967 Ferrari, 2013). Increasingly, private collectors are bequeathing their collections to museums or creating museums to share them with the public, the latest being the LeMay America's Car Museum in Tacoma, Washington which houses part of the collection of Harold and Nancy LeMay's reputedly largest private car collection in the world (Museum History, n.d.).

Organization of the book

This volume is organized thematically in parallel with the three themes discussed above, namely people, places and products relating to motoring heritage and tourism. The book is divided into sections reflecting the principal focus of each chapter consistent with the three themes. However, elements of the three themes can be found throughout the volume; as is the case with the field of motoring heritage, the interests of people and organizations in historic vehicles inevitably includes a more widely focused consideration of place and product as well as people. In this first chapter, we have presented the rationale for this book within the context of it being the first volume to focus on the relationship of motoring heritage to tourism, well as the theories behind it.

The first section on people is made up of four chapters (two from North America and two from Europe) that focus not only on people's experiences of motoring heritage but which also profile the heritage left by two automotive entrepreneurs on opposite sides of the Atlantic, both of whom produced cars bearing their name: the Bricklin in New Brunswick, Canada and the DeLorean in Northern Ireland.

In Chapter 2 Nostalgic Automotive Yearnings on the Road to the Museum, Gary Best explores the nature of automobile heritage as presented through a number of private and individually developed museums in Southern California. This is an appropriate beginning to our exploration of motoring heritage given the importance of the Southern California lifestyle beginning after World War Two and continuing on to the present for the development of a lifestyle which encourages and fosters the prominence of the automobile. Lee Jolliffe's chapter on the efforts of Malcolm Bricklin to manufacture a sports car in North America draws attention to the challenges of attaining success in the automobile industry and the consequential devotion which iconic designs and stories cause among the motoring cognoscenti. So while Bricklin's business venture was ultimately a failure, his design and the story surrounding it live on among his admirers and in the place where it all took place.

Greg Ramshaw's Chapter 4 entitled entitled Assembling Heritage Tourism: The BMW Museum and Factory Tour examines how organizations seek to capitalize on the interest and indeed, obsession which enthusiasts have for performance oriented historic brands, in this case the BMW. In his discussion, Greg looks at how heritage and contemporary culture intersect in the case of this particular factory tour experience. Given the growth of manufacturer sponsored or owned museums, which is also discussed at length in Brad Hudson's Chapter 13 titled The Role of Corporate Vehicle Museums in Consumer Brand Engagement, this is an important examination. Finally in this section focusing on people, Chapter 5 examines the fascinating story of John DeLorean, a one-time major player with General Motors whose dream to manufacture his own sports car failed in somewhat dramatic circumstances leaving the motoring heritage world with a car and a memory that has become a major element in the world of classic cars. Gordon Ramsey in his chapter titled DeLorean Dreams: Back to the Future in Titanic Town, traces DeLorean's story, full of drama, massive egos, political machinations, and international intrigue to its current place of prominence in motoring heritage. Ramsey expertly juxtapositions the historical interest in the DeLorean saga with Northern Ireland's other historical drama, namely the story of the Titanic. And to top this all off, the story is set against the backdrop of The Troubles, Northern Ireland's civil war between the United Kingdom and the Irish Republican Army. In doing so, Ramsey traces the entrepreneurial story of the production of the DeLorean in Belfast, Northern Ireland and examines its role in contemporary heritage tourism there.

The second section focuses on places of historical importance in motoring heritage and their links to the development of tourism. It includes chapters on places related to development of heritage motoring tourism around the globe with contribution from Europe (Italy and England), the Caribbean (Barbados) and Asia (Sri Lanka). These chapters make it is evident how automobile heritage can contribute to and reflect place identities through the holding of related events and the collection of historic automobiles, two activities that parallel the intense interest in the automobiles of the past. The economic impact of historic motoring events is also evident.

In Chapter 6, Ilenia Bregoli examines the use of motoring heritage to reposition an industrial city through automobile heritage, namely the role of the *Mille Miglia* race in the tourism development of Brescia, Italy. The *Mille Miglia* is one of those truly iconic events that began as a test for automobiles, their manufacturers, and their owners and eventually became an important piece of motoring heritage. As such, it is the perfect example to illustrate the linkage between motoring heritage and tourism planning. Turning to Chapter 7, The Economic Impact of Historic Vehicle Events: the Case of the 2010 London to Brighton Veteran Car Run, Paul Frost, Jaime Kaminski and Geoff Smith demonstrate the economic impact that this major heritage motoring event has for the City of Brighton and Hove. This discussion is a natural extension of the previous chapter, namely the impact of singularly iconic motoring events. In Chapter 8, Heritage Motoring and Tourism in Barbados, Cristina Jönsson and Lee Jolliffe look at how this Caribbean island nation is using a variety of motoring heritage events, activities, and collections to discuss their emerging role in both heritage and sports tourism on the island. In Chapter 9, M.S.M. Aslam examines motoring heritage in Sri Lanka. The Potential for Heritage Motoring Tourism discusses the colonial legacy of the interest in motoring heritage on this exotic island, identifying the challenges faced by collectors of heritage vehicles and discussing the potential role of historic motoring for heritage tourism to the country. Interestingly, this chapter along with the previous one on Barbados and the final chapter on Jordan, demonstrate the pervasiveness of motoring heritage around the world including places one might not normally think of in this field.

The third section includes six chapters that focus broadly on motoring heritage events and collections. Although motoring heritage is first and foremost about automobiles, the way in which the field manifests itself, particularly in a touristic way, is through museums and events. As with the other sections in this book, these six chapters highlight the pervasiveness of motoring heritage around the world with chapters discussing museums in Australia, North America, Italy, and Jordan and events in Australia and North America.

Both Chapter 10 and 11 focus on Australia. In Chapter 10, Racing Back in Time: Victoria's Historic Racing Scene, Matt Harvey traces the development and significance of historic racing in Victoria, Australia. As discussed at the opening of this chapter, the 'racing' of vintage automobiles has become an important part of motoring heritage as evidenced by the success and profile of events such as the Rolex Monterey Motorsports Reunion in the United States and The Goodwood Festival of Speed in England. What Harvey expertly demonstrates is how vintage racing can and does become an activity with national proportions, one that captures in this case, an entire continent. It also underscores how relevant this activity is to tourism in a destination or a region. This Australian love of automobiles is reinforced by Leanne White's Chapter 11, The Motor Museum of Popular Culture: Exhibiting the Patriotic Heritage of 'Australia's Own Car'. White examines how the two historically important Australian motoring brands are portrayed through museums, contributing to and forming part of the national identity of the country.

Moving to the other side of the world, Jerry Epperly and Asli Tasci examine the world renowned Amelia Island Concours d'Elegance held annually in Florida. In Chapter 12 titled Significance of Amelia Island Concours d'Elegance, Florida, USA, Epperly and Tasci examine both participation and impact in the case of this well-known automobile event. Like most concours events, participants enter historically important vehicles that are judged on a range of criteria focusing on authenticity. Like vintage racing, concours events are a more narrowly focused aspect of motoring heritage and participants, in many cases, are from higher socio-economic strata within their societies, reflecting the sometimes enormous cost of restoring and caring for vintage automobiles. Nonetheless, concours events do attract a lot of enthusiasts for whom ownership of vintage automobiles at the 'concours' level will always be but a dream. Attendance at the premier event, the Pebble Beach Concours d'Elegance in California, has grown dramatically since its inception in 1950 to the point where attendees vastly outnumber exhibitors. And this can be seen at most major concours event around the world. In Chapter 13, The Role of Corporate Vehicle Museums in Consumer Brand Engagement, Brad Hudson examines the influence of museums established and operated by contemporary vehicle brands in engaging visitors and reinforcing brand recognition with consumers. Another museum case study is presented by Antonella Capriello in Chapter 14, Product Innovation for Repositioning and Destination Development Marketing Strategies: The Museo Nazionale dell'Automobile, Turin, Italy. Capriello focuses the value of the museum for marketing this automotive city. And finally in Chapter 15 entitled The Role of the Royal Automobile Museum in Tourism and Heritage Education in Jordan, Salem Harahsheh and Rafa Haddad not only profile the national museum as a key player in education but as instrumental in using the car collection of the royal family of the country to reinforce national identity.

These authors expertly portray a niche of industrial and cultural heritage that has for many years been a significant component of tourism in many destinations, regions, and even countries and continents. They demonstrate clearly the complexity of motoring heritage, its challenges and its rewards, and most importantly, its role in developing and supporting tourism. So the future for motoring heritage is bright. The challenge is to determine how bright and relevant it is for motoring-related tourism.

References

Belk, R.W., 1995. *Collecting in a consumer society*. Psychology Press.

Berger, M.L., 2001. *The automobile in American history and culture: a reference guide*. Santa Barbara, CA: Greenwood Publishing Group.

Clark, J., 2013. Peopling the Public History of Motoring: Men, Machines, and Museums. *Curator: The Museum Journal*, 56, 279–287.

Clark, J., 2012. 15 Objects of subversion. Narrat. Objects Collect. Stories 221.

Clark, J., 2010. The 'rough and tumble': displaying complexity in the motor museum. *Museum Management and Curatorship*, 25, 219–234.

Clark, J., 2008. Challenging motoring functionalism: Roadside memorials, heritage and history in Australia and New Zealand. *The Journal of Transport History*, 29, 23–43.

Conlon, R.M., and Perkins, J., 2001. *Wheels and deals: the automotive industry in twentieth-century Australia*. Farnham: Ashgate Pub Limited.

Divall, C., and Scott, A., 2001. *Making histories in transport museums*. London: Continuum.

Doolittle, J.R., 1916. *The romance of the automobile industry*. New York: The Klebold Press.

Eckermann, E., 2001. *World history of the automobile*. Warrendale, PA: Society of Automotive Engineers Inc.

Firth, T.M., 2011. Tourism as a means to industrial heritage conservation: Achilles heel or saving grace? *Journal of Heritage Tourism*, 6, 45–62.

Hospers, G.-J., 2002. Industrial heritage tourism and regional restructuring in the European Union. *European Planning Studies*, 10, 397–404.

Jakle, J.A., and Sculle, K.A., 2008. *Motoring: the highway experience in America*. University of Georgia Press.

Jakle, J.A., and Sculle, K.A., 2006. *Signs in America's auto age: signatures of landscape and place*. University of Iowa Press.

Jeremiah, D., 2003. Museums and the history and heritage of British motoring. *International Journal of Heritage Studies*, 9, 169–190.

Jeremiah, D., 1995. The motor car from road to museum. *International Journal of Heritage Studies*, 1, 171–179.

Kaminski, J., and Smith, G., 2013. 15 'Mobile heritage'. *Contemporary Issues in Cultural Heritage Tourism*, 218.

Martin, K., and Clark, L., 2013. *Strange but true tales of car collecting: drowned bugattis, buried belvederes, felonious ferraris and other wild stories of automotive misadventure*. Minneapolis, MN: MotorBooks International.

McKercher, B., Cros, H. du, and McKercher, R., 2002. *Cultural tourism: the partnership between tourism and cultural heritage management*. London: Routledge.

Merriman, P., 2009. Automobility and the Geographies of the Car. *Geography Compass*, 3, 586–599.

Mom, G., Trischler, H., and Zeilinger, S., 2003. *Tackling Transport*. East Lansing, MI. Michigan State University Press.

Muensterberger, W., 1994. *Collecting: an unruly passion: psychological perspectives*. Princeton, NJ: Princeton University Press.

Oddy, N., 2005. Tackling transport. *J Hist J. Des. Hist.* 18, 305–307.

Sachs, W., 1992. *For love of the automobile: looking back into the history of our desires*. Oakland, CA: University of California Press.

Timothy, D.J., and Boyd, S.W., 2006. Heritage tourism in the 21st century: Valued traditions and new perspectives. *Journal of Heritage Tourism*, 1, 1–16.

Urry, J., 2004. 'The "system" of automobility'. *Theory, Culture and Society*, 21, 25–39.

Xie, P.F., 2006. Developing industrial heritage tourism: A case study of the proposed jeep museum in Toledo, Ohio. *Tourism Management*, 27, 1321–1330.

Web References

Chatham Kent Tourism (n.d.): http://www.chatham-kent.ca/tourism.

Cite de L'Automobile: http://citedelautomobile.com/en/home

Classic Car Database: http://classiccardatabase.com/museums.php

Coventry Telegraph (2013): http://www.coventrytelegraph.net/news/local-news/festival-motoring-stoneleigh-park-hailed-5784569

1967 Ferrari sells for 27.5 million dollars (2013). MSN Autos. Retrieved at http://editorial.autos.msn.com/blogs/post--1967-ferrari-sells-for-275-million-dollars

Fox Sports, January 19, 2015 Barrett-Jackson reaches historic highs at 2015 Scottsdale auction http://www.foxsports.com/motor/story/cars-barrett-jackson-arizona-historic-highs-at-2015-scottsdale-auction-011915

Henry Ford Museum Annual Report (2000). Retrieved at https://www.thehenryford.org/docs/default-source/default-document-library/2000-annual-reporte28b4984d30d6b-61be8bff000073bae4.pdf?sfvrsn=0.

London Motor Museum - http://www.londonmotormuseum.co.uk/

Museum History (n.d.). LeMay American's Car Museum. Retrieved at http://www.lemay-museum.org/page.php?id=65

Peachland World of Wheels. http://www.peachlandcarshow.com/

The Haggerty Company (n.d.) https://www.hagerty.ca/valuationtools

The Independent. Ralph Lauren car collection goes on display in Paris (2011). Retrieved at   http://www.independent.co.uk/life-style/motoring/ralph-lauren-car-collection-goes-on-display-in-paris-2275889.html

Vintage Racing Association, (n.d.) http://www.vintagemotorsport.com/

Vintage Automobile Club of Canada, http://varac.ca/

World Forum for Motor Museums http://worldforumformotormuseums.com/

http://autoweek.com/article/car-news/great-garages-ralph-lauren-looking-look-finding-next-cool-car-gets-harder-every-day

Part II
People and automobile heritage

2 Nostalgic automotive yearnings on the road to the museum

Gary P. Best

Saturday night's all right ...

The first Saturday night of each month of 2013 saw *Bob's Big Boy* in Burbank return more completely to its former automotive glory with a 1950's costume theme Trophy Night and Cruise-In. Awards? You bet: Best Hot Rod; Best Cruiser; Best Custom; Best Classic; Best Muscle Car; and Manager's Choice. Behaviour? Very 2013 community conscious: 'No Alcohol ... No Loud Exhausts ... No Burn Outs ... No Kidding!!!' Please, tell me it isn't so! Hot rods, customs, and muscle cars are rebels with a cause. The shake, rattle and roll of dangerous Dodge doppelgängers is supposed to put the frighteners on family-friendly Ford Fairlanes, even more so if Mom and Pop's 1958 wins Best Classic.

The 'Big Boy' is where late 1940's coffee shop/restaurant *streamline moderne* architecture meets *Happy Days* and *American Graffiti* on a daily basis. Designed and built in 1949, the Burbank *Bob's* is the oldest surviving example of the chain and in 1993 was designated a California Point of Historical Interest (Lewis, 2000: 132). At Bob's, the past *is* the present and a big serve of nostalgia comes with every burger. So, what's with nostalgia for old burger joints and old cars, and old movies with old cars and drive-in dining? Perhaps, more significantly, why nostalgia at all? Is nostalgia only a cyclical craze, like fashion, or is it a more profound phenomenon, one that offers the reassurance of a simpler, more innocent past that distracts from fear of a nuclear fallout future?

Nostalgic yearnings

Nostalgic yearnings, frequently taking the form of a desire to escape an alienating present, have contributed to the growth of a car culture that, in many ways, looks to the past in an attempt to redress the manifold automotive deficiencies of that present. One site providing a constructed past is that of the automotive museum but a diversity of founding (and funding) rationales, collections, spaces, curating practices and politics highlight the fact that what constitutes any given museum is almost always a work in progress. The primary challenge for most automotive museums, however, may be to attract return visitation when many visitors could consider such museum collections to be static, and that one visit may suffice.

This is, of course, at odds with new museum exhibitions and regular re-focusing of current collections.

In the case of the tourist, automotive obsessive or otherwise, many major international cities have automotive museums that may be linked to a specific marque – The Porsche Museum and The Mercedes-Benz Museum, both in Stuttgart, Germany; The BMW Museum in Munich, The Henry Ford in Dearborn – while others offer an experience that have a broader charter of displaying different marques and models such as Beaulieu National Motor Museum and Haynes International Motor Museum, both in the UK. Both instances, however, are profoundly linked to a cultural tourism imperative; the automobile is both a major technological and cultural phenomenon of the twentieth century, as well as a complex and enduring cultural construct contributing to the realization of a broad range of touristic outcomes. Even if a museum display consists of only a few vehicles in an otherwise empty space, a cultural resonance is generated in terms of both individual and collective engagement, as well as the promulgation of an implied, if not stated, automotive heritage construct.

Four museums in Los Angeles and environs are dedicated to the history and heritage of automotive experience. Each museum is named after its founder and offers a distinctive experience, focus, narrative arc, and heritage construct that can be very informally characterized as:

Petersen Automotive Museum, Los Angeles:
US automotive nostalgia through a Southern Californian lens
www.petersen.org

The Nethercutt Museum, Sylmar:
an immaculate, nostalgic veteran and vintage automotive past
www.nethercuttcollection.org

Mullin Automotive Museum, Oxnard:
European automotive nostalgia as high art
www.mullinautomotivemuseum.com

The Murphy Automotive Museum, Oxnard:
automotive nostalgia as jumble sale
www.murphyautomuseum.org

All four museums are the legacy of individuals not only passionate about the automotive experience, but also possessing the financial wherewithal to create dedicated spaces that formalize collections reflecting personal passions and histories in a museum context. That the museums are located in, or close to, a city that is a major international tourist destination in its own right as well as a profoundly traffic-choked metropolis adds another layer of significance to automotive museums that ostensibly revere and celebrate that nemesis of the natural environment, the fossil-fuel burning automobile. Despite its darker side, Mottram emphasizes that 'the automobile is … embedded in whatever is American' (1989: 41).

Los Angeles is a multi-dimensional tourism heritage site par excellence: the climate, the movie industry, the theme parks, the prospect of a quaky San Andreas Fault frisson, and the roads north to San Francisco, south to the Mexican border, and east to the desert cities all deliver on their promise. Los Angeles (LA) has always been about modernity, with its constant flow of newcomers and never-ending renewal and transformation but many others saw only the flipside, that of a cultural backwater and intellectual wasteland that was the antithesis of civilization with Hollywood as the epitome of vulgarity and philistinism (Brook, 2013: 107). Bahr proposed that these 'two competing mythologies' were a possible means of negotiating the city's 'complex psychological, sociocultural and philosophical tensions' (2007: 36).

Complex tensions notwithstanding, the tourist nostalgic for an uncritical, mediated childhood version of LA can, however, drive along the boulevards and freeways and connect to memories of TV's *Highway Patrol* (1955–1959) and *77 Sunset Strip* (1958–1964), not to mention a lifetime of LA in the movies; driving past the Hollywood sign is always resonant. Print media also contributed to this author's Antipodean childhood, with the car advertisements in *Look*, *Life*, *The Saturday Evening Post* and *The New Yorker* stimulating automotive yearnings for a '58 Cadillac Eldorado Biarritz or '61 Lincoln Continental, ownership never realized but the desire still burning undiminished. This tourist's gaze in LA is forever seeking tangible remains of that constructed automotive past and, perhaps not surprisingly, extant examples are frequently evident. The streets of LA regularly reward the eagle-eyed car-spotter but it is in the museums where the in-the-metal encounters breathe life into those still bright double-page magazine spreads of the annual new car releases.

Chase and Shaw's (1989) three conditions: a secular and linear sense of time, the failed present, and evidence of the past, and Margalit's assertion that nostalgia distorts past reality, and idealizes its object whilst locating it in a time of purity and innocence (2011) will be utilized to investigate nostalgic forms and processes in the four automotive museums examined here presenting alluring and distinctively constructed takes on automotive heritage. First, though, some backstory is presented to set the scene.

LA: movies and automobility

The year 1896 saw two momentous events that would profoundly impact the cultural landscape of 20th century America in general and Los Angeles in particular. On April 23, 1896 Thomas Edison's 'Vitascope' was presented at Koster and Bial's Music Hall, New York City, and is commemorated by a plaque on Macy's wall: 'Here the Motion Picture began' (Brownlow, 1968: 2). Like those earlier brave pioneers, the movie industry that began way back east soon made its dusty way west and set up camp in the endless sunshine of Los Angeles. Less than two months after the 'Vitascope' sensation, Henry Ford drove his 'Quadricycle' down Bagley Avenue in Detroit in the early hours of June 4, 1896, the first Ford of the empire that was to rapidly follow (Lacey, 1986: 66) and the second invention that would soon also characterize Los Angeles, albeit negatively with the passing of decades as the sunshine disappeared behind a poisonous orange smog.

The emergence and rise of Hollywood and the ascendency of the automobile are two remarkably enduring cultural and profoundly nostalgic Los Angeles experiences. Hollywood, both industry and construct, continues to survive despite the golden years of the 'Dream Factory' ending more than a quarter of a century ago. Similarly, by the end of the twentieth century, the glory of US automotive production, the other 'Dream Factory', was long over but, for those weaned on the regular new releases of both industries, the formative pleasures can be sustained, albeit through significantly altered forms.

Perhaps the first material intersection of the two great American institutions may have been that between the newly wealthy movie stars and their inclination to be seen in the latest automobiles. Period publicity shots reveal that some were modest: Roscoe 'Fatty' Arbuckle sitting on the running board of his 1919 Pierce-Arrow; some were perky – Joan Crawford with her 1929 Ford Town Car; and some were fabulous – Marlene Dietrich with her 1935 Cadillac Fleetwood Town Cabriolet (Author's collection). Deals brokered by managers, agents and stars themselves also resulted in a synergy adding further to both star power and car power, not to mention flocks of fans emulating their screen gods and goddesses behind similar steering wheels.

The rise of custom automobile builders developed along with not only the new wealth of Hollywood but new wealth in general. Demand for bespoke bodies and svelte styling increased when mass produced Model T Fords poured off the production lines, flooding roads with uniformity. The formerly exclusive cachet of automobile ownership diminished, so those with the means to do so found consolation with exotic and expensive European brands such as Isotta-Fraschini, Hispano-Suiza, Mercedes and Rolls Royce (Gartman, 1994: 49). The economic boom of the 1920s, however, saw cashed-up clients less engaged by manufactured luxury and more attracted to custom-built bodies where the buyer could specify as many styling details, exotic woods and rare fabrics as could be conceived and acquired. The movies, of course, relied upon the automobile for its utility as well as serving narrative functions that consolidated embedded perceptions of class consciousness.

Another obvious intersection is movies with a period setting requiring period-correct cars. For the majority of Hollywood productions, cars were, and still are, a necessary but largely incidental means of narrative mobility. Mottram proposes that while cars have been evident in the movies since the medium began, their use and semiotic function are frequently other than transport (1989: 67), one example being in *films noir*. Noir cars became 'amoral spaces where laws and social arrangements such as marriage and class hierarchies are suspended' (Osteen, 2008: 184), with cars instrumental in realizing narrative outcomes destined to shatter lives. *Films noir* reflect post-World War II disillusionment as well as future uncertainty. *Gangster Squad* (2013), on the other hand, was Ruben Fleischer's recent *noirish* take on LA circa 1949 when crime lord Mickey Cohen and the mob 'ruled'. Skilful art direction, use of extant locations and period correct cars evoked a mood of mobster madness despite chronological errors reporting Cohen's life. Leslie Kendall, chief curator of LA's Petersen Automotive Museum observed: 'These cars, they're as important as the buildings and clothes and makeup in establishing the time and place' (Cohen, 2013: D5). Hollywood's promise, it seems, still appears to be delivering the goods in flawlessly constructed versions of the past.

Ridin' along in my automobile …

Movie Mecca, playground of the stars, organized crime capital, racial melting pot, and palm-fringed pleasure dome, Los Angeles promised infinite mobility but instead delivered dystopian downtown delays. LA's population almost doubled between 1919 and 1929 but a far more significant growth was the 550 percent increase in automobile registrations (Kunstler, 1993: 211). Little more than a decade later the frenzy of automobility was further consolidated by the opening in 1940 of the Arroyo Seco Parkway that one year later morphed into the Pasadena Freeway (Kay, 1997: 206); the stranglehold of automobility was already tightening.

Producing 650,000 vehicles annually, the Los Angeles auto industry was, during the 1950s, the second largest automobile manufacturing centre in the world after Detroit (Morales, 1986: 289). This momentum continued until a flood of cheap imports beginning in the early 1970s, coupled with two energy crises that same decade, contributed to buyers rejecting domestic 'gas-guzzlers' for supposedly more fuel efficient vehicles, either imports or under-engineered local subcompacts such as the much-derided Ford Pinto or Chevrolet Vega. Automobility took a deep breath, then stepped back on the gas. Crisis? What crisis? By then, however, the glory days were already junkyard bound.

Relocating business to newer developments in outlying suburbs had not only further consolidated dependency of the automobile but also contributed to the abandonment of former downtown business districts. Dimendberg identified an LA-specific symptom of automobility in the city's suburbanization and decentralization: its unique centrifugal [outward directed] spatiality (2004: 116). For most of the post-war 1940s and until the mid-1950s Hollywood presented the old LA downtown as a shadowy noir nightmare of dark alleys and mob corruption, a dramatic counterpoint to advertising of the period showing orange groves and endless beaches. The sun still shone on the tourist dollar but who'd drive downtown? Robert Aldrich's atomic assignation *Kiss Me Deadly* (1955) has LA as: 'a city without pedestrians … post-war freeways and … broad boulevards stream, night and day, with unending lines of moving cars, whose drivers and passengers … are in shadow, invisible … throughout the film' (Christopher, 1997: 21–22). It should also be noted that car crazy cool cat P.I protagonist Mike Hammer drove a Jaguar XK 120 until its untimely, but fortunately simulated, end over a cliff, replacing it with a 1954 Chevrolet Corvette.

Kay observed that as downtown died: 'Corporate flight … made every structure a servant to the automobile, a highway adjunct and car park alike' (1997: 264). A corollary was the emergent imperative of the two-car family. In June, 1950

Ford advertising proposed '*Now thousands own two fine cars ... and they're both '50 Fords*', and by 1955 it was '*First we had one FORD ... now we have two*' (Author's collection).

Cowan confirmed that: 'by mid-century the automobile had become, to the American housewife of the middle classes ... the vehicle through which she did much of her most significant work, and the work locale where she could be most often found' (1983: 85). Significance and engagement notwithstanding, missing from Cowan's notion of satisfying and independent mid-century mobile motherhood is consideration of the dislocation and isolation that must have characterized life for many women in the suburban sprawl, particularly those without two Fords.

Television, however, counterpointed the reality of suburban isolation with constant narrative high-jinks and automobility in foregrounded sponsor's vehicles set in busy neighbourhoods: *Father Knows Best* (1954–60) with multiple Mercurys; *Leave It to Beaver* (1957–1963) with plenty of Plymouths; and *The Donna Reed Show* (1959–66) with a flurry of Ford wagons: 1958 Edsel Bermudas, 1959 Ford Country Sedans, and 1960–63 Mercury Comets. In the early evening, these television shows presented privileged baby-boomer narratives as morality plays with reassuring resolutions, as well as sponsor commercials. Watching the shows again now in digitally refreshed detail, the automobiles have showroom sparkle, generating nostalgic yearning for times that were only ever fictional constructs but now glorified as 'the good old days' when such new cars were annually the stuff of viewers' dreams. The significance of the sitcoms now is not so much their narrative content but the larger contemporary socio-cultural commentary that is conspicuously absent. Home improvement, commodity acquisition (such as a new car or TV), educating the kids, dealing with crazy teenage angst, and balancing the budget were foregrounded as primary components of the daily American dream; the atomic future did not make the final script.

Considering nostalgia

Chase and Shaw proposed three different conditions as prerequisites for what they termed a 'popular mood of nostalgia': 'a secular and linear sense of time, an apprehension of the failings of the present, and the availability of evidences of the past' (1989: 4). They further propose that nostalgia does not preclude considerations of Utopia, as: 'the counterpart to the imagined future is the imagined past' (1989: 9). Views of automotive futures have always been thrilling, with Detroit regularly promising tomorrow today but, by the day after, it was yesterday's news. The 1942 De Soto had 'tomorrow's style today' and 'Suddenly It's 1960' was the advertising claim for the 1957 Plymouth but, annually, the future quickly became the past when the new cars were released, sometimes with slight cosmetic updates; other times, like the 1959 Chevrolet it was, without apparent irony 'All new, all over again'.

Chase and Shaw also note that, in conjunction with the sense that the present is manifestly deficient, evidence of the past must be available in order to construct nostalgic, 'retro' tributes to the original. VW's revisiting of its iconic Beetle with the New Beetle (1997–2011), Chrysler's 1930s–1940s inspired PT Cruiser (2000–2010), and BMW's 'new' MINI (2001–) utilized nostalgic, yet distinctly contemporary styling cues that evoked each company's past glories (Devine, 2014: 211). Ransacking design archives, however, may appear a brazen, cynical exercise in both creating and manipulating consumer demand through the uncritical reassurance of carefully (re)constructed visions emphasizing selected past pleasures. Consequently, historical challenges, such as former European enmity and atrocity, and 1930's Depression hardships didn't feature in new advertising, but Kaempfert and Gabler's schmaltzy 'L-O-V-E' (1965) provided a safe, smooth jazz soundtrack for a reassuring 2001 PT Cruiser US TV commercial (Author's collection).

Songs with an automotive theme as well as advertising jingles heard long after their initial broadcast often stimulate a nostalgic resonance by addressing ownership, driving, brand and/or model preference, the pleasure and promise of the road, aspiration, sex, and fantasy: Chuck Berry's 'Maybellene' (1955) and 'No Particular Place to Go' (1964); The Beach Boys' 'Little Deuce Coupe' (1963); The Beatles' 'Drive My Car' (1965); Wilson Pickett's 'Mustang Sally' (1966); Prince's 'Little Red Corvette' (1983); Bruce Springsteen's 'Pink Cadillac' (1984); and Billy Ocean's 'Get Out Of My Dreams, Get Into My Car' (1988). Lubar observed that: 'Popular songs are both personal and general; they provide a structure for specific memories, yet at the same time tell universal stories' (1997: 401).

Nostalgia is often understood as a sentimental yearning for the past beyond one's living memory (Kim, 2005) and, as Margalit noted, distorts past reality, and idealizes its object whilst locating it in a time of purity and innocence (2011: 273). The effects of early experience on consumer preferences for automobile styles was investigated by Schindler and Holbrook who noted that a common factor of past studies of nostalgic preferences appears to be the experience of a period of intense affective consumption (2003: 279). Utilizing 80 photographs of automobile styles (69 US manufacturers, 11 other), they found men but not women show evidence of nostalgic attachment to the styles experienced in their youth.

Finally, for Devine: 'the role of nostalgia does not mean a complete fabrication of previous events or … smoothing out the rough edges of history … it helps us to understand how people make sense of both their individual and collective pasts and what they judge as important to them' (2014: 214). Whilst the public experience of nostalgia may keep the edges rough, privately a little smoothing out is probably not unknown to many.

Automotive museums: past, present, future

Paving the road

Given the preceding discussion exploring nostalgia and its constituent elements, museums dedicated to the automotive experience are almost inevitably going to rekindle personal memories of automobility when visitors encounter vehicles directly linked to their past. Whilst visitors to motor museums are frequently attracted through their love of the automobile, generally and specifically, as well as its technological environment (Clark, 2010), many may simply enjoy seeing automobiles of the type they grew up with, learned to drive in, dated and cruised in, got a speeding ticket in, raised their kids and took vacations in, and have cherished photographs of. Divall also emphasizes that: 'Personal and collective memories meld, making and reproducing the shared identities that help to define us all as social beings' (2003: 261). Automotive museums, however, must have as a central, founding tenet, namely the expectation of some degree of connectivity to, or at least familiarity with, the phenomenon of automobility.

Heritage can also take multiple forms in the automotive museum context, three broad themes which are discussed by Jeremiah (1995). 'The motoring landscape' is rich with possibilities, given both literal and/or metaphorical readings. More specifically, 'the road' continues to be a significant, recurring trope in literature and cinema, frequently offering a subversive reading on 'landscape' and how it is understood and experienced. 'The pursuit of performance', Jeremiah's second theme, immediately calls to mind Richard Sarafian's *Vanishing Point* (1971), when the pursuit of performance necessitated by a race against time becomes itself the target of pursuit by 'the law'. Peary observes that *Vanishing Point*: 'shows a finer aspect of the sixties-seventies counterculture, for which I have nostalgic feelings' (1983: 160). Museum exhibitions now regularly provide an aligned film program intended to further illuminate displayed themes and can present: 'vehicles as objects of art, speed and prestige to be admired and cherished by enthusiasts' (Clark, 2010: 219).

'The cult of ownership' suggests an obsessive compulsive disorder that has deified the car far beyond its fundamentally quotidian *raison d'etre*. Jeremiah proposes, however, given that the history of the motor car and motoring is: 'complex in its multi-disciplinary character, ephemeral in its products and experiences, it needs to be presented as a democratic and popular culture that is both educational and entertainment' (1995: 171). He also notes that Britain's first motor museum opened in London, May, 1912 and while it was a pioneering venture that challenged the conventions of the museum world, more significantly it introduced an operational model barely changed in just over a century (Jeremiah, 1998).

Critical issues

Writing on The Henry Ford (THF) in Dearborn, Bandt proposed that the primary limitation of the visitor experience is the attempt to make history tangible through display and re-enactment strategies that privilege nostalgic reflections on: 'the transition from pre-industrial ways of living to industrial society' (2007: 385). A better, selective future was, in fact, the focus of Ford's third advertising campaign of 1944, with *'There's a Ford in Your Future'* becoming the immediate post-war era's best known automobile slogan (Lewis, 1976: 382–383).

A deeper, more complex story of motoring is possible through a museum utilising motoring's material culture to engage visitors (Clark, 2010). Clark (2013) further emphasised that people are the main players in motoring's story but that very public, shared history is still problematic in museum spaces. Divall (2003) advocated audience engagement with familiar objects, asserting that the pull of the 'real thing' is very strong, proposing that the ideal transport museum allows visitors to traverse three routes to the past: those of material reminders (relics); personal and collective memory; and history.

Hatton investigated the complexities of serving multiple purposes supported by multiple masters (2012: 129). Visitors value museums because they have usually consciously selected the activity over many others. The decision making process is often aligned with what Pekarik and Schreiber termed 'scripts' that are informed by both what visitors intend to do and the form that their visit will assume (2012: 495). Such experience seeking in museum contexts is also often linked to memories, with museums ... often being described as 'memory institutions' (Robinson, 2012: 414).

The road ahead

Clark has recently identified that stories of personal mobility in social, economic and environmental systems need to be told; displays refocused, spaces reimagined creatively, and compelling 'lost' people are needed to reanimate motoring history (2013: 286–287). Jeremiah also asserted that collections be re-evaluated in light of the emergence of new meanings, as well as further reconsideration of outdated museum narratives that obscure rather than enhance visitor engagement with ... motoring's history and heritage (2003). Similarly, Lubar (1997) identified that the formerly complacent public now expects to contribute to creating meaning in museums, and that museums must address the rich interplay of history and memory, reminiscence, and research.

Müller also identified the benefits of museums broadening definitions, so that: 'the presentation, as well as the message communicated, must be in line with the experience and knowledge of today's visitors' (2012: 16). Pekarik and Schreiber, however, warned that: 'museum personnel who believe that a museum's mission is to communicate or transmit specific messages, feelings, or other experiences will need to appreciate that ... only visitors already attuned to seeking these experiences are likely to find them' (2012: 495).

Tickets to ride: four SoCal automotive museums

Petersen Automotive Museum: 6060 Wilshire Blvd., Los Angeles, CA. 90036: US nostalgia as through a SoCal lens

The Petersen Automotive Museum in Los Angeles employs a nostalgic southern Californian lens to begin the visit, and then further emphasizes its LA location with a Hollywood Gallery and at least two changing exhibitions. It has a very contemporary and techno-savvy vibe, but in a nod to the past has been offering tours of its *Vault* (read: basement storage) collection of vehicles for an extra $25.00. The 90-minute tour is, for the enthusiast, well worth it but those who have visited the museum previously may recognize more than a few vehicles that have previously been on display in the upper galleries. There is no pomp, or ropes, in the Vault, but often there is Hollywood provenance, such as Steve Mc Queen's 1957 Jaguar XKSS, and compelling histories, like that of the elusive 'Round Door Rolls' (Hennigan, 2012).

Robert E. 'Pete' Petersen (1926–2007), founder of Petersen Publishing, began his company with *Hot Rod* magazine in 1948, and later beginning *Rod and Custom* and *Motor Trend* magazines. With his wife Margie (1935–2011), Petersen opened the Petersen Museum in 1994. In June 2014 The Petersen Automotive Museum will celebrate its 20th anniversary of providing an engaging and inclusive visitor experience for the automotively-inclined as well as those along for the ride.

At the Petersen

After purchasing an admission ticket, the visitor turns right and immediately enters 'The Streetscape' which offers *The Car and the City in Southern California*, a constructed, one-way stroll through a historical chronology of vignettes and vehicles that together constitute a fragmented narrative of twentieth century LA automobility. Despite the specificity of LA 'locations', there is a reassuring, pre-dictably nostalgic universality of mobility in the display themes, especially in the US context: early motoring challenges; early auto racing; gas stations; the garage becoming attached to the home; billboards; auto showroom; *Speed Shop*; grocery store; diner/ malt shop; and just getting away from it all. Car culture is carefully curated but more focused exhibits, often with direct links to LA/ SoCal heritage, constitute both permanent and temporary exhibitions.

Beginning with Chase and Shaw's second condition, the failed present, there is little in the Petersen to indicate that the automotive present is wanting, although it could be argued that selective provision of content privileges soulless, manipula-tive consumerism as well as more than a century of questionable industrial and environmental legacies. One counterpoint is the permanent exhibition *Alternative Power: Lessons from the Past, Inspiration for the Future* that acknowledges other forms of the internal combustion engine such as the turbine (a '50s and '60s Chrysler Corporation research focus, and a 'back to the future' moment; see Lehto, 2010) as well as fuel cells, electric, and petroleum alternatives.

In 2013, the Corvette's 60th anniversary exhibition displayed every generation as well as other important historical examples. Sixty continuous years of produc-tion provided significant evidence of the past as well as the opportunity to respond to the flawless examples of *America's Sportscar*, which may be consistent with Margalit's 'distortion of past reality' as well as uncritically locating the Corvette 'experience' in a time of purity and innocence. Evident also was Lubar's 'rich interplay of history and memory, reminiscence, and research' (1997: 405); each Corvette's story contributed to the exhibition's composite interplay of fact and factoid, embellished and otherwise.

One final exhibition for brief consideration: *Southern California: Vacationland USA* (September 2003 to March 2005) in which vacationers' vehicles in the

25 years after WWII such as 'cars, trucks, station wagons and other types of vehicles' really delivered with a range of vehicles in stagey settings. An immaculate black '57 Chevy Nomad looked as though it had done little campfire duty but was the most gorgeous conceit; in fact, the pristine cars and campsites in the faux great outdoors was quite a stretch, but the fun of camping it up won on the day. A distortion of past reality? Yep. A time of purity and innocence? You better believe it. Such limitations notwithstanding, the late '40s and '50s vacations were nostalgically realized and communicated, and while the construct provided brief information on each vehicle, any real challenges facing tourism automobilities were edited out, replaced with a genuinely child-like quality, similar to that of playing with toy cars in home-made dioramas but this time for children-at-heart.

The Nethercutt Collection and Museum, 15200 Bledsoe St., Sylmar, CA. 91432: a nostalgically immaculate veteran, vintage, and classic automotive past

The Nethercutt Collection and Museum, Sylmar, is about a 20–30-minute drive north of LA on I-5. According to its brochure it is a: 'world class treasure trove of prize-winning automobiles', but the Museum's vast exhibition hall is row upon row upon row of more than 100 significant, immaculate automobiles that overwhelms simply due to the scale of the display as well as the fact that it is self-guided. The Collection nearby requires a pre-booked guided tour and offers the Lower Salon (25 vehicles, 1900–1940s), the Grand Salon (30 vehicles, 1910–1930s), and the Mezzanine (automobilia).

J.B. Nethercutt (1913–2004) and his wife Dorothy (d. 2004) shared a love of classic automobiles and opened the Museum, which has always had free admission, in 1971. Nethercutt's fortune was made through working with his aunt Merle Nethercutt Norman's cosmetics business. The website notes that Nethercutt once observed somewhat ambiguously: 'It would suit me well if what people remembered about me was 'Where he went, he left beauty behind'.

At the Nethercutt

Entering The Nethercutt Collection (not The Museum) is rather like walking into an aircraft hangar full to overflowing with immaculate old cars parked on bad floral carpet. When asked about marque or model order, or sequence, or the availability of a plan of the layout, the desk attendant observed airily 'There isn't any – start wherever you want'. Not exactly a promising, or courteous, beginning.

A single automobile on the left after entering was a spectacular 1934 Packard Le Baron Phaeton with 'Hussy' licence plates. Long story short, 'Hussy' is an abbreviated version of 'Hussey', the family name of the owner of a '34 Packard J.B. wanted to acquire but the owner would not sell. J.B. found a Packard of his own, restored it, and had it painted a rich red that eventually formed the basis of a Merle Norman cosmetic range of the same name. Along from the 'Hussy' Packard was a spectacular 1930 Rolls Royce Phantom II Town Car that exemplified the

Gatsby-esque excesses of the period. It is probably no surprise that the Collection is all about a flawless past. The only patina evident is the high gloss of expensive restoration on vehicles that were stratospherically expensive in the midst of a shattering economic crisis. There is no broad historical address at the Nethercutt; the Collection has been hermetically sealed.

One unexpected but engaging echo of the Petersen's *Southern California*: *Vacationland USA* was a 1937 Pierce-Arrow Enclosed-Drive Limousine (read: sedan) ($4953.00 new) towing a 1936 Pierce-Arrow Travelodge Trailer ($1282.00 new) but, once again, this was not vacationing for the masses but further privileging already privileged narratives. There is some attempt at contextualizing the majority of vehicles but the information plaques only provide manufacturer details and a few descriptive sentences on each vehicle's history and Nethercutt ownership. Margalit's notion of nostalgia being located in a time of purity and innocence can only be infrequently applied at the Nethercutt simply because there is a predominantly jaded air of fetishizing each fabulous object; the idealizing has already been taken care of. Similarly, Chase and Shaw's notion of the failed present is pertinent; the automotive present simply cannot compete with the glories of the Nethercutt past.

The Nethercutt Museum across the way from the Collection has a smaller cohort of cars over two levels in very ornate interiors that celebrate columns, chandeliers, and ceiling frescoes in a Sylmar Sistine Chapel of sorts. The observations above can also be applied to the extraordinary marques of the Museum – more of the same, really, except now in a marble mausoleum. The reverential importance of the Museum setting and its automobiles means that entry is only via a pre-booked, two-hour-guided tour, so no unruly walk-ins allowed.

Perhaps the most spectacular Museum exhibit is the 1933 Duesenberg Model SJ Arlington Torpedo Sedan that cost $20,000 in the depths of the Depression, and was 'the hit' of the 1933–1934 Chicago World's Fair. No mention of the Depression is made on the Duesy's information plaque – unemployment and homelessness are the stuff of nightmares, not dreams, and might distract the visitor from the Museum's constructed core business of selective nostalgic automotive enlightenment. Lubar's proposal that museums must address 'the rich interplay of history and memory, reminiscence and research' (1997: 405) appears to have been overlooked due to sustaining the single Nethercutt narrative. Jeremiah (1995) also emphasized that collections need to be continually re-evaluated in light of new meanings; alas, at the Nethercutt, no such light shines.

Mullin Automotive Museum, 1421 Emerson Ave., Oxnard, CA. 93033: European automotive nostalgia as high art

The Mullin Automotive Museum's primary charter is to present the great craftsmen-built automobiles of the Art Deco era – Bugatti, Delage, Delahaye, Talbot-Lago and Voisin – in a purpose built space that permits the visitor maximum proximity, with information plaques identifying the vehicles and providing a couple of background paragraphs. French furnishings and decorative arts, many from the Museum's Carlo Bugatti collection, are also on display. The Mullin collection focuses on the elegance and luxury of a bygone era but also offers, as a counterpoint, a number of 'barn finds' – classics unearthed in a state of neglect and displayed as found – as well as a 1925 Bugatti Type 27 Brescia Torpedo recovered from Italy's Lago Maggiore in 2009 shown in a dedicated, darkened gallery that illuminates the drama of its skeletal metallic remains.

Peter Mullin, a retired Los Angeles financier, is chairman emeritus of Mullin TBG and developed a passion after his first sighting of a Delahaye. He opened the Museum, which has a car collection and a decorative art collection, in April 2010. Mullin lives with his wife Merle (another Merle) in Brentwood.

At the Mullin

The Mullin's display space is basically one big gallery, and a mezzanine filled with all things Bugatti, and both are energetic and exhilarating – nostalgia here is about creativity and passion and exemplary design that thrilled in the past, and still pulses with life; automotive artisans rule at the Mullin.

The museum's layout and arrangement of vehicles is intended to evoke the Paris Auto Salons (Mason, 2011: D1) which means enough space for inspections at close proximity. The Mullin, according to the museum's brochure is: 'an homage to … Art Deco and (the) machine age – eras that produced exquisite art and magnificent automobiles'. Quite a charter, and one that is thoroughly fulfilled. The informing spirit of French Art Deco has shaped the collection and the cars and art are, without exception, extraordinary. Chawkins' (2010) by-line was 'Oxnard car collector exhibits more than 100 vintage French luxury vehicles with histories as exotic as their looks' which nailed it completely. The Mullin is about *automobiles de luxe sans barrières* in a dedicated space informed by a spectatorial *esprit de corps*. If there are eagle eyed attendants they epitomize discretion, but visitors observed by this author have always been suitably reverent towards all of the museum's collections on exhibit

Where to start with the automobiles? Why not with *Le Vision de Voisin*, an exhibition that offered an impressive overview of Gabriel Voisin (1880–1973) and his career. On exhibit were seventeen Voisin vehicles including the 1935 Avions Voisin C25 Aerodyne, winner of the Best of Show trophy, 2011 Pebble Beach *Concours d'Élégance*. Regular floor talks illuminated the remarkable diversity of the displayed Voisins and, judging by those present, what may have seemed a rather esoteric theme was attracting large, enthusiastic crowds. Voisin's relative obscurity may have had an appeal that was consolidated by the Pebble Beach win, so those keen to see the C25 Aerodyne had to experience the exhibition as well. Voisin's annotated drawings and sketches, illuminating personal correspondence, family memorabilia, photography and some film, as well as scale models further enriched the broad range of vehicles, six of which were from the Mullin collection.

Le Vision de Voisin was a nostalgic reflection on, and tribute to, Voisin's lifetime commitment to realizing his innovative and creative automotive vision through a critical lens. There was no sense of a distorted past, but instead more of a tacit understanding that visionaries such as Voisin are less evident in the contemporary automotive milieu.

One final Mullin moment must revere the bold exhibition of the 1925 Bugatti Type 27 Brescia Torpedo recovered from Italy's *Lago Maggiore* in 2009. The Brescia display strategy could not be simpler, but is so richly resonant that it deserves more than a footnote. The Mullin version of the story has the Brescia submerged (but attached to a float) in 1936 to avoid fees and taxes. The float perished, the car sank to the lake bottom and lay on its side in the mud for 73 years, was duly raised, sold on, and now fascinates those who behold the dimly-lit wreck in Oxnard. Whilst the Mullin is an undisputed automotive treasure trove, there is something indefinably compelling about the remains, the side buried in mud intact-*ish*, the other, exposed to the water for three quarters of a century, a rusted, skeletal ghost of all Bugattis past. If you visit the Mullin, don't miss it.

The Murphy Auto Museum, 2230 Statham Blvd, Oxnard, CA. 93033: automotive nostalgia as garage sale

A two-minute drive from the Mullin is the Murphy Auto Museum, the approach of which is much more garage sale than Mullin high art chic. Admittance to the Murphy was via a modest payment to an elderly gentleman sitting beside an only slightly more elderly Model T Ford. Once inside it becomes apparent that the randomness of the display – apart from a posse of posh Packards – most resembles a time–warp car park rather than a carefully curated collection. There is, however, appeal in the casual approach to display – some vehicles were for sale, giving the impression that it is more of a storage facility than a museum.

Retired neurosurgeon Dr Dan Murphy founded the non-profit museum in Ventura in 2002, moving to the current Oxnard location in 2005. According to the refreshed website, the museum's ownership and administration was, however, recently transferred to: 'Ventura County business owner and car enthusiast, David Neel. His love of automobiles and his commitment to the Museum's mission statement will ensure its existence into perpetuity'.

At the Murphy

Driving into the Murphy car park an embellishment on an external wall is perhaps an early indicator of the Museum's quirky, informing spirit. A six inch 'slice' of a red 1955 Packard Clipper's passenger side 'floats' on the white painted wall rather like an ascending saint, with mother looking out the front window, and two youngsters beaming from the rear. Neither mother nor children appear distressed, which is a relief, so maybe the rising Packard hints at a museum charter aiming to 'elevate' the automobile to greater heights. Maybe.

The Murphy has an engaging, almost endearing 'collection' of vehicles that run the gamut from a 1903 Curved dash Oldsmobile to a 2008 Ford Mustang Shelby 500KR, although not all vehicles are on display at once due to space restrictions.

Many on display, however, have a lived-in patina, such as the Continental Mark II with a large dent and missing paint on the rear left panel and a puddle of what appeared to be transmission fluid leaking from underneath. The display also includes randomly placed life-sized, faceless mannequins decked out in a range of period clothing, perhaps to encourage historical verisimilitude but only adding a slightly unsettling, frisson.

It becomes apparent upon entering the Murphy that despite the specific title of 'Auto Museum' it is more a multi-purpose venue, consolidated by the 'Vintage Clothing' and 'Model Trains' content; yes, the 'huge model railroad display is certain to enthral' but it didn't; show me the cars.

The overall ambiance is rather garage-sale like, with vehicles displayed in more of a random than chronological order, although some linkages can be made. A red and white '60 Corvette began the Murphy encounter, accompanied by a face-less, tough guy mannequin in a trench coat and fedora which tends to counterpoint the *Route 66* TV show moment evoked by the Corvette.

The vista from the entrance into the museum is fluorescent bright, model trains to the left and cars ahead and to the right that included a couple of Cadillacs, more Corvettes, a coral and white '57 Ford Fairlane 500 Sunliner Retractable and '50 Ford Woody, the aforementioned Continental Mark II and a '58 Lincoln Continental Mark III, a fine '60 Imperial Le Baron, and nine or so Packards from a '37 V12 sedan to a pair of '55 Caribbeans. Other, quirky content included a '24 Chevrolet 'Housecar', literally a cobbled together shack on wheels, and a '55 Bentley R Type. Each vehicle in the collection was nostalgically resonant, an inevitability given their respective histories and marque heritages, but perhaps it was the lack of display linkages and limited space precluding close inspection that may have contributed to a degree of frustration. Apart from the Packard posse there was little thematic connectivity, hence the jumble sale analogy.

The Murphy collection is not without nostalgic appeal and whilst an idealization of sorts is evident – the vehicles are privileged through display, indicating decisions have been made relating to the museum context – there is little attempt to specifically locate the collection in either a historical or temporal sense. There is significant evidence of the past, as Chase and Shaw require, but nothing that suggests such an outcome is a result of the failed present; some of the outfits of the faceless mannequins, however, indicate the past also has its share of fashion failures.

The lack of any automotive narrative at the Murphy, focused or otherwise, is conspicuous by its absence. There is no evidence of critical interrogation of any aspect of automobility, nor any attempt at locating or contextualising mobilities in local, state or national contexts. Assumptions about nostalgic motivation and response generating connectivity between museum and visitor would be misplaced as no consideration of socio-cultural and economic impacts, or industrial legacy, is provided. There is also no indication at the Murphy of Clark's noting that a minimum expectation of the museum sector now is dynamic engagement (2013: 286–287) nor is there any evidence of Müller's assertion that current visitors have experience and knowledge that must not only be considered but also acknowledged when the museum 'message' is being constructed (2012: 495).

Finally, the Murphy website has had a recent makeover and reports that there is now a promising program of upcoming 2014 exhibits and events that include 'Pickups and Station Wagons'; 'Glamping (glamorous camping) and Vintage Trailer Show'; 'Modernism at the Murphy'; and 'Big American V8 Power'. At the Murphy change, finally, seems to be afoot.

Back on the road again …

Each of the four automotive museums discussed offer opportunities for the visitor to engage with various approaches to, and constructs of, exhibiting automobility. The single and shared informing spirit in the four contexts is, however, the multiple influences and processes that together constitute what is collectively experienced and understood as nostalgia. In the context of automobility the nostalgic response can be generated by a glimpse of tailfin, rusted remains, exquisite coachwork, or a spill of transmission fluid on a linoleum floor. Nostalgia can be deeply felt when recalling family cars, or the turning of an ignition key for the first time, or just driving through Hollywood and seeing bright swathes of chrome on insolent chariots sparkle, just like the old days, in real Los Angeles sunshine.

References

Bahr, E. (2007) *Weimar on the Pacific: German Exile Culture in Los Angeles and the Crisis of Modernism*. Berkeley: University of California Press.

Barndt. K. (2007) Fordist Nostalgia: History and Experience at The Henry Ford, *Rethinking History* 11 (3), 379–410.

Brook, V. (2013) *Land of Smoke and Mirrors: A Cultural History of Los Angeles*. New Brunswick: Rutgers University Press.

Brownlow, K. (1968) *The Parade's Gone By …* London: Abacus.

Chase, M. and Shaw, C. (1989) The Dimensions of Nostalgia. In C. Shaw and M. Chase. (eds) *The Imagined Past: history and nostalgia* (pp. 1–17). Manchester: Manchester University Press.

Chawkins, S. (2010) Auto museum displays the crème of the crop – Online document http://articles.latimes.com/print/2010/may/08/local/la-me-automuseum-20100508

Christopher, N. (1997) *Somewhere in the Night: Film Noir and the American City*. The Free Press: New York.

Clark, J. (2010) The 'rough and tumble': displaying complexity in the motor museum, *Museum Management and Curatorship* 25 (2), 219–234.

Clark, J. (2013) Peopling the Public History of Motoring: Men, Machines, and Museums, *Curator: The Museum Journal* 56 (2), 279–287.

Cohen, S. (2013) Beloved vintage cars in 'Gangster Squad', *The Atlanta Journal-Constitution*, January 14th, D5.

Cowan, R. (1983) *More Work for Mother: The Ironies of Household Technology from the Open Hearth to the Microwave*. New York: Basic Books.

Devine, K. (2014) Removing the rough edges? Nostalgia and storytelling at a UK museum, *Consumption Markets and Culture* 17 (2), 208–214.

Dimendberg, E. (2004) *Film Noir and the Spaces of Modernity*. Cambridge, MA: Harvard University Press.

Divall, C. (2003) Transport museums: another kind of historiography, *The Journal of Transport History* 24 (2), 259–265.

Gartman, D. (1994) *Auto Opium: A Social History of Automobile Design*. London: Routledge.

Hatton, A. (2012) The conceptual roots of modern museum management dilemmas, *Museum Management and Curatorship* 27 (2), 129–147.

Hennigan, W. (2012) Vaulting into car history at the Petersen museum – Online document http://articles.latimes.com/2012/dec/25/business/la-fi-petersen-auto-vault-20121226

Jeremiah, D. (1995) The motor car from road to museum, *International Journal of Heritage Studies* 1 (3), 171–179.

Jeremiah, D. (1998) The Formation and Legacy of Britain's First Motor Museum, *Journal of the History of Collections* 10 (1), 93–112.

Jeremiah, D. (2003) Museums and the History and Heritage of British Motoring, *International Journal of Heritage Studies* 9 (2), 169–190.

Kay, J. (1997) *Asphalt Nation: How the Automobile Took Over America and How We Can Take It Back*. Berkeley: University of California Press.

Kim, H. (2005) Research Note, *Nostalgia and Tourism Tourism Analysis* 10, 85–88.

Kunstler, J. (1993) *The Geography of Nowhere: The Rise and Decline of America's Man-Made Landscape*. New York: Simon and Schuster.

Lacey, R. (1986) *Ford: The Men and the Machine*. London: Pan Books.

Lehto, S. (2010) *Chrysler's Turbine Car: The Rise and Fall of Detroit's Coolest Creation* Chicago: Chicago Review Press.

Lewis, L. (2000) *Roadside America: The Automobile and the American Dream*. NY: Harry N. Abrams, Inc.

Lubar, S. (1997) Exhibiting Memories. In A. Henderson and A. Kaeppler (eds) *Exhibiting Dilemmas: Issues of Representation at the Smithsonian* (pp. 15–27). Washington: Smithsonian Institution Press.

Margalit, A. (2011) *Nostalgia Psychoanalytic Dialogues* 21, 271–280.

Mason, D. (2011) Paris via Oxnard: Museum houses collection of French automobiles, *Santa Barbara News-Press*, July 13, D1, D8.

Morales R. (1986) The Los Angeles automobile industry in historical perspective, *Environment and Planning D: Society and Space* 4 (3), 289–303

Mottram, E. (1989) *Blood on the Nash Ambassador: Investigations in American Culture*. Hutchinson Radius: London, UK.

Müller, R. (2012) Museums designing for the future: some perspectives confronting German technical and industrial museums in the twenty-first century, *International Journal of Heritage Studies* 19 (5), 511–528.

Osteen, M. (2008) Noir's Cars: Automobility and Amoral Space in American Film Noir, *Journal of Popular Film and Television* 35 (4), 183–192.

Peary, D. (1986) *Cult Movies 2*. London: Vermilion.

Pekarik, A. and Schreiber, J. (2012) The Power of Expectation, *Curator: The Museum Journal* 55 (4), 487–496.

Robinson, H. (2012) Remembering things differently: museums, libraries and archives as memory institutions and the implications for convergence, *Museum Management and Curatorship* 27 (2), 413–429.

Schindler, R. and Holbrook, M. (2003) Nostalgia for Early Experience as a Determinant of Consumer Preferences, *Psychology and Marketing* 20 (4), 275–302.

3 The Bricklin

From automobile to place narrative

Lee Jolliffe

Automobile production inevitably becomes part of the narrative of a place. The stories of specialty automobiles produced for a short period have thus become part of the local lore, legends and character of many places. Once out of production automobiles are valued for their heritage, becoming collectable by private individuals who may use or display them as well as by public institutions such as museums where they may be exhibited (Clark, 2010). The unique narrative of a place can have local appeal developing a sense of community around a shared history and can in addition play a role in destination development and marketing. A number of authors have acknowledged the power of narrative in shaping places as tourist destinations. Jamal and Hill (2004) discussed the role of place, or placeness in developing authenticity in cultural and heritage tourism. Graham and Howard (2008) observed that heritage is one of the main means of establishing identity. These authors indicate that heritage can be shaped into a cultural resource. Heritage is also now widely seen as a resource for economic development (Ashworth, 2014).

In Canada the narrative of place and heritage related to automobile production includes the historical production of cars such as the LeRoy, the Russell, the Tudhope, the Thomas, the Galt and others, including the Bricklin (White, 2007). This chapter focuses on the narrative related to the Bricklin, a sports car produced briefly in the province of New Brunswick in the 1970's. The emphasis of the chapter is on examining the story of this car in relation to place, tracing its transition from a specialty car to a collectable car to part of the local narrative commemorated in various ways. The story of the Bricklin in relationship to that of the DeLorean is also briefly considered.

The place

New Brunswick, is one of Canada's three Maritime provinces, located just north of Maine (United States of America) and bordering the provinces of Quebec and Nova Scotia. The rural economy of the province has been known for forestry, mining, mixed farming and fishing whereas the industrial economy has historically, been dominated by shipbuilding, oil refining, forestry production, and food production. In the 1970's the Premier of the province, Richard Hatfield was looking to attract investment to the province to boost the economy (Fredericks and Chambers, 1977). One of his initiatives was to invest in the production of the

Bricklin, advocated by entrepreneur Malcolm Briklin, in hopes of establishing an auto industry in the province. Bricklin had been responsible for introducing the Subaru to America and had a dream of establishing his own automobile company. He sold the New Brunswick government of the time, led by Premier Richard Hatfield on granting generous government subsidies (1974–1976) into the production of the Bricklin SV-1 automobile in New Brunswick, a location not know for automobile production (Fredericks and Chambers, 1977).

The car

In 1974 Entrepreneur Malcolm Bricklin had persuaded the New Brunswick government to invest in a scheme for the production of his gull-winged luxury automobile, the Bricklin (White, 2007). The possibility of economic development and the lure of producing an automobile in the province were attractive to the young premier, Richard Hatfield. The main plant was officially opened in Saint John August 6, 1974. The cars were designed in Michigan, assembled in New Brunswick (plants in both Saint John and Minto) and marketed in the United States. However, the unique sports automobile with gull-wing doors and an acrylic body was only produced in New Brunswick, Canada for a short period from 1974 to early 1976. As sales did not meet projections the company went into receivership in 1976 after producing only 2,854 vehicles costing the New Brunswick government almost $25 million (Andrews, 2013).

The collapse of the project can be attributed in part to world conditions for automobile production and start-up problems as well as the inefficiencies of the Bricklin organization (with cars designed in Michigan, produced in NB, financial records kept in New York and the organization directed by Bricklin from Phoenix, Arizona) as well as the incompetence of management (Fredericks, 1977). Bricklin himself, the flamboyant entrepreneur reportedly underestimated the cost of launching a new car brand, did not understand the problems involved in the engineering of a car and went into production without a completed production model. White (2007) indicates that the cars were technically flawed and were never taken seriously. Projections for sales of the Bricklin were also not achieved (Fredericks, 1977).

The story of the Bricklin Car Company has been studied as a case of failed entrepreneurship within a mature sector of the economy (Anastakis, 2010). Canada has a long history of car production, but mostly in terms of assembling cars in partnership with producers in the United States (White, 2007). As noted above the shortcomings of the firm in terms of lack of experience and poor organization crippled the company. Government investment in the car also reportedly represented poor decision making on the part of the Province of New Brunswick and its Premier, Richard Hatfield (Anastakis, 2010).

The Bricklin in the place narrative

Culture related to cars includes not only the cars but also documentation and expressions of related histories such as oral and written histories expressed through songs and the popular media (books and magazines etc.). With the production of any car and then its subsequent collection (tangible) and interpretation (intangible) the automobiles and their history become part of the heritage that defines a sense of place that can be employed in tourism development.

Various categories of material and oral local culture are related to the Bricklin. This includes the cars themselves that form the main artefact held in both public and private collections, materials commemorating the Bricklin, souvenir objects that might be associated with the car, and events that celebrate the Bricklin, such as the Bricklin collector events that bring together the owners and others interested in the car. The events serve to pass on oral history and create new experiences related to the Bricklin. This reflects the shaping of heritage into cultural products (Graham and Howard, 2008).

This material culture related to the Bricklin, like that of other automobiles, has the potential to expand the interpretation of motoring beyond production into the use of the autos by people (Clark, 2010). There is thus the possibility for the traditional exhibits of heritage vehicles to be expanded beyond the focus on the automobile itself, to incorporate its ownership and use, thus potentially engaging with new audiences and telling new stories. In the case of the Bricklin, exhibitions related to this automobile could be used to tell the story of the New Brunswick Government of the day and their urgent desire for economic development, as well as to interpret the challenges of entrepreneurship (Anastakis, 2010). As Clark (2013) notes this would require a dramatic shift in the curatorial attitudes towards the exhibition of the automobile. In the case of New Brunswick and the Bricklin the story is also to some extent a political one, interwoven with the Progressive Conservative party and their Premier of the time, and the only institutions in the province capable of telling this story (New Brunswick Museum in Saint John and Automotive Museum in Edmundston) are part of the provincial system of museums, primarily funded and administered by the province.

Ownership of the Bricklin, which was somewhat advanced in terms of its design can also be seen as part of contemporary mobility (Merriman, 2009). Clark (2010) notes that motor museums are traditionally conservative in style, exhibiting cars in a static mode, while operationally they were all about motion and mobility. The complex history of motoring and its relationship to people is thus not often interpreted in a comprehensive manner (Kaminski and Smith, 2013).

The Bricklin as artefact

According to (Clark, 2010) motor vehicles in museums are presented either as symbols of speed, art and prestige, or in a social history context. Automobiles may be presented in specialized museums dedicated to motor vehicles, or in the context of more general science and technology or history museums (Jeremiah, 1995). At a number of museums around the world the Bricklin automobile is found as part of the collection (See Table 3.1).

Table 3.1 Bricklin cars in museums

Museum	Location	Details
New Brunswick Museum	Saint John, New Brunswick, Canada	This white Bricklin is part of the permanent collection of the provincial museum.
Museum of Science and Technology	Ottawa, Ontario, Canada	This fully restored white Bricklin is part of the museum's permanent collection.
Haynes International Motor Museum	Sparksford, Somerset, England	This Bricklin is orange.
Western Development Museum	Moose Jaw, Saskatchewan, Canada	This white Bricklin is part of the museum's permanent collection.
America's Car Museum	Tacoma, Washington, USA	An orange Bricklin is on exhibit.
Ontario Science Centre	Toronto, Ontario, Canada	In 1976 as part of the promotion for the Bricklin a model cut in half was exhibited to showcase design features.

Source: Adapted from various sources including the web pages of the Bricklin International Owners Club at http://www.bricklin.org/index.htm and Bricklin SV-1 from http://en.wikipedia.org/wiki/Bricklin_SV-1.

Why do museums hold the Bricklin automobile in their collections? In a few cases (i.e. the Ontario Science Centre) museums were given the automobile as a promotion during the period that the car was being marketed to the public. In other cases, the Bricklin automobile is integral to the story of economic development and politics in New Brunswick, for example referring to the holdings of the provincially owned Automobile Museum in Saint-Jacques (the car that Richard Hatfield probably used in the 1974 election campaign in the province) the car has reportedly been at the museum since the beginning of the tourist season in 1980. The New Brunswick Museum has at times also exhibited a white Bricklin in their Transportation Gallery.

These museum exhibits encapsulate some of the appeal of the Bricklin, as a car and an icon of progress in New Brunswick where it was manufactured, and as Clark (2010) indicates such heritage related to the automobile exhibited in museums can encapsulate the sense of motoring in the past. They also provide a focus for interpreting to visitors the story of the Bricklin and especially its place in regional economic development at a certain point in Eastern Canada. It is also part of a provincial political story of a particular era. The Bricklin was featured in one of Richard Hatfield's political campaigns, with the Premier pulling up in a flashy Bricklin being symbolic of the economic development priorities of his government. As part of the place narrative of New Brunswick two provincially owned museums in the province thus have Bricklin's in their collection, the New Brunswick Museum in Saint John and the Automobile Museum in Saint-Jacques.

Commemorating the Bricklin

The Bricklin has become part of the oral history and popular culture of New Brunswick. A number of documentary films have been made about the Bricklin, and its place in the history of New Brunswick and indeed Canada. There have been numerous press articles with a focus on the Bricklin (for example, Holloway, 2003). As an icon the car has had cameo appearances in a number of films, although none with as much impact as The DeLorean car had as a key part of the film, *Back to the Future* (1985).

The museum exhibitions discussed above to a certain extent commemorate the short history of production of the Bricklin as well as celebrate the activity of collecting the car. In addition, the Canada postal service issued a commemorative stamp June 8, 1996 while the Canadian mint issued a commemorative coin in 2003. These items are also available as souvenirs.

The Bricklin has also thus lived on in a number of media that have documented and interpreted the story of the car. This has included a book, a song, a play, souvenirs and events, that are discussed below. These cultural expressions and items of material culture related to the car can potentially act as resources for interpreting and packaging the story of the Bricklin into a consumable tourism product.

The book

While several books have been written about the Bricklin the most comprehensive, simply called Bricklin (Fredericks and Chambers, 1977) essentially documents the story of the Bricklin, providing a resource not only on the production of the car but on the contemporary political situation that influenced both the establishment and closing down of the Bricklin production.

The play

In 2009 The Fredericton Playhouse (Canada) commissioned a play about the story of the Bricklin. As part of Fredericton's 2009 Cultural Capital of Canada designation the Playhouse received both Federal and Provincial funds to commission the writing of the play about the made in New Brunswick car (Fredericton Tourism, 2011). The play, entitled 'The Bricklin: An Automotive Fantasy' was premiered in the summer of 2010, traces the rise and fall of efforts to build the car in New Brunswick. The play had short theatre runs in both the summers of 2010 and 2011, attracting the interest of media and tourists. However, as a tourism product, it was somewhat limited, as indicated by a representative of Fredericton Tourism interviewed for this chapter, there is interest in the story of the Bricklin, however to build a consistent tourism product focusing on motoring heritage other components would have to be available, such as exhibitions and events. Fredericton does have some other car events organized by local car clubs, but most of their focus is on local and regional collectors and as such they lack a broad appeal to tourists.

Examining the relevance of the theatrical performance to place and the ability of New Brunswick to export products around the globe (Andrews, 2013) concludes that 'The Bricklin: An Automotive Fantasy thus becomes a model of local and provincial self-sufficiency that employs nostalgia and historical economic failure to create a potentially brighter future' (p. 44). A link to the global export of the local story of the Bricklin is also reflected by the Fredericton Playhouse's March 2013 agreement for rights to perform The Bricklin with the Old Timers Garage Theatre and Musical Club in Katowice, Poland. This is only one indicator that the cultural impact of the story of the Bricklin resonates beyond its origins in New Brunswick. This perhaps reinforces and is reflective of the international interest in the Bricklin by collectors.

The song

In addition there has been a satirical song 'The Bricklin by Charlie Russell' (Rosenberg, 1978). First published in 1975 'The Bricklin' was a satirical folk song by local radio personality and performer Charlie Russell, reflecting the popular culture of the time regarding the Bricklin. It was recorded by Russell and was featured in the background of many of the news stories about the car. As quoted at the beginning of this chapter the song encapsulated the story of the appeal of the car to then premier Richard Hatfield in terms of local economic development but also the fears of the locals that production would be short lived.

The souvenirs

At the collapse of the company in 1976, only 2,854 cars had been produced. From this point the cars, due to their uniqueness and limited supply became collectable, and could be viewed as souvenirs or mementos of that short-lived production of this specialty automobile. This trend is now best represented by the presence of the Bricklin International Owners Club. The club has also produced and made available Bricklin related souvenirs, the web site classifies Bricklin paraphernalia as 'Bricklinalia'. Proceeds from souvenir sales support the activities of the club. The 'Bricklinalia' available includes for example: shirts and caps, coffee cups and champagne glasses, key rings, posters and watches as well as reproduction Bricklin Owners ID cards and service manuals (Bricklin International Owners Club, n.d.). These are particular objects that identify those using these objects as either owners or aficionados of the car. Besides being available on-line the souvenirs can be purchased at Bricklin related events. However, unlike the DeLorean souvenirs for a time available at a specialty shop in Belfast (see Chapter 5) the Bricklin souvenirs are not widely available in New Brunswick.

The events

Events focused on the Bricklin include annual meet-ups of owners, for example the 'Back to the Nest' event scheduled for July 31, and August 1–5, 2014 in

Saint John, New Brunswick to celebrate the 40th anniversary of the start of production of the car in the city. These events are of some value to tourism as they do bring Bricklin owners and their families back to New Brunswick and to Saint John in particular, while attracting visitors who are interested in car related events. Jeremiah (1995) identifies three themes through which the history of the motorcar and motoring heritage can be accessed as heritage: motoring landscape, pursuit of performance and cult of ownership, so Bricklin owners are contributing to the public access to motoring history. However, they require marketing beyond a local and fan market (such as the Bricklin International Owners Club) in order to be effective as tourism products (McKercher *et al.*, 2006).

Connections to the DeLorean

The Bricklin is also linked, if only through folklore to the DeLorean, another distinctive sports car produced briefly in Belfast, Northern Ireland (see Chapter 5). Vance (2011) observes that the similarities between the stories of the two cars and their promoters are inescapable. Both had flamboyant promoters (Malcolm Bricklin and John DeLorean) who had associations with the Detroit automobile industry. It is not clear if the two entrepreneurs met, but the timing of their production ventures (Bricklin prototype 1972 and production 1974–1976, DeLorean prototype 1976 and production 1981–1983) indicates that there may have been some synergies through common knowledge. White (2007) even indicates that John DeLorean considered setting up production in Eastern Canada for his gull-winged sports car, but found more generous subsidies in Northern Ireland and thus set up his operations there. The two proponents had dreams of creating their own sports car brand and both found economically depressed maritime jurisdictions (albeit on different sides of the Atlantic) that were keen to take up production on the hopes and dreams of the car production bringing prosperity to the local economies. The political leaders at both locations were keen to find 'good news' for the development of their respective economies.

What the Bricklin and the DeLorean owners do have in common now is a love of their gull-winged door sports cars, celebrated at joint events such as the Bricklin National Meet and DeLorean Car Show and Convention 2014 nicknamed, 'The Big Gullwing Super Show' scheduled for June 11–15, 2014 in Dayton, Ohio. According to the web site of the Bricklin International Owners event 150 DeLoreans and 40 Bricklins were expected to attend the event which will include a show of the cars, a visit to the Packard Museum and also to a private car collection as well as many social occasions (dinners and receptions) where DeLorean and Bricklin owners can swap stories and anecdotes about their collectable cars.

Discussion

When the Bricklin production ceased in 1976 the cars produced (as object and artefact) and the stories connected with the short-lived production became the stuff of heritage and part of the place narrative of the province of New Brunswick.

Expressions of that narrative are readily found within the province and sometimes beyond in the form of various media (documentaries, a play, a book, a song as well as souvenirs and events). That the two provincially owned museums telling the story of transportation and automobiles in the province each hold a Bricklin in their collections is significant, not only as part of the entrepreneurial story of the place, but as a reflection of the politics of the time of production, when the then Premier used the Bricklin as his campaign car and a sign of progress within his jurisdiction. The collectors of the Bricklin have also contributed to keeping the legend alive, through their clubs and meets, often in collaboration with owners of the DeLorean with whom they share common interests in collecting, using and exhibiting these two cars, both with gull-winged doors.

However, for heritage as a commodity to be transformed for consumption by both locals and tourists requires both interest and resources. The Bricklin, with its rich folklore surrounding its production certainly has potential to be transformed into a product for heritage tourism, however so far the story has only been transformed into museum exhibits and a play, the latter which has had several limited runs, one within the province and one internationally. The potential for product development related to the Bricklin may also be limited by its political connections to a story of failed entrepreneurship within the province (Andrews, 2013) and by the limited market of automotive enthusiasts willing to consume heritage related Bricklin products and experiences.

Conclusion

The legend of the Bricklin in relation to New Brunswick politics and entrepreneurship lives on, in part reflected by the exhibition of the Bricklin in provincial museums. There is potential for special tours using a Bricklin, particularly in Saint John, which was the major production centre for the car. This could appeal to the cruise market as a unique shore excursion. For Bricklin enthusiasts there would also be potential for a tour of the places in Saint John and Minto, New Brunswick associated with the production of the car, culminating with a visit to the New Brunswick Museum, where a Bricklin is sometimes on exhibit. The Bricklin car on exhibit at the Automobile Museum in Edmundston, New Brunswick could also be a focal point for a future expanded Bricklin exhibit at the museum and or a Bricklin festival that could draw car history enthusiasts and Bricklin collectors to visit. Being part of the story of New Brunswick a Bricklin exhibit could also be used to engage local visitors with other issues related to automobiles, such as safety as suggested by Clark (2010).

The Bricklin makes for an interesting case in terms of the contribution of a local automobile to the place narrative. It certainly is part of the story of New Brunswick, but is a relatively small part of the place narrative, with only small reminders of its existence. Nonetheless, the fact that the Bricklin is collectable with an international club of collectors forms a subtle link to the place of assembly, New Brunswick, whenever the cars are exhibited at events.

References

Anastakis, D., 2010. Hubris, Nepotism, and Failure: The Bricklin Car Company and the Question of Inevitability. *Business and Economic History On-line*, Volume 8, http://www.thebhc.org/sites/default/files/anastakis.pdf

Andrews, J., 2013. Reading The Bricklin: Narrating the Place of Dreaming in an Era of Self-Sufficiency. *Journal of New Brunswick Studies/Revue d'études sur le Nouveau-Brunswick* 4, 31–46.

Ashworth, G., 2014. Heritage and Economic Development: Selling the Unsellable. *Heritage & Society* 7, 3–17.

Clark, J., 2010. The "rough and tumble": displaying complexity in the motor museum. *Museum Management and Curatorship* 25, 219–234. doi:10.1080/09647771003737331

Clark, J., 2013. Peopling the Public History of Motoring: Men, Machines, and Museums. *Curator: The Museum Journal* 56, 279–287.

Fredericks, H.A., and Chambers, A., 1977. *Bricklin*. Brunswick Press, Fredericton, N.B.

Fredericton Tourism, 2011. What's New in Fredericton 2011–2012 (Spring 2011). Accessed at http://www.tourismfredericton.ca/en/ June 2, 2014.

Graham, B. and Howard, P., 2008. *The Ashgate Research Companion to Heritage and Identity*. Farnham: Ashgate.

Holloway, A., 2003. Live and learn Meet Malcolm Bricklin, the man behind the Bricklin sports car. *Canadian Business*, 76, 28–29.

Jeremiah, D., 1995. The motor car from road to museum. *International Journal of Heritage Studies* 1, 171–179.

Kaminski, J., and Smith, G., 2013. 15 'Mobile heritage'. *Contemporary Issues in Cultural Heritage Tourism* 218.

McKercher, B., Mei, W.S., and Tse, T.S., 2006. Are short duration cultural festivals tourist attractions? *Journal of Sustainable Tourism* 14, 55–66.

Merriman, P., 2009. Automobility and the Geographies of the Car. *GEC3 Geography Compass 3*, 586–599.

Rosenberg, N.V., 1978. Goodtime Charlie and the Bricklin: A Satirical Song in Context. Presented at the Oral History Forum d'histoire orale. 3(1) http://www.oralhistoryforum.ca/index.php/ohf/issue/view/31.

White, R., 2007. *Making cars in Canada: a brief history of the Canadian automotive industry, 1900–1980*. Canada Science and Technology Museum, Ottawa.

Vance, B. (2011) Bricklin: Dreams and Disaster in New Brunswick. Accessed April 7, 2015, http://www.autos.ca/classic-cars/bricklin/

4 Assembling heritage tourism

The BMW museum and factory tour

Gregory Ramshaw

Introduction

The role of the backstage in tourism has taken on a significant and applied function in recent years. Goffman's (1959) notion of performance of front and back stages in personal and industrial settings are pertinent, as are MacCannell's (1973) views of how there are multiple constructs of the backstage in touristic locations. However, beyond their social/spatial construction, a revelation of the backstage is both a commercial and a quality concern for contemporary businesses. Many venues have commodified backstage spaces, providing tourists and other interested parties an opportunity to see and experience locations normally hidden from public view. Backstage tours are particularly prominent at sporting venues (Gammon and Fear, 2007; Ramshaw and Gammon, 2010) and in the brewing/distillery industry (Plummer *et al.*, 2005), but they have become commonplace in other industries as well. In part, this may also be part of a broader notion of truth, morality, and honesty at the corporate level (MacCannell, 1973). In other words, potential customers – whether they be tourists or not – may also be current or potential clients, and the 'backstage' can provide a connection and intimacy with the product.

Backstage tours may also produce and disseminate particular heritage narratives, such as corporate achievements and history, and product development – that are meant to address contemporary needs and circumstances – be they longevity and gravitas, ties to the local community, distinctiveness from rivals, and quality assurance. In particular, heritage can connect the product to a place, particularly in an age of mobile and flexible capital (Morely and Robbins, 1995). Though tour patrons may already be 'fans' – and, therefore sympathetic to corporate/heritage narratives – many visitors may simply be curious or looking for a unique cultural or educational experience. In essence, by employing heritage narratives in a backstage tour, a company can foster loyalty, provide a subtle sales presentation, and demonstrate ties to region, all under the umbrella of a heritage-based tourist attraction. As discussed in Ramshaw and Gammon's (2010) article regarding tours of Twickenham Stadium in London, the tour acted as a lure for the stadium's commercial products including the souvenir shop, the rentals/catering department, and match tickets. Furthermore, the tour solidified the stadium as an authentic attraction for both die-hard rugby supporters and those merely looking for a glimpse of English sporting culture.

However, backstage tours are one way in which an organization might lure tourists. Frequently, tours are also operated in tandem with a museum where artefacts, exhibitions, and displays are meant to supplement the tour or be a standalone attraction in their own right. Although not all facilities operate a museum and tour, a museum has the potential to act as a Janus-head for the organization, demonstrating both corporate history and future developments, in addition to acting as a kind-of interpretive centre for the tour and facility, helping to make the facility a more interesting full-day attraction, and providing as a commodifiable rental space for special events.

An examination of this heritage attraction – the backstage tour and the corporate museum – is the focus of this chapter with particular attention paid to how both the tour and museum constructs and produces heritage narratives. In other words, this chapter examines what types of heritage narratives are told at the tour/museum and what contemporary purposes – both touristic and otherwise – those heritage narratives serve. The location for this examination is the lone US-based automobile manufacturing plant for BMW, located in Spartanburg, South Carolina, which features both a museum and a backstage tour experience. This examination identified three themes from the tour and museum narratives: plant and production history, quality assurance, and connecting the world to South Carolina and South Carolina to the world. Ultimately, these themes produce three outcomes: creating a sense of aspiration for visitors, that is for the visitors to the tour and museum to aspire to own a BMW vehicle; creating confidence in BMW's products for potential and existing customers; and providing a sense of stability, both in the company's future and in its commitment to South Carolina.

Heritage and cultural production – museums and tours

The notion that cultural products are produced and administered to meet particular corporate outcomes and agendas is not new (Adorno, 2001; Power and Scott, 2001). Heritage, as a cultural product, is also administered to meet current aims, ambitions, and outcomes – be they social, economic, or political (Timothy, 2011). As tourist attractions, heritage sites may propagate – or ignore – specific narratives that help to address current agendas; as tourist attractions, these narratives are also disseminated to a global audience. For example, Ramshaw (2010) examined the narratives at an Olympic sports museum, noting that heritage narratives were manipulated to address two key concerns: attracting and retaining the international tourist market and a dissemination of the organization's current exploits (and thereby place the organization as a present concern) rather than its past feats. Together, these narratives met current economic and political agendas rather than those that were simply historically or culturally significant. Similarly, tours disseminate narratives that are meant to address contemporary concerns. Gammon and Fear's (2007) analysis of a stadium tour in Wales discovered that the tour helped to position the facility as the 'legitimate' home of a team and a certain kind of national identity, particularly as it had replaced a beloved historic stadium that possessed a potent and pervasive cultural symbolism.

The result of heritage being produced to meet certain contemporary ends has, of course, applications for the commercial and corporate world. Many commercial industries use heritage – and, in particular, heritage tourist attractions – as a means of self-celebration, establishment of history and cultural *gravitas*, and local/regional relevancy. It is perhaps no surprise, then, that many heritage attractions in this area are either sport-based or food-based. Sport-based heritage attractions have long been positioned as economic products as well as organizational boosters (Phillips, 2011; Ramshaw and Gammon, 2005) although sport heritage attractions can also act as catalysts for social and political change (Schultz, 2011). Food-based heritage attractions often have the dual role of producing heritage narratives and having tourists see the product of production. Breweries, wineries, and distilleries commonly host tourists, though other types of food/beverage organizations have similar attractions, such as the *World of Coke* display in Atlanta – which does not have a backstage factory tour, but rather is the touristic entry point in a city known for that particular beverage. Both sport and food have an experiential component as well; the visitor can 'try' a sport or a beverage while at the attraction, for example, which makes them of particular interest to tourists. Less common are tours/museums of factories, where tourists cannot necessarily participate in the production, however some do exist – for example, the US mint offers tours. Of course, there must also be demand for these attractions to exist; if no one wanted to see 'backstage' or see a corporate museum, these attractions would not exist. Although some tours/museum attendances can be modest, others – such as the tour/museum for FC Barcelona and visitation to Fenway Park in Boston – can attract significant numbers of visitors (Gammon, 2011). As such, heritage tourism can provide a corporation a vehicle for disseminating particular messages, can help attract and maintain customers, and perhaps even provide additional revenue.

Study site

The BMW US Factory, located in Spartanburg, South Carolina, opened in 1994. It is the company's lone US manufacturing plant, and has produced several different BMW models over its history, including the 318i, Z3, X5, Z4, and X6 ('Plant History', 2013). The plant offers six-to-eight public tours on weekdays for a fee of US$7 with advanced bookings strongly recommended. The tour lasts nearly two hours, and is promoted as:

> BMW's only American factory is a marvel of the blending of modern engineering and design aesthetics. See for yourself how the ultimate driving machine is built during a guided plant tour … For the enthusiast, it's the ultimate backstage pass.
>
> ('Guided Factory Tour', 2013)

The tour begins and ends at the BMW Zentrum Visitors Center (Figure 4.1), a museum that exhibits many BMW vehicles (both contemporary and historic),

Figure 4.1 BMW Zentrum Visitors Center in Spartanburg, South Carolina. Photo by Gregory Ramshaw.

its motorsport heritage, its connections and commitment to safety, environmental sustainability, and to culture and economy of the Greenville-Spartanburg region. The museum also has a BMW art display, a café, and a gift shop. Admission to the Zentrum is free. According to Zentrum staff, the museum hosts approximately 50,000 visitors annually, with most visitors also taking a factory tour. The Zentrum and factory tour are promoted regionally as a tourist attraction and, according to Zentrum staff, visitation to the Center/tour comes from four main sources: tourist's driving past the plant and stopping to see the site (the plant is located on the I-85 interstate and the Visitors Center is well-marked on the highway), customers who have purchased a BMW vehicle and are at the plant for their test drive/training (BMW offers a one-day driving course – including a time-trial on their nearby test track – to all customers who have purchased a new BMW made at the Spartanburg plant), local school groups, and through corporate/private functions held at the Zentrum. Finally, according to Zentrum staff, the tour and Zentrum exhibit narratives rarely change, normally only incorporating information about new products.

Methodology

For this chapter, three forms of data were used: observations of factory tours and museum displays, analysis of factory tour and museum display materials such as brochures, website copy, and text of the Zentrum virtual factory tour, and informal conversations with tour and museum personnel. The data collection took place between December 2011 and November 2013, and included two factory tours, three visits to the Zentrum Visitors Center. According to Patton (2002), 'using a combination of observations, interviewing, and document analysis, the fieldworker is able to use different data sources to validate and crosscheck findings' (p. 306). As this research study focused entirely on the supply-side of the tour narrative, the views and actions of tour patrons were not recorded nor solicited. Data from this study were coded manually, as the amount of raw data was manageable enough to not require a software program. Open coding, using a word processing program and coloured flags on data sources, was used to group the data into manageable segments. Following the open coding, themes were developed for analysis and informed more focused coding of the data (Bailey, 2007).

Themes

Analysis of the BMW factory tours and Zentrum exhibits produced three main themes: plant and production history, quality assurance, and connecting the world to South Carolina and South Carolina to the world.

History

The BMW factory tours and Zentrum Visitors Center espouses a Janus-headed approach – or, what the museum/tour marketing dubs 'The Ultimate Look Back' and 'The Ultimate Look Ahead' (BMW Zentrum Visitors Centre, n.d.). As is the case with many corporate heritage entities, the history is selective and celebratory, and is primarily interpreted as a progressive and inevitable path to the present and future. For example, the exhibits did not focus on the company's creation in post-Versailles Treaty Germany, nor include its role in the production of jet engines for the *Luftwaffe* during the Second World War (Pavelec, 2007). Rather, the history displayed is primarily about changes in production models and design, historical development of engineering and mechanical features of BWM products, and a history BMW's other activities, particularly in motorsport (Figure 4.2). The factory tour primarily discusses the history and development of the plant and the various models that have been produced at the plant over the years. Similarly, both the exhibitions and tour point to the historical development of BMW engineering, performance, and production, espousing a corporate legacy of continued innovation and improvement. For example, one of the exhibits at the Zentrum shows the progression of BMW engine development through to the present, with the understanding that there would be improvement and changes to come. Furthermore, the motorsport displays not only demonstrate the history of BMW in other arenas (and make for captivating sport heritage displays in their own right), they also suggest an ongoing commitment to performance at the highest and most competitive levels – particularly in comparison to rival companies. Ultimately, the historical narratives in the museum exhibits and on the tour provide a sense of *gravitas*

Figure 4.2 BMW motorsport history display. Photo by Gregory Ramshaw.

in that BMW is a contemporary company, but with a long history and legacy that suggests constant and consistent improvement and modernization.

Quality assurance

Quality assurance in terms of production, durability, and safety are significant narratives in both the tour and museum narratives and displays. The focus on the quality of BMW products is not surprising, given that the tour/museum's audience is both current and potential BMW customers. The tour, for example, features many narratives about the innovative modes of production, the training and expertise of workers, the multiple inspections throughout the production process, and the quality of the parts used in production. Furthermore, the tour strongly suggests the individuality and uniqueness of production, stressing the handcrafted aspects of production and the fact that each model is special ordered – and, therefore, not simply mass-produced for dealerships. The museum further reinforces the tour through the many displays about contemporary production features, particularly in terms of vehicle safety (Figure 4.3). Beyond the celebratory aspects of these narratives, the strong focus on quality production not only provides current customers confidence in their purchase – and any future purchases – but also posits an aspirational narrative to potential consumers, in so far as the tour/museum demonstrates a commitment to safety and quality that, seemingly, are superior to competitors.

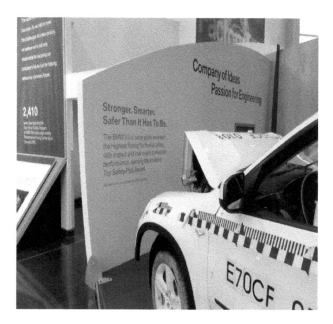

Figure 4.3 Safety display in the Zentrum Visitors Center. Photo by Gregory Ramshaw.

The world to South Carolina and South Carolina to the world

A major theme, both on the tour and the museum exhibits, are the parallel themes that the BMW plant brings the world – in terms of production, culture, and expertise – to South Carolina and, as such, BMW broadcasts South Carolina to the world. The tour and exhibits suggest that the location of the plant to South Carolina's Upstate region was not driven by happenstance or, as was the case, hundreds of millions of dollars of tax credits and incentives (Collins, 2012). Rather, the narratives suggest that the region, its culture, and its workers are strongly compatible with BMW's vision and goals and, in some respects, that the location of the plant to South Carolina's Upstate was inevitable. The virtual factory tour, for example, begins with the following narrative:

> Within the foothills of the Blue Ridge Mountains, where earth and sky merge, and the cool breeze carries the echoes of countless stories, there is a place where dreams fuse with steel and beauty becomes motion as free as the wind. Here, a thousand parts entrusted to a thousand hands begin a journey destined for one purpose: to become the ultimate driving machine.
>
> (Virtual Factory Tour, 2013)

Exhibits in the Zentrum also emphasize how BMW contributes to local education, employment, and charity. Furthermore, the tour emphasizes all of the

Figure 4.4 A map of BMW's global operations. Photo by Gregory Ramshaw.

multinational companies, such as Michelin, that have located to the Upstate region in order to be close to the BMW plant. At the Zentrum, promotional material and exhibits emphasize how the plant has put the region on the global map. Promotionally, the Zentrum positions itself as a global tourist attraction – noting that it attracts visitors from 'near and far' and emphasizing both that it is BMWs only North American plant and, outside of Germany, the only plant that offers a visitor experience through the museum and tour ('Discover the Zentrum', 2013). Exhibits also show how the plant fits into the broader BMW global production landscape (Figure 4.4) and suggests that how much of the overall company production is located in the Upstate region and how much this production contributes to the local economy.

The tour and museum also, simultaneously, describe how the plant broadcasts South Carolina to the world. Tour narratives emphasize that plant production is global and not just domestic, pointing to both the left and right side steering columns as proof of global distribution. The global distribution of products is further emphasized in the Zentrum exhibits, with one exhibit featuring the text 'every X3, X5 and X6 is manufactured for the world right here in South Carolina'. One exhibit further suggests the infamy of the plant's production lines. The initial exhibit visitors' encounter in the Zentrum is the first Z3 roadster produced at the plant, which was used in the James Bond film *Golden Eye* (Figure 4.5). Ultimately, the tour and museum attempt to demonstrate just how much of BMW's global operation, and the benefits that ensue, have been brought to the region, and how the culture and expertise of the region have been globally disseminated.

Figure 4.5 The Z3 'Golden Eye' James Bond car display. Photo by Gregory Ramshaw.

Discussion

Timothy (2011) contends there are several reasons – including revenue generation, brand visibility, public relations, and creation of a regional identity – as to
why heavy industry might position themselves as a tourist attraction. It is clear
that the BMW museum and tour mirror these reasons, as these attractions appear
to produce three outcomes: creating a sense of aspiration for visitors, that is to
have the tour and museum visitors aspire to own a BMW vehicle; creating confidence in BMW's products for potential and existing customers; and providing a sense of stability, both in the company's future and in its commitment to
South Carolina.

The creation of BMW's products as aspirational is clear throughout the museum
and tour experience. Not only does the museum espouse the company's rich legacy both in terms of products and design, the tour reflects these legacies through
exposing visitors to the individual attention provided to every vehicle throughout
the production process. In effect, the total BMW heritage experience reinforces
many preconceived notions about their product – that it is exclusive, luxurious,
cosmopolitan, and exceptional. Although there is not a direct sales-pitch, the
entire experience is meant to drive the visitor to an inevitable conclusion.

Similarly, the tour and museum are meant to both maintain as well as grow
the brand and, therefore, the heritage components are meant to instil a sense of
confidence. At the museum and on the tour, one of the selling features of purchasing a BMW vehicle is that customers are flown to Spartanburg for a full day

'driving school' where they can test their vehicle on a full-length track. Not only does this add to the aspirational value of owning a BMW (after all, how many car manufacturers provide a full-day, expenses-paid, 'driving school' experience?), but also meant to instil confidence in customers that, indeed, they have chosen the correct car. Furthermore, the numerous displays and narratives about quality control, safety, and environmental impact further reinforce that a BMW purchase is a wise purchase.

Finally, the heritage narratives on both the tour and museum exhibit a sense of stability and longevity, which adds *gravitas* to the BMW brand insofar as it has a long and (selectively) distinguished heritage. However, more important is the sense that BMW's heritage and culture is consistent with that of the region, and that the company is committed to South Carolina for the long-haul. Not only do the museum and tour narratives attempt to position BMW as a natural fit with South Carolina heritage, geography, and values, there are also many indicators of BMW's ongoing commitment to the social and economic well-being of the region. This is particularly important in that the company received (and, likely, continues to receive) preferable tax treatment. Whether it is the museum displays that demonstrate all of BMWs local community initiatives, or the 'future heritage' of new production lines that are currently in production, the museum and tour mirror Timothy's (2011) assertion that politics plays a role in why heavy industry may employ tourism.

Conclusion

Heritage is a product of the present, whereby the past is used to address contemporary needs and circumstances (Graham *et al.*, 2000; Lowenthal, 1998). BMW appears to use its heritage assets in several ways, not only to educate tourists about the company's history and current initiatives but also to promote products, provide an additional revenue stream, and demonstrate a synergy between the region and the corporation. The combination of the museum and tour provides both an interesting attraction providing both a frontstage/backstage experience that – at the very least – provides an entertaining and immersive diversion, but may also provide the company several forms of capital, be it through new sales or customers, or through positioning themselves as committed to the holistic well-being of the region. In an age of mobile capital – whether it be consumer brand loyalty or transnational corporations – it is worth noting that heritage tourism appears to play a central role in these broader economic and political initiatives.

References

Adorno, T.W. (2001). *The Culture Industry*. London: Routledge.
Bailey, C.A. (2007). *A Guide to Qualitative Research* (2nd ed.). London: Sage.
BMW Zentrum Visitors Center [Brochure] (n.d.). Greer, SC: BMW Manufacturing Co, LLC.
Collins, J. (2012, December 23). BMW at 20: Plant exceeds hopes, tax debate ongoing. *Associated Press*. Retrieved online November 29, 2013 from http://bigstory.ap.org/article/bmw-20-plant-exceeds-hopes-tax-debate-ongoing

Discover the Zentrum (2013). Retrieved November 29, 2013 from https://www.bmwusfactory.com/zentrum/exhibits/discover-the-zentrum/

Gammon, S. (2011). 'Sporting' new attractions? The commodification of the sleeping stadium. In: R. Sharpley and P. Stone, (Eds.), *Tourism experiences: contemporary perspectives* (pp. 115–126). London: Routledge.

Gammon, S. and Fear, V. (2007). Stadia Tours and the Power of Backstage. In S. Gammon and G. Ramshaw (Eds.), *Heritage, Sport and Tourism: Sporting Pasts – Tourist Futures* (pp. 23–32). London: Routledge.

Goffman, E. (1959). *The Presentation of Self in Everyday Life*. New York: Doubleday.

Graham, B., Ashworth, G.J., and Tunbridge, J.E. (2000). *A Geography of Heritage: Power, Culture & Economy*. London: Arnold.

Guided Factory Tour (2013). Retrieved November 29, 2013 from https://www.bmwusfactory.com/zentrum/tours/guided-factory-tour/

Lowenthal, D. (1998). *The Heritage Crusade and the Spoils of History*. Cambridge: Cambridge University Press.

MacCannell, D. (1973). Staged Authenticity: Arrangements of Social Space in Tourist Settings. *American Journal of Sociology* 79, 589–603.

Patton, M.Q. (2002). *Qualitative Research & Evaluation Methods* (3rd ed.). Sage: Thousand Oaks.

Pavelec, S.M. (2007). *The Jet Race and the Second World War*. Westport: Greenwood Publishing.

Phillips, M. (2011). *Representing the sporting past in museums and halls of fame*. London: Routledge.

Plant History (2013). Retrieved September 30, 2013 from https://www.bmwusfactory.com/manufacturing/plant-history/

Plummer, R., Telfer, D., Hashimoto, A., and Summers, R. (2005). Beer Tourism in Canada along the Waterloo-Wellington Ale Trail. *Tourism Management* 26, 447–458.

Power, D. and Scott, A.J. (2001). A prelude to cultural industries and the production of culture. In D. Power and A.J. Scott (Eds.), *Cultural Industries and the Production of Culture* (pp. 3–16). London: Routledge.

Ramshaw, G. (2010). Living Heritage and the Sports Museum: Athletes, Legacy and the Olympic Hall of Fame and Museum, Canada Olympic Park. *Journal of Sport Tourism* 15 (1), 45–70.

Ramshaw, G. and Gammon, S. (2005). More than just Nostalgia? Exploring the Heritage/Sport Tourism Nexus. *Journal of Sport Tourism* 10 (4), 229–241.

Ramshaw, G. and Gammon, S. (2010). On Home Ground? Twickenham Stadium Tours and the Construction of Sport Heritage. *Journal of Heritage Tourism* 5 (2), 87–102.

Schultz, J. (2011). Lest We Forget: Public History and Racial Segregation in Baltimore's Druid Hill Park. In M. Phillips (ed.), *Representing the sporting past in museums and halls of fame* (pp. 231–248). London: Routledge.

Timothy, D.J. (2011). *Cultural Heritage and Tourism: An Introduction*. Bristol: Channel View.

Virtual Factory Tour (2013). Greer, SC: BMW Manufacturing Co, LLC.

5   DeLorean dreams

Back to the Future in 'Titanic Town'

Gordon Ramsey

Introduction

The building of the DeLorean factory in Belfast during a period of intense communal conflict, the production of the distinctive gull-winged DMC-12 by a mixed Protestant and Catholic workforce in the violent west of the city, the ultimate collapse of the project and arrest of John DeLorean on drugs charges, and the revival of the car as a global icon by the Hollywood movie, *Back to the Future*, is a dramatic story. However, today's tourist in Belfast, Northern Ireland, is unlikely to hear that story told.

Drawing on documentary sources, a survey of DeLorean owners worldwide, and interviews with DeLorean enthusiasts, tourist industry representatives and former DeLorean workers, this chapter considers the significance of the DeLorean as part of Belfast's history and heritage, exploring the part the DeLorean story currently plays in Belfast's tourism product, and considering to what extent further development may be possible.

John Zachary DeLorean

John DeLorean was central to the drama that unfolded in Belfast between 1978 and 1981. Born in Detroit, then known as Motor City, in 1925, DeLorean was the eldest of four sons of immigrant parents who both worked in the car industry. His Romanian father, Zaharie, whose name he was given in anglicised form, was kept in low-income employment by his poor English, and his wife sometimes took her sons to her sister in Los Angeles to escape his violent behaviour. John DeLorean's parents divorced in 1942, and his father became a chronic alcoholic.

Despite this troubled background, DeLorean did well in school and eventually gained a BSc in Industrial Engineering in 1948, whilst working part-time at Chrysler. Gaining access to Chrysler's education program, he obtained an MSc in Automotive Engineering in 1952, and worked for Chrysler for a short time as an engineer before moving to Packard, where he had a successful four years, before being headhunted by General Motors (GM).

At GM, DeLorean initially worked in Pontiac where he took most of the credit for the development of the GTO, often described as the first 'muscle-car', developing

Pontiac's identity as GM's 'performance' brand. In 1965, DeLorean, then aged 40, became GM's youngest ever division head when he took leadership of Pontiac, where he went on to develop the successful Firebird in 1967, and Grand Prix in 1969. How much of DeLorean's success was a product of his undoubted engineering skills and how much to his talent for self-promotion is a subject of debate. DeLorean did not conform to the conservative image of the automotive industry at the time, dressing fashionably, travelling to exotic locations for promotions, socialising with celebrities from the entertainment world and building something of a celebrity profile himself. Whilst this did not endear him to the older generation of executives, it may well have appealed to those who made up the market for sports cars in the 'swinging sixties', and his sales success could not be challenged.

In February 1969, DeLorean took charge of GM's most prestigious brand, Chevrolet, which was suffering production problems with a range of models at the time. By 1971, he had turned the division around and achieved record sales, which led to a further promotion, this time to Vice-President of GM Cars and Trucks. Whilst many saw him as a future President, DeLorean's often abrasive approach had made enemies within both management and the unions, and many within GM were strongly opposed to such a move. In 1973, DeLorean announced that he was leaving GM to 'do things in the social arena'. In 1979, in collaboration with journalist Patrick Wright, he published *On a Clear Day You Can See General Motors,* a scathing attack on what DeLorean saw as complacency and corporate inertia within the company (Wright and DeLorean, 1979). In the book, he suggested that rather than focusing on superficial annual styling changes, automotive companies should direct their energies to such issues as safety, reliability and environmental impact.

Fallon and Srodes (1983), whose work is a source for this account of DeLorean's life up to this point, suggest that DeLorean's social and environmental concerns were largely a strategic tuning in to the social currents of the time, and note that his rise was characterised by insensitivity to the feelings of others and a ruthless approach to those he saw as rivals or obstacles. They also assert that DeLorean's departure from GM was not a matter of choice – that he had not 'fired General Motors' as parts of the automotive press subsequently suggested, but had been forced out after losing a corporate power struggle (Fallon and Srodes, 1983: 55–7).

From dream to prototype – the DeLorean sports-car

DeLorean remained in the public eye – seen by some of the press as a potential saviour of the auto-industry following the 1973 energy crisis resulting from war in the middle-east (Fallon and Srodes, 1983: 58–65). In April 1974, he announced in a speech in Dallas that:

> The ideal thing that I would like to do with my life right now would be to build the American equivalent of the Mercedes-Benz. A car with high quality, where you wouldn't have to worry about the price, just build the best car you could.
>
> (Fallon and Srodes, 1983: 65)

At the time, DeLorean was himself driving a Mercedes 300SL, a classic sports-car featuring gull-winged doors, also a feature of the Bricklin which was then being produced in Canada (see Joliffe this volume). In September 1974, he met Italian designer Giorgetto Guigiaro at the Turin Motor Show, and commissioned him to design a gull-winged sports-car, which would also feature a stainless-steel shell, and a rear-mounted engine. DeLorean intended to make the vehicle slightly more exclusive and expensive than Chevrolet's Corvette, competing with Porsche in the American market. DeLorean signed off on Guigiaro's design in March 1975. He also intended the chassis to be moulded from fibreglass through a new process known as Elastic Reservoir Molding (ERM), which would make it not only light, and therefore, fuel-efficient, but also crash-resistant. Other safety features would include airbags and a centrally mounted fuel-tank. DeLorean described his project as an 'ethical' car, and these features were so appealing to car-insurance company Allstate that they funded a significant part of the research and development process, and a prototype was produced in early 1976 (Fallon and Srodes, 1983: 74,79).

The DeLorean Motor Company (DMC)

The DeLorean Motor Company (DMC) was set up in October 1975, and DeLorean put together a management team and offered stock to dealers interested in selling the car, raising substantial funding, although still insufficient to actually build the car. DeLorean retained control by the use of complex shadow companies. As the money became available, DeLorean's lifestyle became more extravagant. Initially considering production in Pennsylvania, DeLorean was dissatisfied with the financial package he was offered, and entered into 18 months of negotiation with Puerto Rico, which finally turned him down. DeLorean then entered negotiations with the Irish government in Dublin. After 3 months, they too walked away. Only then did DeLorean turn to Northern Ireland, then mired in some of the most violent years of the 'Troubles'.

The 'Troubles' was the understated term by which people in Northern Ireland described the guerrilla war which had raged since 1969 between Irish republicans, mostly Catholic, who hoped to unite Northern Ireland with the rest of the island; Ulster loyalists, solidly Protestant and determined to keep Ulster British; and the British state, whose forces were nominally there to keep the warring sides apart, but which also had its own political agenda. By the end of the 1970s, over 1200 had died in gun battles, bombings, riots and sectarian assassinations, the presence of the army on the streets was routine, and the economy was in meltdown (Bew and Gillespie, 1999; McKittrick *et al.*, 1999). The British government was desperate to bring jobs to the province, and it took DeLorean only 45 days to secure an offer of $121 million to build a factory in West Belfast, one of the most deprived and violent areas in the country. Here he would produce his dream car, to be named the DMC-12 (Fallon and Srodes, 1983: 117–23).

The dream comes to life: from building the factory to building the car

DeLorean had secured the investment from the Northern Ireland Development Agency (NIDA) on the promise that he could bring the car to production within 18 months – an impossibly short timetable considering that he was starting with nothing more than a boggy field between Belfast and Lisburn in a country which had never built a car. DeLorean brought American engineers to build and run the factory. The design of the vehicle itself he largely sub-contracted to the English sports-car company, Lotus, who swiftly dispensed with many of the features that were supposed to make the car 'ethical', including the ERM chassis and the airbags.

On October 2nd 1978, DeLorean came to Belfast for the ground-breaking ceremony at the new factory location. The event was attended by a host of local dignitaries including a British government minister and the Lord Mayors of both Belfast and Lisburn. Fallon and Srodes (1983:183) recount how during 1979:

> Men who had never worked in their lives were enthusiastically seizing the opportunity they had thought would never come. From the Catholic estate of Twinbrook on one side to the Protestant enclave of Seymour Hill on the other, they watched as a small river was diverted and the steel framework began to appear.

By July 1980, however, the car's launch had been postponed until February 1981, DeLorean was running low on funds and had convinced the British government to invest a further £14 million. On December 3rd 1980, the first car came off the production line. DeLorean had already spent the £14 million and was now demanding a further £10 million, which Margaret Thatcher's government, despite its commitment to cutting government spending, felt unable to refuse. On April 20 1981, the first 400 cars were shipped to California, where they were snapped up by customers keenly awaiting the opportunity to 'Live the Dream', as DeLorean's advertising slogan had promised them.

The dream unravels

During 1981, one of the pivotal events of the Troubles led to violence impacting directly upon the DeLorean factory. A hunger-strike for political status by prisoners from the Irish Republican Army (IRA) led to the death in the Maze prison of IRA man Bobby Sands on May 5th 1981. Sands' family lived in Twinbrook, the Catholic estate adjoining the factory from which many DeLorean workers came. Less than an hour later, the DeLorean factory was attacked by rioters and a temporary office close to the perimeter was burned out. On the day of Sands' funeral in Twinbrook, a third of the DeLorean workforce were absent. Initially shaken by these events, DeLorean swiftly turned them to his advantage, exaggerating the damage and using the British government's fear of escalating violence in West Belfast to convince them to provide him with a further £7 million (Fallon and Srodes, 1983: 280–288).

DeLorean would receive no more money from the British taxpayer, however. On September 22nd 1981, his English former personal secretary, Marion Gibson, who had become disillusioned with DeLorean's unscrupulous approach, met Conservative MP, Winterton, and revealed to him massive abuses of the money the British government had supplied to DeLorean. Winterton took the evidence to Margaret Thatcher personally, and on October 2, she ordered a police investigation. On the following day, the story was broken in the media. By this time, it was already clear that DeLorean was building twice as many cars as he was able to sell – in part because quality-control issues resulting from the inexperience of the Belfast workforce had resulted in bad publicity – for instance when a visitor to a car-show was trapped in a DeLorean due to the refusal of the gull-wing doors to open (Fallon and Srodes, 1983: 288,357–358). More fundamentally DeLorean's projections had always been over-optimistic, oil-price rises had significantly changed the sports-car market between the car's conceptualisation and its production, and a deep recession in the USA had diminished even that remaining market.

DeLorean angrily denied the allegations against him, remained publicly optimistic, talking of unidentified new investors, and continued to live an extravagant lifestyle, regularly flying the Atlantic on the supersonic airliner, the Concorde, using the most exclusive hotels and clubs, maintaining plush offices and an art collection, and paying high salaries to staff. Regardless of DeLorean's optimism, in January 1982, the factory went on to a three-day week, and subcontractors in Belfast started laying off workers. The following month, DeLorean having failed to produce the new investors of which he had spoken, the British government put DMC into receivership. Reluctant to see the factory close, the government receiver put together a deal with investors – telling DeLorean it was dependent upon him investing £20 million of his own money, the deadline being October 20. DeLorean, however, was already so short of cash that his offices were running out of envelopes and coffee.

The most bizarre chapter was yet to come. On October 19, DeLorean boarded a flight from New York to Los Angeles. That afternoon, he was arrested in his LA hotel by an FBI sting operation and charged with trafficking in narcotics. In court, the FBI produced video evidence in which DeLorean was heard describing a suitcase full of cocaine as 'good as gold'. Nevertheless, in 1984, DeLorean was found not guilty, after convincing the jury that he had been the victim of entrapment by FBI agents who had persuaded him to raise the money to save his company through drug smuggling.

DeLorean's arrest spelt the end of the factory. The receiver moved to close it down, laying off all workers. A workers' sit-in was organised, initially in hopes of saving the factory, but ended after seven weeks, ultimately settling for better redundancy terms. The dream, it seemed, was over.

The car's the star: the DeLorean goes to the 'Dream Factory'

It has often been suggested, not least by John DeLorean himself, that his story was worthy of a movie. In fact, it was the 1985 science-fiction fantasy, *Back to the*

Future, that made his car a global icon once again. Steven Spielberg's blockbuster, released within a year of John DeLorean's acquittal on drugs charges, used a heavily modified DMC-12 as the time-machine central to the movie's plot. The film was followed by two blockbuster sequels, together capturing the imagination of a generation, and John DeLorean personally wrote to Spielberg to thank him for immortalising the vehicle. The movie had no apparent benefits for Belfast, however. In 1988, the DeLorean factory was acquired by Montupet, a French company manufacturing cylinder-heads, who still occupy the site, employing around 600 people.

Tourists entering Belfast who are unaware of the DeLorean story will find little to awaken their interest. Rather, they are likely to find their experience focused on an older aspect of Belfast's industrial heritage – the huge cranes of the Harland & Wolff shipyard which still dominate the city, and the brand new visitor attraction: Titanic Belfast, which commemorates and commodifies the tragic story of the yard's most famous product.

Tourism in post-conflict Belfast

In Belfast, as in other post-industrial cities, tourism, and in particular heritage tourism, has been seen as an essential part of a strategy of urban renewal (see Zukin, 2008). In Belfast, the task has been complicated by the legacy of thirty years of sectarian conflict, which has certainly given the city a global profile but not one obviously attractive to tourists. Neill, Murray and Grist (2014: 12) note that 'the relaunching of Titanic as a Belfast brand (was) at the forefront of marketing the new Belfast'. The global success of James Cameron's blockbuster film, *Titanic*, was used as a springboard to rebrand Belfast as 'Titanic Town', the home of the doomed liner. The 'signature building', Titanic Belfast, opened in 2012 on Queen's Island, the site of the old shipyard now relabelled the 'Titanic Quarter'. Easily accessible to visiting cruise ships, the building was to be the centre of a large-scale urban regeneration project. Much of the planned development, including the provision of affordable social housing, was never completed due to the global financial crisis of 2008 from which Northern Ireland still shows little sign of emerging (Bronte, 2012: 55; Neill, 2014: 71–73). Rather than standing surrounded by 'urban villages' as planned, therefore, the glass-covered signature building, ironically nicknamed 'the Iceberg', stands somewhat isolated, overlooking the historic but still derelict Drawing Offices in which the White Star Liner was designed.

The attempt to both celebrate and sell the legacy of a disaster in which 1500 people died created dilemmas for planners and marketers, which have been discussed by a range of scholars, notably in Neill, Murray and Grist's (2014) edited volume. In some ways, the selling of the Titanic story complemented 'Troubles tourism', another form of 'dark tourism' in Belfast, in which people are given tours of paramilitary murals in working-class areas of the city, whilst being sold the story of the 'peace process' – a task complicated by the fact that the city is still bitterly divided and occasionally erupts into violence. At the same time, writers such as Hill (2014), Kelly (2012) and Bronte (2012) have detailed how the 'Titanic experience' seeks to push the conflicts which permeate the history of the city, and indeed of the shipyard, to the fringes of the visitor's awareness. The attempt to sell Titanic as part of a shared heritage is made more difficult by the fact that in Belfast, the ship is still widely perceived as having been built by an almost entirely Protestant workforce, from which Catholics were excluded. A walk through the working-class neighbourhoods of loyalist east Belfast reveals many murals commemorating the ship including one describing it as a 'Ship of Dreams'. Such memorials are much rarer in nationalist neighbourhoods. Where then, does the DeLorean fit into Titanic Town? At first, glance, the answer seems to be, hardly at all.

DeLorean in Belfast today

DeLorean's production site has not become a tourist icon, but remains a factory making car components. The test track still exists but is overgrown and largely disused. There is no 'signature building' to which the DeLorean aficionado can gravitate; the DeLorean does not feature in advertising promoting tourism in Northern Ireland and the gift shops of Belfast city-centre, overflowing with Titanic memorabilia, offer little to the DeLorean fan. Nor does the DeLorean feature on wall murals anywhere in the city. Unlike the Titanic, the memory of the DeLorean appears to have been embraced neither by the tourist industry nor by the working-class communities who built it. The DeLorean is not completely forgotten, however.

For the tourist wishing to actually see a DeLorean, the destination must be the Ulster Folk & Transport Museum, located at Cultra, a few miles from Belfast. The museum has on display a car acquired directly from the factory. Known as an 'endurance car', it was a high mileage test vehicle and is displayed unrestored as such. Alongside it is a complete rolling chassis, with a display board behind it telling the story of the factory, alongside *Back to the Future* posters featuring the car. The museum also has a wooden mock-up of the car produced by Guigiaro during the design process. This is currently displayed separately, but the museum's Director of Transport, Mark Kennedy, has plans to create an integrated display.

There was one other DeLorean on display in the city – in a gift shop named The DeLorean Experience which opened in June 2012 close to the city centre, where visitors could pay to have their photo taken with a car customised to resemble the time-machine of *Back to the Future*. A banner outside the shop claimed to have the only DeLorean exhibit in Europe, and in addition to Titanic, Guinness and DeLorean souvenirs, offered tours of the DeLorean Factory and DeLorean's house (which he rarely visited), as well as tours of the city in a DeLorean DMC-12. The enterprise closed in early 2014, although the Facebook page can still be found (DeLorean Experience Belfast, 2012).

Whilst the DeLorean has not become a significant part of mainstream tourism in Belfast, there is a global community of DeLorean enthusiasts for whom Belfast has become something of a Mecca, thanks largely to the efforts of Belfast

DeLorean enthusiast Robert Lamrock: a DeLorean owner, two of whose relatives worked in the factory. Every five years, Lamrock organises the Eurofest – a gathering of DeLorean owners and cars which sees DeLorean's driven to Belfast from all over Europe, as well as owners flying in from across the globe to participate. Events during the Eurofest have included a visit to the Ulster Folk & Transport Museum, a tour of the former factory, an opportunity to drive on the test track with its banked turn, the chance to meet former factory workers, an autocross competition in the Titanic Quarter, and the opportunity to drive the scenic Causeway Coastal Route. Participants are housed in Belfast's best-known hotel: the Europa, which has an indoor carpark and was once famous as the most bombed hotel in Europe (Heydari, 2007). Many Eurofest participants take the opportunity for a longer holiday exploring Ireland more widely.

The initial Eurofest, held in 1993, attracted 90 people from 10 countries, with 12 cars present. Subsequent events in 1997, 2001, 2006 and 2011 grew steadily, with the 2011 event bringing in eighty cars and about 300 people from 21 countries, the furthest travelled car being driven from Hungary. Early events received a small financial grant from the Northern Ireland Tourist Board, whilst in 2011, the Autocross event was financed by the Laganside Corporation, a public body established to regenerate the Belfast waterfront, and sponsorship was also received from *Autotrader* magazine and Lisburn City Council.

Outside the Eurofests, Robert Lamrock has derived occasional income from his car through using it for weddings and photoshoots, as has another Northern Irish DeLorean owner, Mark Lenny of Cookstown, who is hoping to give up dentistry to devote himself fully to tourism and publicity featuring the car.

If the DeLorean has not become a mainstream tourist icon like the Titanic, then, it can at least be seen as having developed a small but significant 'niche' in the market, although this is largely due to the efforts of DeLorean enthusiasts themselves rather than to the tourist industry. Is there any potential for the DeLorean to move beyond this niche to become a mainstream icon of the 'new' Belfast comparable to the Titanic? Both possibilities and pitfalls present themselves.

Back to the Future again?

The publicity given to the Eurofest may be one element in a willingness within Belfast to look past the shock and disillusionment of the company's collapse to consider the DeLorean as a positive element in the heritage of the city. There are some signs of this happening. In February 2014, Belfast's new Music and Arts Centre (MAC) held a 'prom dance' modelled on the high-school dance scenes in *Back to the Future*. A DeLorean formed a major element of the promotion. The following month, the Belfast St. Patrick's Day parade included a float featuring a mock-up of the *Back to the Future* DeLorean, The Eurofest always receives news coverage, and the 2001 event was featured in Ulster Television's documentary *DeLorean Fever*, whilst independent film-maker Owen Gormley is currently working on a new documentary on DeLorean owners in Ireland, which he aims to release in time for the 30th anniversary of *Back to the Future* in 2015.

There are some striking similarities in the stories of the Titanic and the DeLorean. Both were cutting-edge industrial products produced in Belfast and seen as icons of their age, both ended in disaster and disillusion, and both were then reborn as global icons thanks to Hollywood movies. In some ways, however, the DeLorean may seem more suitable as a symbol of post-conflict Belfast than the Titanic. The sinking of the DeLorean did not involve any loss of life, tragic as it was for many of the workers who struggled to find other employment in the devastated city. Moreover, whilst the Titanic is still widely seen as the property of the Protestant community, the workforce in DeLorean was deliberately recruited from both Protestants and Catholics, and according to all the workers to whom the author of this chapter has spoken, there was a genuine camaraderie which transcended sectarian divisions, even during the dark days of the early 1980s, and which enabled co-operation, both in building the car, and later, in the workers' sit-in which followed the factory closure.

The former workers interviewed for this chapter all remembered their time at DeLorean with affection. All said that they 'loved it' and more than one described it as 'the best job I ever had'. Moreover, they were proud of their achievements in building such a radical vehicle in such a short time with no previous experience. All agreed that it was an important part of Belfast's history which should be remembered positively. In this regard, it could be pointed out that, like the Titanic, the disaster that befell was not the fault of the workers who built it (see Hill, 2014: 36, 40).

From a practical point of view, Robert Lamrock, who has an extensive collection of memorabilia and original documents relating to the DeLorean, feels that such material should ideally be displayed at a visitors' centre at the test track. In 2013, Lamrock wrote to the planning authorities to express concern at plans by Montupet to develop a heavy-goods parking area which would have destroyed part of the test track. Planning permission for this development was refused, and Montupet withdrew their application. As a result, the track remains intact. To date, no other stakeholders have bought into the concept of a visitors' centre, however. There are obvious reasons for such caution.

After the 'peace dividend': austerity Belfast

The development of the Titanic Quarter was supposed to deliver a 'peace dividend' that would create a new middle-class urban community (Neill, 2014: 70). On the neo-liberal understanding that a rising tide lifts all boats, it was also supposed to bring prosperity to the impoverished surrounding neighbourhoods that had once supplied workers to the shipyard, and which had been at the heart of the violence of the 'troubles' when those jobs disappeared (Neill, 2014: 70). This conceptual 'ship of dreams' sank as rapidly as the original after the 2008 financial crash led to massive withdrawals of investment, negative equity for those unlucky enough to have paid high prices for unbuilt apartments, and increasing desperation in the surrounding working-class neighbourhoods which manifested itself in the traditional way – sectarian rioting. The disintegration of the neo-liberal peacebuilding model (Kelly, 2012) was symbolised by a widely published photograph of a masked youth launching a petrol bomb in front of the 'Ship of Dreams' mural. As this chapter is written (Summer, 2014), sectarian tensions remain high in several working-class areas of Belfast, including the interface between the Catholic Short Strand and Protestant Newtownards Road where the 'Ship of Dreams' mural is located. In the financial climate resulting from the recession and associated social unrest, there is likely to be a cautious response from both public and private sectors in regard to new investments with uncertain returns. Moreover, given the loss of government money in the original DeLorean project, there is likely to be a particular aversion to presiding over the creation of a second 'money-pit' with the same branding. What evidence, exists, then, of interest in DeLorean as a tourist product? There is one group amongst which there is a very clear interest – DeLorean owners. They are a small group, but the reasons for their enthusiasm for the car may offer insights into the way the DeLorean might become a tourist product with much wider appeal.

DeLorean owners – car enthusiasts or relationship enthusiasts?

The author of this chapter distributed questionnaires online to DeLorean owners through DeLorean owners clubs and other DeLorean oriented websites. There were 32 completed questionnaires received from DeLorean owners, and five from club secretaries. The geographical spread of the response was global, ranging from Donegal to Arizona, and from Hungary to Japan. The results suggest that DeLorean owners are overwhelmingly male and mostly aged 30–50, with a minority in their 20s and an even smaller number over 50. Since DMC-12s rarely change hands for less than $30,000, it may be assumed that they are part of an affluent demographic group. Strikingly, over half the respondents had visited Northern Ireland, mostly to attend the Eurofest, and over 80%, including all those who had previously visited, expressed an active desire to visit in the future. Two, however, expressed reservations about visiting due to concerns about recent violence and political instability.

All respondents seemed passionately attached to their cars. Every owner agreed that ownership had lived up to their expectations and many emphasized that it had far exceeded their expectations. Only one would consider selling his car – the response of many to this question was 'No Way!' or 'Never!'.

When asked what had attracted them to the car, the most commonly expressed themes were looks and styling, uniqueness, and *Back to the Future* (many considered this the only answer necessary). Asked what they most enjoyed about owning the car, the themes of looks and uniqueness emerged strongly again, but were outstripped by a new theme – the effect the car had on other people, mentioned by 66% of respondents. The driving experience was referred to by 33%, but even this was talked about more in terms of reactions to the car by others rather than in terms of performance, which many owners acknowledged was lacklustre even by 1980s standards. Some of the answers to the question

'What are the most rewarding aspects of owning a DeLorean?' shed light on the special appeal of the car:

> 'talking to other people about it' (UK).
> 'great community' (UK).
> 'enthusiasm it gains from others' (Belgium).
> 'It almost confers celebrity status' (USA).
> 'It makes you 10% rock star' (Canada).
> 'It makes people smile!' (USA).
> 'Smiles everywhere!' (USA).
> 'connecting with people in a positive way' (Canada).
> 'The joy it gives to other people who see the car and experience a bit of their childhood too' (Canada).

It is clear from these and many more comments that owning a DeLorean is valued first and foremost as a social experience and that the experience is inextricably associated with the DeLorean's role in *Back to the Future*. It is the association with the film that confers celebrity status, makes people smile, and takes them back to their childhood. Whilst one owner commented that he had never been a car enthusiast before the DeLorean, another wrote that he had owned many unusual cars, but none had generated the enthusiasm from others he experienced in the DeLorean, whilst a third observed that at car shows, his car attracted far more attention than more expensive vehicles such as Ferraris and Maseratis.

It is clear then from the survey results, that unlike ownership of most prestige cars, owning a DeLorean is more than a statement of status and exclusivity – it is a social experience, because it is not just car-owners or enthusiasts who feel a sense of ownership towards the car. Everybody who was emotionally impacted by the films in their youth can feel a connection with car and driver. DeLorean owners are able to 'live the dream' – a phrase a number of them used – precisely because it is a dream that is shared with so many others.

Many DeLorean owners who had attended the Eurofest event commented that this wide sense of public ownership is particularly marked in Ireland, where people readily identified their vehicles as 'Belfast built', 'Northern Irish' or 'Irish' cars, and enthusiastically engaged with the visiting owners. Many owners had feared that the negative associations of the DeLorean factory's collapse might provoke resentment or hostility from local people, and they expressed their delight at such positive interactions, particularly when they were approached by people who had worked on the car, or had family connections to the factory. The wide public sense of connection to the DeLorean, then, both within and outside Ireland, may offer possibilities to extend its appeal as a tourism product beyond those who actually own the vehicles.

Dreams and possibilities: forward to the future?

The construction of the DeLorean factory in Dunmurry was financed by the British government in the hope that employment would bring peace to Belfast. For a time, the factory did appear to create a peaceful oasis within the wider turmoil, but the investment did not ultimately return the hoped for dividend. Much the same can be said about the creation of the Titanic Quarter. Kelly (2012: 45) notes that the project has failed to deliver even the most minimal benefits to local working-class communities, and claims that 'The Titanic project illuminates in an especially crass manner the free market fundamentalism underpinning the 'new' Belfast, and epitomizes the convergence of local and global capital in remaking the whole of Northern Ireland in a neo-liberal mode'. Kelly (2012: 45) goes on to assert that:

> The stark social inequalities that fuelled the Troubles remain deeply entrenched: the very same districts that suffered the brunt of the violence from 1969 onward remain at the bottom in poverty, unemployment, and social deprivation; public funding is being cut to the bone, with hospital patients dying on trolleys and schools facing closure; low-paid public sector workers whose wages make up a large portion of income in every working-class community across the North are threatened with redundancies by the thousands.

In these circumstances, another 'flagship project' is clearly the last thing Belfast needs, nor is there likely to be any appetite in government to fund more 'lipstick on the gorilla' (Neill, 1995). The DeLorean seems to be barely on the radar of major tourism agencies in Northern Ireland which gave little or no response to queries from this author.

Whilst the grandiose dreams of tourism as a driver of regeneration in Northern Ireland are no longer credible, tourism does make a significant contribution to the Northern Ireland economy, and by 2013, tourist numbers had returned to the levels experienced before the 2008 financial crash at just over 4 million (Fáillte Ireland, 2014; Dept. of Enterprise, Trade & Investment, 2014). If 'flagship' projects may be prone to that sinking feeling, the widespread interest in, and positive feelings towards the DeLorean described by the cars' owners, both inside and outside Ireland suggest that there could be scope for more modest and perhaps, sustainable uses of the DeLorean as a visitor attraction in Belfast. There are three existing dynamics which could be capitalized upon to achieve this. The first is the strong community of DeLorean owners and enthusiasts, many of whom have already visited Northern Ireland and developed a strong affection for the country, and nearly all of whom have a considerable knowledge of Northern Ireland's role in the car's construction. The second is the considerable pride and feelings of ownership within Belfast for the car, revealed both by my interviews with former workers, and by the accounts of visiting DeLorean owners. The third, which is intertwined with the first, is the public affection for the DeLorean deriving from the *Back to the Future* films. It is the films that make this perhaps the most democratic of two-seater sports-cars – in that it is associated with positive experiences by a mass-audience rather than just by an exclusive group of affluent owners.

Several options have been suggested as to how DeLorean tourism in Belfast might be developed. The test-track still exists in Dunmurry, and Robert Lamrock has made a compelling case that it should be preserved for its historical significance, and has mooted the possibility of a visitors' centre on the site, much of which could be filled with his own collection of memorabilia. Both Robert Lamrock and Mark Lenny suggested that DeLorean's former residence, Warren House, adjacent to the test track, would be an ideal location for such a centre. Warren House has served as a guest-house in recent years and was recently advertised for sale at £425,000. It is currently off the market, but there is ample space for the construction of a small visitors centre within the area of the test track. Such a project would require cooperation with the site's current owners, Montupet, and might be possible within a modest budget. There is a precedent for such a project in the Studebaker test track, which is linked to the Studebaker Museum in South Bend, Indiana, and is used to host automotive events related to the museum (see 'Bendix Woods', n.d.). An alternative location suggested by Mark Lenny is in the Titanic Quarter, where it would fit the theme of industrial heritage and could benefit from the large numbers of tourists visiting Titanic Belfast.

Jeremiah (2003: 176–177) has pointed out that many vehicle displays can appear more like garages or storage spaces than museums whilst Clark (2013) has highlighted the need to bring people into displays of automobiles by setting them in a social context and telling stories. A DeLorean attraction could be an ideal opportunity to put people at the centre of the display by exploring themes including social, industrial, economic and political history through the stories of the workers, engineers, politicians, car-owners, film-makers and fans whose lives have become entangled with the DeLorean in different ways.

A further potential strand of development lies in the direction of DeLorean associated events. A DeLorean Visitors' Centre situated on a spacious site, whether in Dunmurry or currently disused parts of the Titanic Quarter, could serve as a central location not only for automotive events such as car-shows or autocross, but for events associated with the film *Back to the Future*. In early 2014, for example, the Dungannon Film Club organised a one-off 'drive-in' showing of the film, at which Mark Lenny's DeLorean was present as an atmospheric prop. Lenny has suggested that the Titanic Quarter would be an ideal venue to stage such events in Belfast, and is currently seeking funding to develop this and related ideas. Significantly, 2015 will be the 30th anniversary of the release of the original movie, which will be widely celebrated by film fans and marked by cinema showings of the original film, new DVD releases and a stage musical in London's West End, bringing the show to a new generation.(see 'Back to the Future Fan Celebrations: We're Going Back' 2011–; McNally, 2014) The fact that the shipyard's former Paint Hall is now a major film studio could be seen as adding to the appropriateness of developing events related to film history in this location.

The presence of an actual DeLorean was also considered essential to setting the atmosphere at the MAC's Back to the Future 'Prom Dance' and musical events associated with the film could be developed on a larger scale, with potential venues being available in the Titanic Quarter's Odyssey Arena Complex, or elsewhere in Belfast.

Summary

The DeLorean story is an extraordinary saga including elements of hope, pride and despair, personal ambition and frailty, engineering setbacks and achievements, communal conflict and peace-making, and the ultimate production of a vehicle which has become a global icon. Until recently, this story has not been fully embraced by the city of Belfast, and its potential as a tourist attraction has been under-exploited.

This research suggests that both the global community of DeLorean owners, who understand the significance of Belfast to the story, and the former workforce in Belfast regard the building of the DeLorean as an achievement deserving of pride and worthy of celebration. In this it is often compared to the Titanic, and reference could also be made to the Concorde aircraft, another product whose financial failure was not seen as compromising its iconic status as an engineering achievement. The global popularity of the DeLorean as a result of the *Back to the Future* film trilogy offers possibilities outside those normally available in the world of motoring heritage, and the 30th anniversary of the original film's release in 2015 offers a particular opportunity to raise the profile of the DeLorean in Belfast.

In the current climate of austerity, initiatives are unlikely to come from government, but government support is likely to be crucial to the success of projects developed from the bottom up. Whilst some possibilities have been suggested in this paper, these will need detailed business plans to ensure viability. This work has revealed that there is some awareness of the potential of the DeLorean as a tourism icon, if only at the grassroots level.

Tourism projects cannot be expected to provide solutions to Belfast's deep-seated economic and social problems. Northern Ireland continues to have higher poverty levels and greater levels of inequality between rich and poor than the rest of the UK (Kelly, 2012: 45–46) and as long as the most deprived communities are forced to compete for inadequate resources, there is no reason to suppose that sectarian tensions will decrease. Projects such as Titanic Belfast have done little to address these issues (Kelly, 2012; Neill, Murray and Grist 2014).

Nevertheless, to do nothing is not an answer to these problems either. The DeLorean factory did provide a genuine respite from economic desperation and communal conflict for one of the most bitter periods of the conflict in Northern Ireland between 1979 and 1982. This experience is still valued by the workers who built the car, and appreciated by the owners who bought them. The production of the DeLorean is an important element in the industrial history of Belfast, and indeed, the workers sit-in that followed the factory's closure is a significant episode in the city's labour history. Whilst *Back to the Future* may provide a 'hook' that will attract tourists to DeLorean themed exhibits, a focus on the experience of the workers may enable them to connect to the city at a deeper level. In this regard, it is noteworthy that the reason so many of the DeLorean owners who have attended the Eurofest event express a desire to return is the connections they made, through the car, with Belfast people. The focus on 'connection' by Eurofest participants echoes the Canadian DeLorean owner who stated that what he valued most about the car was 'connecting with people in a positive way'. As a result of its extraordinary history, the DeLorean does seem to offer this connection to many people, particularly in Belfast. And something which enables such positive connection may be of more than just economic value in this still troubled city.

References

'Back to the Future Fan Celebrations: We're Going Back' (2011–) Facebook page, accessed 15/7/14. https://www.facebook.com/weregoingback.

'Bendix Woods' (undated), Wikipedia article, accessed 8/8/14. http://en.wikipedia.org/wiki/Bendix_Woods.

Bew, P. and Gillespie, G. (1999) *Northern Ireland: A Chronology of the Troubles 1968–1999*. Dublin: Gill & Macmillan.

Bronte, J. (2012) *Rebranding Belfast through the Titanic Quarter*. Unpublished MSc. Dissertation, Queen's University Belfast.

Clark, J. (2013) 'Peopling the public history of motoring: men, machines and museums', *Curator: The Museum Journal* 56 (2), 279–287.

DeLorean Experience Belfast, (2012) Facebook page, accessed 5/7/14. https://www.facebook.com/DeLoreanExperienceBelfast.

Dept. of Enterprise, Trade and Investment. (2014) 'Northern Ireland Tourism Statistics April 2013 to March 2014', accessed 8/8/14. http://www.detini.gov.uk/publication_january_march_2014.pdf?rev=0

Fáilte Ireland: National Tourism Development Authority (2014) 'Tourism Barometer', accessed 8/8/14. http://www.failteireland.ie/FailteIreland/files/48/48b8176c-6aae-4d79-b36a-b59e1ee2ef3d.pdf.

Fallon, I. and Srodes, J. (1983) *DeLorean: The Rise and Fall of a Dream-maker*. London: Hamish Hamilton.

Heydari, F. (2007) 'Ten Hotels that Made History' in Forbes Traveller, accessed 5/7/14. http://www.today.com/id/20731411/ns/today-todaytravel/#.U7gDABy236Y.

Hill, J. (2014) 'The relaunching of Ulster pride: The Titanic, Belfast and film', in Neill, W., Murray, M. and Grist, B. (eds) *Relaunching Titanic: Memory and Marketing in the New Belfast*. London: Routledge.

Jeremiah, D. (2003) 'Museums and the history and heritage of British motoring', *International Journal of Heritage Studies* 9(3), 169–190.

Kelly, B. (2012) 'Neo-liberal Belfast: disaster ahead?' *Marxist Review* 1(2), 44–59.

McKittrick, D., Kelters, S., Feeney, B. and Thornton, C. (1999). *Lost Lives: The Stories of the Men, Women and Children Who Died as a Result of the Northern Ireland Troubles*. Edinburgh: Mainstream.

McNally, K. (2014) 'Back to the Future to hit West End for 30th anniversary' in *Express: Home of the Daily and Sunday Express*, accessed 15/7/14. http://www.express.co.uk/news/showbiz/457254/Back-To-the-Future-to-hit-the-West-End-for-30th-anniversary.

Neill, W.J.V. (1995) 'Lipstick on the gorilla? Conflict management, urban development and image making in Belfast' in Neill, W.J.V., Murtagh, B. and Fitzsimons, B. (eds) *Reimaging the Pariah City: Urban Development in Belfast and Detroit*. Aldershot: Avebury.

Neill, W.J.V. (2014) 'The debasing of myth: the privatisation of Titanic memory in designing the 'post-conflict' city' in Neill, W., Murray, M. and Grist, G. (eds) *Relaunching Titanic: Memory and Marketing in the New Belfast*. London: Routledge.

Neill, W.J.V., Murray, M and Grist, B. (2014) 'Introduction: Titanic and the New Belfast' in Neill, W., Murray, M. and Grist, G. (eds) *Relaunching Titanic: Memory and Marketing in the New Belfast*. London: Routledge.

Wright, P. and DeLorean, J.Z. (1979) *On a Clear Day You Can See General Motors*. Grosse Point, MI: Wright Enterprises.

Zukin, S. (2008). 'Foreword' in Cronin, A.M. and Hetherington, K. (eds) *Consuming the Entrepreneurial City: Image, Memory, Spectacle*. London: Routledge.

6 Repositioning an industrial city through automobile heritage

The role of the *Mille Miglia* in the tourism development of Brescia, Italy

Ilenia Bregoli

> A museum in motion, unique and charming, in a beautiful framework of jubilant visitors.
>
> (Enzo Ferrari, founder of Ferrari talking about the historical re-enactment of *Mille Miglia*)

Events are one of the attractions a destination can develop to increase tourist flows, together with other offers. Visitors tend to consume different types of services, for instance, event goers tend to be involved in activities that are not just event-related, such as visiting museums, shopping, etc. (Chalip and McGuirty, 2004; Marzano and Scott, 2006). Although it is clear that there is a relationship between events and tourism destinations, this has been rather neglected in research. In this area, researchers have primarily focused on the analysis of the economic impacts of events on a destination (Mair and Whitford, 2013). One aspect in particular has received little attention, i.e. the contribution of events to the development of the destination brand and the factors that allow a positive link between an event brand and the destination brand. There are few studies on this topic, but of those that do exist, most have focused on sport events (Chalip and Costa, 2005; Jago *et al.*, 2003; Lee and Arcodia, 2011; Xing and Chalip, 2006). There is also lack of attention to this topic on the part of practitioners – event organizers and destination managers – who fail to work together and do not cross-leverage events with other attractions of destinations (Chalip and McGuirty, 2004).

This chapter focuses on the contribution of events to the development of destination brands. The aim is to identify the challenges that destination marketers and event organizers face when adopting an historic car race to reposition, brand and promote a city. The chapter focuses on the case of the city of Brescia which is located in the Lombardy region in the north of Italy. The city is well known for the development of its industrial activity, contributing to the city's title of Italy's 'capital of iron rod'. Brescia is also the place where the *Mille Miglia* (which means 'one thousand miles') was established and it is here that the historical re-enactment begins and ends every year (Figure 6.1). The original race began on the roads of Italy from Brescia to Rome and back to Brescia, covering a distance of one thousand miles. The actual competitive race took place between 1927 until

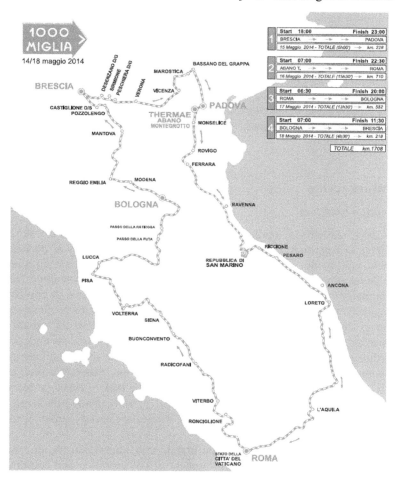

Figure 6.1 Mille Miglia route (2014 edition).

1957. Then, in the 1980s a historical re-enactment of the race was brought to life as a regular race between the models of cars that took part in the original race. Similar to the original *Mille Miglia*, the historical re-enactment takes place on the roads of Italy from Brescia to Rome and back to Brescia, covering a total of one thousand miles.

This research comprises a case study examining factors that might influence the strategic use of the *Mille Miglia* in branding and repositioning the city of Brescia. The study explores the perspectives of destination marketers and event and attraction managers through the analysis of secondary data (websites of the organizations involved, reports, etc.) and primary data obtained through interviews with four key stakeholders working for the destination marketing organization (Brescia Tourism; one person interviewed), the event organizers

(1000 Miglia S.r.l.; one person interviewed) and the *Mille Miglia* Museum (two people interviewed).

The rest of the chapter is structured as follows. The literature review covers destination management and branding and the link between branding and events. Following this, there is a brief introduction to the city of Brescia and the *Mille Miglia*. The factors facilitating the strategic use of the *Mille Miglia* for the branding and repositioning of the city and challenges in doing so are then analysed. The chapter concludes with a discussion and presentation of the managerial implications and limitations.

Literature review

Destination branding

These days, similarly to traditional products and services, tourism destinations face fierce competition, in the latter case from the high number of destinations available worldwide. As a result, destinations are paying increasing attention to the development of brands made up of both tangible and intangible features (de Chernatony and Dall'Olmo Riley, 1998), which are a source of competitive advantage (Dwyer and Kim, 2003). However, destinations are difficult entities to manage for a number of reasons: first, they involve different stakeholders who provide a diverse range of products and services to tourists; second, politics can influence the decisions taken within the destination; third, the Destination Management Organisation (DMO) does not own all the resources consumed by tourists, resulting in lack of control; fourth, there is a lack of financial resources available to DMOs (De Carlo and D'Angella, 2011; Morgan and Pritchard, 2010; Ooi, 2004; Pike, 2005). For all these reasons, destination brands cannot be treated like product or service brands.

To develop a successful destination brand, it is crucial that the governance of the destination facilitates the development of collaboration and coordination among stakeholders working within the destination, so that their actions convey a unique message to current and potential visitors and provide them with a unique and coherent experience (Bregoli and Del Chiappa, 2013; De Carlo and D'Angella, 2011; Laws *et al.*, 2011; Ritchie and Crouch, 2000).

Furthermore, a set of brand values and a brand identity representing the essence of the place must be identified (Giles *et al.*, 2013; Morgan and Pritchard, 2010; Zenker, 2011). Only if this happens will local stakeholders and residents support the destination brand and bring it alive through their behaviours. Hence a bottom-up approach to destination branding is preferred over a top-down strategy which is less likely to be successful (Ooi, 2004).

When developing a brand, it is also essential to identify the positioning to be achieved (Ries and Trout, 2001). Decisions relating to a destination brand and its positioning are closely linked to the existence of a strategy for the tourist development of the destination. For example, in the case of the city of Milan, the development of a strategy for the destination was useful in deciding how to reposition the city and improve the visitors' perceived image of it (De Carlo and D'Angella, 2011). More specifically, when the city won the bid to hold the 2015 Expo exhibition, many stakeholders felt the need to redefine the positioning of the city and improve its international image. In order to do so, the City Council set up a Department of Tourism and a DMO representing the interests of a diverse range of stakeholders. Subsequently, a strategy for the city was set and a marketing plan identifying the actions that needed to be carried out was developed. Following this, the city's brand values were identified on the basis of an internal and historical analysis of the city. Finally, the brand values and the marketing plan guided the development of the city's brand architecture (De Carlo and D'Angella, 2011).

Event brands and destination brands

Research on the link between events and tourism destinations has focused primarily on the study of the economic impacts of events on the hosting destination (Mair and Whitford, 2013). However, it has been recognized that events can also contribute to repositioning a destination in visitors' minds, changing its perceived image and increasing its salience (Jago *et al.*, 2003; Xing and Chalip, 2006). One aspect in particular has received little attention in the research literature, namely the relationship between events and destination branding. For example, the lack of understanding of how events can be used strategically to build destination brands has been highlighted (Chalip and Costa, 2005; Jago *et al.*, 2003). Although there is a dearth of research in this area, six factors that facilitate the use of events for destination branding purposes have been identified (Jago *et al.*, 2003):

1 Support should be gained from the local community, which should feel a sense of ownership of the event, in turn resulting in positive perceptions on the part of visitors concerning the event and the destination.
2 There should be a good fit between the event and the destination.
3 The event should facilitate the differentiation of the destination through distinctive features that competitors do not possess.
4 The event should have been held for a long time (at least five to 10 years). In research on some Australian food festivals, researchers found that festivals which had been running for at least 10 years or more helped in creating or changing a destination brand (Lee and Arcodia, 2011).
5 The extent to which the different stakeholders from both the event and the destination collaborate and their actions are coordinated carries weight.
6 Media coverage must be obtained by both the event managers and the destination. In particular the DMO and the event organizers should cross-communicate with each other.

(Chalip and Costa, 2005)

Current literature acknowledges that a destination brand cannot be developed only by using a single event; rather, it is necessary that the destination hosts a mix of events that can be of different types (such as sports, cultural, etc.) and that smaller events are organized as augmentations of a main event (Chalip and Costa, 2005; Jago *et al.*, 2003).

The city of Brescia

A brief history

The city of Brescia is situated in the north of Italy in the Lombardy region. It is located approximately 82 km from Milan and approximately 180 km from Venice. Its history dates back to the Bronze Age (1200 BC), but it was only with the Roman occupation that it became an organized town known as Brixia. With the dissolution of the Roman Empire, Brescia was invaded by barbarians and in 569 AD it fell to the Lombards who established it as one of their most important dukedoms. Over the following centuries, the city was controlled by the Milanese family of Visconti, the Malatesta family, the Venetian Republic, the French and the Austrians. The city became part of unified Italy in 1861. After World War II, the city embarked on major industrial development, resulting in it becoming one of Italy's most important economic centres (Comune di Brescia, 2012).

Economic indicators

Brescia is a city that is particularly famous for the development of its industrial sector. This sector has had a pivotal role in the local economy, such that in the past the city was also known as the 'capital of iron rod'. However, the recent global economic crisis which started in 2008 had put the industrial sector under pressure and this especially is the case for those businesses not involved in specialized production.

The development of the industrial sector is not only linked to the city of Brescia, but also relates to different areas of the Province of Brescia, for example the Val Trompia, a valley located to the north of the city. From the provincial economic data – which considers the city and other areas – it is apparent that by the end of 2012 overall industrial production had decreased by 6.4% compared to 2011 and compared to the first quarter of 2008 – the peak of activity before the global economic crisis – industrial production fell by 30% (AIB, 2013). If the city of Brescia alone is taken into consideration, the opposite trend can be observed between the manufacturing and hotel and restaurant sectors, with the latter showing growth in the period 2008–2012 (Table 6.1).

The *Mille Miglia*: historical overview

The relationship between the city of Brescia, automobiles and the racing world started well before the first *Mille Miglia* was organized in 1927. Indeed, from the end of the 19th century, races were organized in the city, such as the first *Coppa Florio* in 1905 and the first Italian Grand Prix in 1921 (moved to the Monza circuit the following year) (1000 Miglia S.r.l., 2014a). Not only was the city of Brescia linked to the racing world, but also to the manufacture of cars. In

Table 6.1 Number of firms and employees in the industrial and hospitality sectors of the city of Brescia

Years	Industrial sector		Hotels and restaurants	
	Number of firms	Number of employees	Number of firms	Number of employees
2008	2,518	22,470	1,350	4,387
2009	2,194	21,492	1,577	5,105
2010	2,143	21,283	1,645	5,900
2011	2,131	20,426	1,688	6,498
2012	2,096	20,868	1,715	7,061

Source: Camera di Commercio Industria Artigianato e Agricoltura Brescia.

effect, within the Province of Brescia eight different companies were involved in the production of cars, although some of these only produced prototypes for a short period of time, one such company being Beretta, the weapons manufacturer (1000 Miglia S.r.l., 2014b). Although the route of the *Mille Miglia* was changed over time (as new towns or cities which could be passed through were added to the route each year), the race always centred around the city of Brescia as it was here that the race started and ended, and Rome (1000 Miglia S.r.l., 2014c).

Over time the race became known worldwide and famous drivers, such as Nuvolari, Ascari, Fangio and Moss, participated. Furthermore, car manufacturers from all over the world included their cars in the race, for example Alfa Romeo, Ferrari, BMW, Mercedes-Benz, Porsche, Jaguar and Aston Martin, to cite just a few. The original race was organized from 1927 until 1957 when a car had an accident, running over and killing 10 spectators (1000 Miglia S.r.l., 2014d).

The race came back to life at the beginning of the 1980s, when a group of passionate people decided to organize an historical re-enactment of the *Mille Miglia*. The first edition took place in 1982, but it is only since 1987 that the event has taken place annually in May. According to the *Mille Miglia* website, cars that are eligible to participate are 'those of which at least one specimen took part in one of the speed editions (1927–1957), or completed the registration formalities for one of these editions' (1000 Miglia S.r.l., 2014e), thus just the cars that have a link with the race can participate.

To give an idea of the size of the event nowadays, in the 2013 edition, the organizers received 1,575 requests for participation and of these only 415 cars took part; 76 car manufacturers and 33 countries were represented (68.5% of participants were foreigners) (1000 Miglia S.r.l., 2014f).

Stakeholders linked to the *Mille Miglia*

Before analysing the role of *Mille Miglia* in the repositioning of the city of Brescia it is worth providing a brief description of three organisations that are in some way linked to the *Mille Miglia* and that will be considered in the subsequent analysis. These are the Brescia Automobile Club, the 1000 Miglia S.r.l. and the *Mille Miglia* Museum.

Brescia Automobile Club

This was established at the beginning of the 20th century and since the very first *Mille Miglia* it was the owner of the *Mille Miglia* name and trademark (1000 Miglia S.r.l., 2014a). Among the Brescia Automobile Club remits there is the preservation of Brescia's motor tradition and, for this reason, the Brescia Automobile Club is involved in the organisation of other historical races such as the 'Città di Lumezzane' trophy and the 'Brescia-Edolo-Pontedilegno' in addition to modern automobile races such as the 'Rally 1000 Miglia' (1000 Miglia S.r.l., 2014a).

1000 Miglia S.r.l.

This is a company which was begun by the Brescia Automobile Club in 2013 in order to organise and manage the *Mille Miglia* internally. It was set up in order to achieve long-term objectives from which the city could also benefit in future (further details have been included in the analysis of the governance problems).

Mille Miglia Museum

This museum was established in 2004 by a group of people with a passionate interest in historic cars. It is organised into 9 sections: seven relate to the *Mille Miglia* competitive race (1927–1957), one to the period 1958–1961, and one to the historical re-enactment (*Mille Miglia* Museum, 2014). There are no specific links between the *Mille Miglia* Museum and the 1000 Miglia S.r.l. as the two companies are separate entities managed by different people.

The *Mille Miglia* in the repositioning of Brescia

Before analysing the case of *Mille Miglia*, it is important to note that the city of Brescia has not adopted a city brand; hence, the following analysis is centred on the feasibility of adopting the *Mille Miglia* to help the city develop its own brand and reposition itself. From an interview with one of the museum managers, it emerged that the repositioning of the city is now seen as something unavoidable due to the crisis that is affecting many businesses within Brescia. To achieve this, the role that the *Mille Miglia* can play was highlighted. In the following sections the case will be analysed by considering the macro factors identified by Jago *et al.* (2003).

Destination and event fit

It can be argued that there is a perfect fit between the *Mille Miglia* and the city of Brescia, not only because the race was established in Brescia, but also because the city was linked with the automobile world through its own manufacturing companies. The relationship between the city and the event was summarized by one interviewee, who said:

Brescia is known for weapons [being the city where Beretta operates], the steel industry and the Mille Miglia.

Differentiation

Enzo Ferrari (the founder of Ferrari) described the *Mille Miglia* as the 'world's most beautiful race' and the historical re-enactment as 'a museum in motion' (1000 Miglia S.r.l., 2014g). Authentic legends in car racing (such as Tazio Nuvolari who was said by Porsche to be 'the greatest champion of the past, present and future' and the Formula 1 drivers Alberto Ascari and Juan Manuel Fangio) took part in the *Mille Miglia*, contributing to the aura of the event. Thus, the *Mille Miglia* is a unique event among historical re-enactments. In addition, the historic re-enactment travels through some of the most beautiful places in Italy (e.g. Ferrara, Rome, Siena) and cars can access places that are usually closed to normal traffic, such as St. Peter's Square in Rome and the Piazza del Campo in Siena, starting from the Piazza della Loggia in Brescia.

Temporal aspects

According to Jago *et al*. (2003) and Lee and Arcodia (2011), the length of time an event has been organized influences the opportunity to use the event brand for destination branding purposes. The *Mille Miglia* meets the criterion for this factor (more than 10 years being optimal) as the historical re-enactment has been organized annually since the mid-1980s. However, several interviewees highlighted the problem that the event is too concentrated over just few days and the supporting events (such as the 'Notte Bianca of the *Mille Miglia*') happen just before or after the main event. Hence, it is difficult to establish a long-term link between the event and the destination. One destination marketer pointed out that although some businesses make suggestions to the local council concerning events that could be organized, all the ideas relate to events that should take place close to the main event. To overcome this problem, the destination marketer saw the strengthening of the *Mille Miglia* Museum as a way of linking the Mille Mglia to the long-term tourism development of the city.

Media coverage

Media coverage is a factor that presents some positive elements as well as some critical issues. With regard to the former, in the 2013 edition of the *Mille Miglia* 1,300 journalists and photographers from 30 countries were accredited (1000 Miglia S.r.l., 2014f). Articles on the *Mille Miglia* can be found in newspapers around the world, suggesting that there is international awareness of the race. Some examples of recent newspaper headlines are:

- The New York Times: '*Mille Miglia* Celebrates Cars from Motorsports History' (19th May, 2014) (The New York Times, 2014);
- The New York Times: '*Mille Miglia* Reignites Italy's Racing Passions' (11th May 2013) (The New York Times, 2013);
- The Telegraph: '*Mille Miglia*: The Value of Heritage' (27th May 2011) (The Telegraph, 2011).

This media coverage is quite understandable, given the size of the historical re-enactment. It is also in line with Jago *et al.*'s (2003) point that the extent of media coverage depends on the size of the event itself.

With reference to the problem areas, when considering the communications of both the event organizers and the city, there is almost a complete lack of cross-referencing between the city and the event, respectively. For instance, on the event organizer's website there are simply images of the cars in Brescia in the 'photogallery' section, whereas on the website for tourism promotion there is just the logo of the event at the bottom of the webpages; moreover, in the section on events organized within the province it is possible to find only a brief description of the *Mille Miglia*. One of the interviewees criticized the lack of communication, stressing that Brescia is the city of the *Mille Miglia*. Overall, it can be argued that the absence of a city brand is making it harder for the event organizers and destination marketers to cross-reference the event and the destination and to highlight that Brescia is the city of the *Mille Miglia*.

Support from the local community

One of the interviewees reported how the attitude of Brescia's citizens has changed over time: if the event was initially perceived to be the 'plaything' of rich people who owned an historic car, nowadays there is participation from the local community. This change in attitude can perhaps be explained by the fact that the event has been taking place for 30 years and it is now seen as an opportunity to attract visitors to the city. Furthermore, the local council organizes a night event prior to the race ('Notte Bianca of the *Mille Miglia*') in which museums are open and there are concerts and other live shows in the major squares of the city.

Governance

The fragmentation of governance is evident at different levels: event and tourism. With reference to the event organizers, the organization and management of the historical race has changed over time. From the 1980s to 2008, the event was organized by an event organising company (Marva S.r.l.) that was set up for the purpose of organising and managing the race. This organization was also in charge of the management of the event brand. From 2009 to 2012, the race was organized by a group of companies from Liguria and Rome. The final change to the organization was made in the 2013 edition, when the organization and management of the event and its brand was given to a company set up by the Brescia Automobile Club (1000 Miglia S.r.l., na). As stated by the organizers on their website, the aim of this last change was 'for long-term plans to be made that benefit not only the *Mille Miglia* event but also the city of Brescia and Italy as a whole' (1000 Miglia S.r.l., 2014h). Thus, it was acknowledged that contracting out to external companies to organize the historical re-enactment was not the best option for the long-term strategic use of the event for the city. This view was also expressed by one of the interviewees who pointed out that by giving the organization to a company owned by the Brescia Automobile Club, the aim was to ensure that long-term objectives were pursued. In the past, it was found that there was a lack of continuity in the management of the event due to the many private interests that needed to be satisfied.

In relation to the destination level, the first element to note is the fact that there is no Destination Management Organisation for the city itself, although there is a Destination Marketing Organisation that is in charge of the promotion of the Province of Brescia overall. In addition, no strategic plans for the development of tourism exist at either the city or provincial level. For example, one destination marketer noted that the province does not have a strategy for tourism due to financial issues; furthermore, an interviewee from the event organization complained about the complete lack of strategic thinking aimed at the long-term development of tourism. This issue is of particular importance as in the case of Milan, the development of a strategy was shown to be the first step needed in repositioning the city and changing visitors' perceptions (De Carlo and D'Angella, 2011).

Apart from the event organizers and the DMO, within the city there is also the *Mille Miglia* Museum. The museum is a not-for-profit private organization, which does not receive public funds. Its sources of revenue are entrance tickets, merchandizing, a restaurant located in the same building and its meeting rooms, which are rented out.

Stakeholder collaboration and coordination

Another critical element is the extent of collaboration and coordination developed among local stakeholders. Event organizers and destination marketers do not work together and this lack of collaboration is spread to other stakeholders. For example, one of the interviewees noted that even between the organizers of the historical re-enactment and the management of the *Mille Miglia* Museum there is no collaboration. Although the museum has a license to use the *Mille Miglia* brand, which is owned by the Brescia Automobile Club, and the official dinners of the previous editions of the race were held at the restaurant within the museum, these collaborations were not strategic and were not aimed at developing any kind of strategy. Such a short-term approach can also be found when considering the relationship between the museum and the destination marketers, even though the museum participates in events in support of the *Mille Miglia*, such as the 'Notte Bianca of the *Mille Miglia*'. To explain the reason why there is lack of collaboration among the different stakeholders, one of the museum managers suggested that stakeholders struggle to work as a network due to cultural reasons. Indeed, there is a tendency to work individually rather than as a group, which is a common feature of the great majority of Italian destinations. As there is a lack of collaboration among stakeholders, there is a corresponding lack of coordination and this was perceived to be a problem by one of the event organizers.

Discussion and conclusions

From the previous analysis it has emerged that the *Mille Miglia* event could be leveraged to brand the city of Brescia and reposition it. For instance, the event and the destination fit together as the *Mille Miglia* was established in Brescia during a period in which various automobile manufacturers were operating within the city. Furthermore, the historical re-enactment has been going on since the 1980s and thus has sufficient longevity to support the development of the city brand and the event is so unique that it is differentiated from other historical re-enactments. Finally, the *Mille Miglia* enjoys wide media coverage at both national and international levels.

Nevertheless, the use of the *Mille Miglia* for branding and repositioning the city of Brescia presents some challenges which are partly connected to the use of events for destination branding purposes and partly related to destination management issues that all destinations face. With regard to the first aspect, the event is too isolated; it is thus necessary to develop more events (even of different types) and integrate them (Chalip and Costa, 2005). In the past, events such as the International Contemporary Circus Festival of Brescia and major art exhibitions were organized. The latter event in particular drew the attention to the city and for the first time changed the perceptions of people who had previously viewed Brescia only as the city of 'iron rod'. Neither of these events occurs any longer, but the *Mille Miglia* could be leveraged in conjunction with the attractions of the city, such as the Santa Giulia museum, the Capitolium (the Roman temple), its castle, etc., to brand and reposition the city.

The destination management challenges the city must address are the lack of collaboration and coordination among destination stakeholders. These elements are particularly important if destinations want to develop a successful brand and marketing more generally (Bregoli, 2013; Bregoli and Del Chiappa, 2013). Moreover, the lack of a clear strategy for tourism development is affecting the use of the *Mille Miglia* in the branding and repositioning of the city of Brescia. As has been shown, there are cities (for example Milan) that have been able to develop their own brand having developed and implemented a strategy (De Carlo and D'Angella, 2011).

In light of the previous analysis, the actions that destination marketers within the city of Brescia should undertake are: 1) to develop a modern DMO in which both public and private organizations are involved in defining a shared strategy and actions so that, for example, the different elements of the city's product mix are integrated; 2) to identify the best ways of promoting collaboration and coordination among stakeholders; 3) to promote a bottom-up approach aimed at the creation of the city's brand so that the views of destination stakeholders and the local community are heard; 4) to develop a destination brand that reflects the local identity of the place so that all destination stakeholders and residents can adopt it and bring it to life. These actions are necessary preconditions for them being able to exploit the *Mille Miglia* for the city's brand development and repositioning.

As with all research, this study is subject to certain limitations. As the research was based on limited data, further research is needed to deepen understanding of this under-researched topic. For example, it is crucial to hear the views of the local community to understand fully how an event such as the *Mille Miglia* is perceived and whether it is part of the local identity. By doing so, it will be possible to understand the potential for using the event and also decide the values to be communicated through the destination brand. Furthermore, research aimed at studying the perceived image of the city should be carried out to gain an understanding of its current image and thus decide which areas to improve.

References

AIB (2013) Indagine congiunturale trimestrale del Centro Studi AIB. Online document: http://www.aib.bs.it/download/centro_studi/ict%204-2012.pdf

Bregoli, I. (2013) Effects of DMO coordination on destination brand identity: A mixed-method study on the city of Edinburgh. *Journal of Travel Research*, 52 (2), 212–224.

Bregoli, I., and Del Chiappa, G. (2013) Coordinating relationships among destination stakeholders: Evidence from Edinburgh (UK). *Tourism Analysis*, 18 (2), 145–155.

Chalip, L., and Costa, C. A. (2005) Sport event tourism and the destination brand: Towards a general theory. *Sport in Society*, 8 (2), 218–237.

Chalip, L., and McGuirty, J. (2004) Bundling sport events with the host destination. *Journal of Sport Tourism*, 9 (3), 267–282.

Comune di Brescia (2012) Brescia history. Online document http://www.turismobrescia.it/en/percorso/brescia-history

De Carlo, M., and D'Angella, F. (2011) Repositioning city brands and events: Milan. In N. Morgan, A. Pritchard, and P. Roger (eds) *Destination brands. Managing place reputation* (pp. 225–238). Oxford: Butterworth-Heinemann.

de Chernatony, L., and Dall'Olmo Riley, F. (1998) Defining a "brand": Beyond the literature with experts' interpretations. *Journal of Marketing Management*, 14 (5), 417–443.

Dwyer, L., and Kim, C. (2003) Destination competitiveness: Determinants and indicators. *Current Issues in Tourism*, 6 (5), 369–414.

Giles, E. L., Bosworth, G., and Willett, J. (2013) The role of local perceptions in the marketing of rural areas. *Journal of Destination Marketing and Management*, 2 (1), 4–13.

Jago, L., Chalip, L., Brown, G., Mules, T., and Ali, S. (2003) Building events into destination branding: Insights from experts. *Events Management*, 8 (1), 3–14.

Laws, E., Agrusa, J., Scott, N., and Richins, H. (2011) Tourist destination governance: Practice, theory and issues. In E. Laws, H. Richins, J. Agrusa, and N. Scott (eds), *Tourist destination governance: Practice, theory and issues* (pp. 1–13). Wallingford: CABI.

Lee, I., and Arcodia, C. (2011) The role of regional food festivals for destination branding. *International Journal of Tourism Research*, 13 (4), 355–367.

Mair, J., and Whitford, M. (2013) An exploration of events research: Event topics, themes and emerging trends. *International Journal of Event and Festival Management*, 4 (1), 6–30.

Marzano, G., and Scott, N. (2006). Consistency in destination branding: The impact of events. *Global Events Congress and Event Educators Forum* (pp. 196–205). Brisbane: The University of Queensland Press.

Miglia S.r.l. (2014a) The sporting tradition. Online document: http://www.1000miglia.eu/MilleMiglia/The-Original-Mille-Miglia-race/The-sporting-tradition/

Miglia S.r.l. (2014b) Automobile car manufacturers. Online document: http://www.1000miglia.eu/MilleMiglia/The-Original-Mille-Miglia-race/The-sporting-tradition/Automobile-car-manufacturers/

Miglia S.r.l. (2014c) Brescia, città della *Mille Miglia*. Online document: http://www.1000miglia.it/Mille-Miglia/La-Mille-Miglia-di-velocita/Italia-delle-Mille-Miglia/Brescia-citta-della-Mille-Miglia/

Miglia S.r.l. (2014d) La Mille Miglia moderna. Online document: http://www.1000miglia.it/Mille-Miglia/La-Mille-Miglia-di-velocita/La-storia-dal-1927-al-2012/La-Mille-Miglia-moderna/

Miglia S.r.l. (2014e) Eligible cars. Online document: http://www.1000miglia.it/2014-Edition/Eligible-Cars/

Miglia S.r.l. (2014f) Partner. Online document: http://www.1000miglia.it/Partner-2014/

Miglia S.r.l. (2014g) Cos'è la *Mille Miglia*? Online document: http://www.1000miglia.it/Area-Stampa/Presskit/COSE-LA-MILLE-MIGLIA

Miglia S.r.l. (2014h) 1000 Miglia S.r.l. Online document: http://www.1000miglia.it/Area-Media/Presskit/1000-Miglia-S.R.L.

Miglia S.r.l. (na) Storia della *Mille Miglia* dal 1927 al 2012. Online document: http://www.1000miglia.it/attach/Content/Presskit/202/o/storiadellemillemiglia19272012.pdf.

Mille Miglia Museum (2014) Museum. Online document: http://www.museomillemiglia.it/en/museum.aspx

Morgan, N., and Pritchard, A. (2010) Meeting the destination branding challenge. In N. Morgan, A. Pritchard, and R. Pride (eds), *Destination branding. Creating the unique destination proposition* (pp. 59–78). Oxford: Butterworth-Heinemann.

Ooi, C.-S. (2004) Poetics and politics of destination branding: Denmark. *Scandinavian Journal of Hospitality and Tourism*, 4 (2), 107–128.

Pike, S. (2005) Tourism destination branding complexity. *Journal of Product and Brand Management*, 14 (4), 258–259.

Ries, A., and Trout, J. (2001). *Positioning: The battle for your mind.* New York: McGraw-Hill.

Ritchie, J., and Crouch, G. (2000). *The competitive destination. A sustainable tourism perspective.* Wallingford: CABI.

The New York Times (2014). *Mille Miglia* Celebrates Cars From Motorsports History. Online document:

The New York Times (2013). *Mille Miglia* Reignites Italy's Racing Passions. Online document: http://wheels.blogs.nytimes.com/2013/05/11/mille-miglia-re-ignites-italys-racing-passions/?module=Search&mabReward=relbias%3Ar%2C{%222%22%3A%22RI%3A15%22}

The Telegraph (2011). Mille Miglia: the value of heritage. Online document: http://www.telegraph.co.uk/motoring/classiccars/8531452/Mille-Miglia-the-value-of-heritage.html#disqus_thread

Xing, X., and Chalip, L. (2006) Effects of hosting a sport event on destination brand: A test of co-branding and match-up models. *Sport Management Review*, 9 (1), 49–78.

Zenker, S. (2011). How to catch a city? The concept and measurement of place brands. *Journal of Place Management and Development*, 4 (1), 40–52.

Part III

Places and automobile heritage

7 The economic impact of historic vehicle events

The case of the 2010 London to Brighton Veteran Car Run

Jaime Kaminski, Paul Frost and Geoffrey Smith

Introduction

'Historic motor vehicle event tourism' is a process by which individuals and groups travel to take part as participants, competitors or spectators in events focused on heritage motor vehicles. In this context 'historic' and 'heritage' vehicles are defined as those manufactured more than 30 years ago. Such vehicles have usually been retired from the purpose for which they were built and are now being preserved for posterity.

Analysis of the economic and social benefits of the historic vehicle movement in the UK between 2010 and 2011 indicated that historic vehicle enthusiasts spent 855,000 nights away from home in the UK whilst attending historic vehicle events. These enthusiasts spent a further 300,000 nights abroad attending historic vehicle events (Frost *et al.*, 2011: 15). Clearly the historic vehicle movement has significant implications for tourism.

Despite this little academic consideration has been given to the actual impact of historic vehicle events on communities. Such events can be important tourist attractions but appear to exist on the margins of tourism research. In order to understand how historic vehicle events can impact local communities research was initiated to assess and understand the economic impact of the 2010 London to Brighton Veteran Car Run on the City of Brighton and Hove on the south coast of the UK.

The 'Brighton'

The annual London to Brighton Veteran Car Run is thought to be the longest-running motoring event in the world. The Run has been organised by the Royal Automobile Club (RAC) since 1930. The RAC was a logical choice to take over the organisation because of its long association with motoring events. The RAC was founded on 10 August 1897 as the Automobile Club of Great Britain. The Club's support and promotion of the development of motoring events in Great Britain began in 1900 with the 1000 Mile Trial and it soon became the governing body for motor sport in Britain. In 1907 King Edward VII issued the royal command 'that the Automobile Club of Great Britain and Ireland should henceforth be known as 'The Royal Automobile Club'. The Royal Automobile Club is now a separate organisation to the RAC breakdown service which devolved from the Royal Automobile Club in 1999. The RAC breakdown service provides the official back-up service for the Run.

The first Run took place on Saturday 14 November 1896 and was organised by the Motor Car Club, and its controversial president Henry (Harry) J. Lawson (1852–1925), to celebrate the passing of the Locomotives on the Highway Act 1896. The Act was seen by some as the 'Magna Charta of the motor cars' because it reduced the crippling restrictions then imposed on motor vehicles (Anon., 1896c).

The original Locomotive Act 1861 (24 and 25 Victoria, c. 70) whose official title was: 'An Act for regulating the use of locomotives on turnpike and other roads, and the tolls to be levied on such locomotives and on the waggons and carriages drawn or propelled by the same' came from a time before motor vehicles. The 1861 Act limited the weight of self-propelled vehicles on the highways to 12 tons (12 tonnes), and imposed a speed limit of 10 mph (16 km/h) on open roads and 5 mph (8 km/h) in cities, towns and villages (24 and 25 Victoria, c. 70 [s. 11]). The subsequent Locomotive Act passed in 1865 reduced the speed limit to 4 mph (6 km/h) in the countryside and 2 mph (3 km/h) in towns. It is sometimes referred to as the Red Flag Act because it required a 'locomotive on the highway' to have a crew of three, one of whom was to walk no less than 60 yards (55 metres) in front of the machine holding a red flag or lantern to warn horse riders and horse drawn traffic (28 and 29 Victoria, c. 83 [s. 3]).

The Highways and Locomotives (Amendment) Act of 1878 (Victoria, c. 77) made the requirement for the red flag optional under local regulation, although it was still necessary for a person to walk 20 yards (18 metres) in front of the vehicle (41 and 42 Victoria, c. 77 [s. 29]). The need for a three-man crew remained as did the speed limits. Vehicles were required to stop on the sight of a horse and were forbidden from emitting smoke or steam to prevent horses being alarmed. Moreover, a £10 licence had to be obtained for each county the vehicle passed through. Although these Acts were originally designed for steam vehicles, they were applied with equal vigour to the motor cars that were just beginning to appear on the country's roads in the mid-1890s. It was only a decade prior to the 1896 Act that Carl Benz (1844–1929) had received the world's first patent for an integrated motor car.

A campaign was mounted to change the law, which led to the introduction of the Locomotives on Highways Act 1896 (59 and 60 Victoria, c. 36). The so-called Emancipation Act removed many of the strict rules which had restrained the fledgling motor cars. The Act defined a new category of vehicle, the 'light locomotives', which were vehicles under 3 tons unladen weight. These light locomotives were exempt from the three crew member rule and so did not require a man to walk ahead of the vehicle. They were subject to the higher 14 mph (23 km/h) speed limit, although most Local Government Boards had the authority to reduce it to 12 mph (19 km/h). The Act also formalised the 'keep left' rule, required vehicles to have a warning device such as a horn or bell, use lights at night and stop for the police when requested. An excise duty of up to 3 guineas was also applicable (cf. Merkin and Stuart-Smith, 2004: 4).

The Locomotives on Highways Act 1896 passed into law at the stroke of midnight on the night of 13/14 November 1896. Some of the motoring enthusiasts were so eager to taste their new found freedom that no sooner had the clocks chimed midnight that they took their vehicles out for a spin on the streets of the capital. Just over 10 hours later the Motor Car Club's long-awaited tour to Brighton would begin. Although now widely known as the 'The Emancipation Run', the 'First meet of the Motor Car Club' was referred to as the 'Motor Car Tour to Brighton' by the organisers (Anon., 1896d).

The Run was also intended to demonstrate the speed, comfort, and practicability of the new horseless vehicles. But there was no sense of complacency, the official program sent to the participants and published in *'The automotor and horseless vehicle journal'* stated that: 'Owners and drivers should remember that motor cars are on trial in England and that any rashness or carelessness might injure the industry in this country'.

At 10.30 a.m. on that damp Saturday morning in November over 30 vehicles, of two, three and four wheeled design set off from the Hôtel Métropole, on a 'triumphal journey' from London to Brighton. There is considerable divergence of opinion as to the number of cars that started the Run, but most accounts range between 32 and 39 vehicles. This motley collection of vehicles was powered by petrol, steam and electric because at this stage in the development of the motor car it was unclear which propulsion system would gain precedence.

From the start at Whitehall Place the route would take the pioneers onto Northumberland Avenue along the Embankment to Westminster Bridge, along Lambeth Palace Road, the Albert Embankment, Harleyford Road, Kennington Oval, across Clapham Road, then the first right along the Brixton Road. After Brixton the towns and villages of Streatham, Thornton Heath, Croydon, Purley, Merstham, Reigate, Crawley, Hand Cross, Bolney, Albourne, Pyecombe, Patcham, and Preston Park awaited the motorists. In total the Run would cover about 52 miles (84 km) (Anon., 1896c).

At a time when there were less than a hundred motor vehicles in the country this was a significant display of the cutting edge of transport technology (Montagu, 1990). The participants had brought vehicles from both Europe and America. The attraction of so many of the new horseless carriages on the streets of London drew huge crowds of spectators. An Australian observer cautiously estimated that more than half a million spectators watched the Run in the capital, noting that: 'It is very easy to over-estimate crowds, but in South London alone quite independent of the mighty concourse at the Hotel Metropole there must have been fully 500,000 sight seers. At Westminster Bridge it was like a Lord Mayor's day in Fleet-street'. (Anon., 1896e; 1897)

The crowds were so enormous that the progress of the procession was considerably impeded. In some parts of London mounted police were required to clear a path in front of the cars. It would take over an hour for the cars to travel the four miles (6.4 km) to Brixton. Still, even this glacial pace was an improvement on the previous speed limit of 2 mph (3 km/h) in urban areas. It was only when the Run had passed Brixton that the motorists could begin to put on speed.

It was not only the crowds that caused problems, the weather conditions were highly unfavourable that Saturday. It had rained the previous night and the streets were muddy and slippery. The whole capital was shrouded in a heavy fog, and as the day progressed the weather deteriorated considerably. Once the Run passed Reigate the cars had to contend against a strong head wind, driving rain and occasional showers of sleet, all of which tested the capabilities of the fledgling motorcars to the limits (Anon., 1896a). Despite the unforgiving weather, twenty-two of the pioneers would eventually arrive in Brighton during the course of the day.

The first car to enter Brighton was the Bollée steam car (No. 35) which passed the official timekeepers at 2.30 p.m. just four hours after leaving the Metropole Hotel. A second Bollée (no. 37) arrived at the finish at 2.45 p.m. The two Bollée Cars arrived over an hour before the next car to cross the finish line which was the Panhard Omnibus. A further 10 cars led by Harry Lawson's vehicle arrived between 4.52 p.m. and 5.41 p.m. According to Lawson another nine vehicles would arrive between 6.00 p.m. and 11.00 p.m. (Anon., 1896d). However, as with much associated with the Run there is much contention over who arrived and when. Considering the length of the route and the weather conditions it is remarkable, not that so many vehicles retired during the course of the day, but, that so many reached Brighton at all.

In the evening a public dinner took place in the Clarence Rooms at the Metropole Hotel, which was attended by over 200 guests of the Motor Car Club. In his speech, Harry Lawson, the president of the Motor Car Club would confidently assert that 'motors have now passed beyond the range of speculation and doubt'. He predicted, amongst other things, how the age of the car would benefit British industry, transportation, and would affect the growth of the suburbs, and the value of property (Anon., 1896b). Considering how few cars there were in the world at the time, Lawson's predictions at the Metropole that Saturday night proved remarkably prescient. However, even Lawson could not predict the role that the car would eventually play in tourism, both as a means of transport and as a potential attraction in its own right.

Over the coming years the Motor Car Club organised subsequent Runs. On Monday 29 November 1897 44 cars drove to Sheen House, West London. On Monday 13 November 1899 the Motor Car Club once again organised a run to Brighton but this time with 135 entrants, 95 of whom made it to Brighton Anon (1899: 5). The following day, Tuesday 14 November, the Automobile Club of Great Britain organised a run with over 50 cars on a revisit to Sheen House. In 1900 the Automobile Club organised a Run to Southsea. A rerun was made in 1901 with 174 cars that started in Whitehall Place, London. 1902 witnessed a Run to Oxford with 193 cars. Other organisations such as the Automobile Club of Great Britain would continue the tradition of Runs after the demise of the Motor Car Club.

The beginning of the 'London to Brighton Veteran Car Run' as it is known today can be traced to 1927 when 37 vehicles re-enacted the Emancipation Run. This event called the 'Run to Brighton' was sponsored by the *Daily Sketch* and the *Sunday Graphic* in an arrangement that continued until 1930 when Britain's oldest motoring club, the Royal Automobile Club, took over the organisation of the Run. The event has taken place annually since 1927 with the exception of the war years and 1947 when fuel rationing was in force.

In 1927 the Brighton and Hove Motor Cycle and Light Car Club (now the Brighton and Hove Motor Club) assumed the marshalling in Brighton in a role that the club maintains to this day. Around 400 volunteers are now required to marshal the event from Hyde Park to Madeira drive in Brighton.

The first re-enactment of the Run in 1927 was called the 'Run to Brighton'. The following two years the name changed to the 'Old Crocks' Run to Brighton' after which it became the 'Commemoration Run of Veteran Cars'. From 1957 to 1999 a huge variety of names were employed often incorporating the names of the commercial sponsors. From 2000 it has been called 'London to Brighton Veteran Car Run'.

Since 1956, the 'Brighton', as the Run is colloquially known in the historic vehicle world, has taken place on the first Sunday in November. It starts at sunrise from Hyde Park, London. To qualify for entry, the motor vehicles must have been manufactured prior to January 1, 1905 and be of four-wheel, tri-car or motor tricycle design, although the organisers retain the option to invite a small number of vehicles out of period. The route takes the participants across the Thames and through the London suburbs of Brixton, Lambeth and Streatham on the A23 and through Norbury to Croydon where it joins the A235 to Purley. Here the route re-joins the A23 where it takes the participants past Redhill, Horley, Gatwick and Crawley after which the Run follows the A273 through Cuckfield and Burgess Hill before finishing at Brighton. The Run covers approximately 54 miles (87 km) although subtle variations in the route because of new road layouts and road works often mean that the distance travelled is slightly different each year.

There are now two official stops along the way one at Crawley (for coffee) and the official finish at Preston Park, Brighton. The vehicles then proceed to Madeira Drive on the seafront where the majority of the spectators gather to see the arrival of the veterans. The very existence of Madeira Drive is itself tied to the origins of motor sport when in 1905 Sir Harry Preston persuaded Brighton's town council to tarmac the track between the Palace Pier and Black Rock in order to hold motor racing events. Four years later this stretch of road would be named Madeira Drive. This road would host numerous motor events, most famous of which are the Brighton National Speed Trials which are widely held up to be the oldest running motor races in the country (Gardiner, 2004).

Just as with the Emancipation Run the event is not a race. Participants are restricted to an average speed of 20 mph (32 km/h). Those who finish before 4.30 p.m. are awarded a bronze 'finisher's medal'. The medal has the logo of the Motor Car Club and is based on the medals awarded by the Motor Car Club to the first eight finishers of the original Emancipation Run (Munro, 1964).

Today the London to Brighton Veteran Car Run is one of the longest running and largest meetings of veteran cars in the world. The global prestige of the Run is such that in 2010 the Royal Automobile Club won the Fédération Internationale de l'Automobile's (FIA) Founding Members' Club Heritage

Cup for the London to Brighton Veteran Car Run. The Heritage Cup recognises outstanding achievement in the historic vehicle world and was presented to the Royal Automobile Club for its dedicated promotion of the annual London to Brighton Veteran Car Run and its protection of early motoring vehicles.

The 2010 London to Brighton Veteran Car Run

The 2010 London to Brighton Veteran Car Run was the 77th Run and took place 114 years after the Emancipation Run. It was also the 73rd event to be held under the stewardship of the Royal Automobile Club and took place 80 years after the first event organised by the Club in 1930. The 570 cars registered to take part included 150 makes of vehicles powered by steam, electric and petrol which ranged in age between 105 and 116 years old. All the allotted slots for the Run were filled six months prior to the event. 25% of all registrations (141 vehicles) for the 2010 event were from overseas. These included cars from as far afield as Australia, China, USA, Canada, Mexico, Argentina, and South Africa in addition to a large contingent from Europe. Out of the 505 starters 433 vehicles reached the finish at Brighton.

Methodology

In order to assess the impact of the 2010 event on the City of Brighton and Hove the Federation of British Historic Vehicle Clubs (FBHVC), commissioned the University of Brighton and the Historic Vehicle Research Institute (HVRI) to undertake an economic impact study of the Run. Three avenues of enquiry were pursued:

- The research instrument used to gather data from spectators was a questionnaire which sought information about their expenditure in Brighton and Hove and their demographic characteristics. The aim was to count only that expenditure that would not have occurred if the Run had not taken place (cf. Della Bitta and Loudon, 1975; Burgan and Mules, 1992; Mules and Faulkner 1996). Spectators were selected at random and questioned during the event (this yielded 595 usable responses).
- A further questionnaire was administered to the participants of the London to Brighton Veteran Car Run to establish their expenditure in the City during the Run (this yielded 138 responses).
- Additionally, the organisers provided information regarding their expenditure on the event in the City.

Economic impact assessment is reliant on an accurate estimation of the number of spectators and participants because this is the foundation for all other subsequent calculations (Davies *et al.*, 2010). Therefore, considerable effort was devoted to ensuring the estimate of spectator numbers had the greatest possible accuracy. However, one of the attractions of the Veteran Car Run is that it is an entirely free-to-view event. With no tickets, and spectators free to move about the route and City, and mix freely with non-spectators quantifying spectator numbers was particularly problematic. A variety of mechanisms were therefore used to estimate the number of spectators, these included video recording of the crowds watching the run (in order to enable counting under controlled conditions), manual counting and estimation of turnover of spectators during the event. These observations revealed that an estimated *20,300* spectators watched the Run in Brighton.

The spectators

The 2010 London to Brighton Veteran Car Run took place on Sunday 7 November. The day was sunny with few clouds, no rain, a light breeze and temperatures in the low teens centigrade. These fine conditions were conducive to a good spectator turn out in Brighton and Hove. A questionnaire was administered at random to spectators across the entire route through Brighton from the Black Lion Pub in Patcham on the northern outskirts of the city to Madeira Drive on the seafront. 595 usable responses were generated representing 3% of the estimated population (with a 98% confidence level and a 5% margin of error). The survey revealed that 37% (7,600) of the 20,300 spectators who watched the Run in 2010 were residents of Brighton and Hove. The remaining 63% were from outside of the City (12,700) and of these 72% (14,700) had come specifically to see the Run. In total 48% of all spectators were from outside of the City and had come specifically to watch the Run (see Figure 7.1).

Most of the spectators were day visitors (52%) and residents (34%), the remaining 14% staying overnight in the City. This highlights just how accessible the event is to day visitors. Although the Run begins at Hyde Park in London at sunrise, and the first vehicles can potentially arrive in Brighton from 10.00 a.m., most vehicles arrive between 11.30 a.m. and 3.00 p.m. (see Figure 7.2). The good transport links between Brighton and the capital and the wider south-east region means that many spectators can travel to Brighton and return home on the day of the event.

As might be expected the Run attracts most spectators from the south east region. Of those spectators who came to Brighton specifically to watch the Run 39% came from East and West Sussex, 13% from London, 9% from Surrey, 7% from Kent and 5% from Essex. This corroborates research undertaken by the Federation of British Historic Vehicle Clubs and the Historic Vehicle research Institute (HVRI) on the

	In Brighton specifically for the Run	In Brighton but **not** specifically for the Run
Residents	5,000 (24%)	2,600 (13%)
Visitors	9,700 (48%)	3,000 (15%)

Figure 7.1 Estimated size of different spectator groups at the London to Brighton Veteran Car Run.

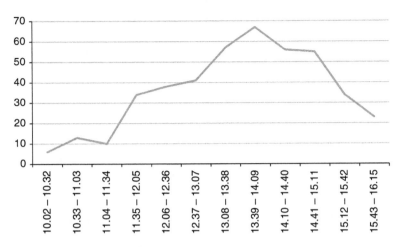

Figure 7.2 Vehicle finishing times recorded at Preston Park during the 2010 London to Brighton Veteran Car Run.

Importance	Very (%)	Important (%)	Neutral (%)	Least (%)
Distance from home	21	47	26	6
Single marque	15	32	35	18
Value for money	13	43	33	11
Multi-marque	8	26	51	15

Figure 7.3 Factors that influenced visits to historic vehicle events (Frost *et al.*, 2009: 4).

activities attended by historic vehicle enthusiasts. In a 2009 survey of the UK historic vehicle movement 68% of respondents indicated the distance from home was an important factor when choosing which events to attend (see Figure 7.3). Moreover research conducted in 2011 indicated that 40% of events attended were within 50 miles (80 km) of home base (Frost *et al.*, 2011: 15). This is clearly reflected in the visitor origins seen in the 2010 London to Brighton Run.

International visitors who came specifically to watch the Run comprised 4% of the spectators (800), with those from Australia and Myanmar travelling the furthest.

Spectator expenditure

The average spend of the spectator's *within the city* was quantified. Non-Brighton residents visiting the city specifically to attend the event spent on average £43.90 per person (see Figure 7.4). As would be expected Brighton residents attending the event spent considerably less averaging £8.90 per person in the city.

	In Brighton specifically for the Run	In Brighton but not specifically for the Run
Residents	£8.97	£8.74
Visitors	£43.87	£98.27

Figure 7.4 Estimated expenditure per person of different spectator groups at the London to Brighton Veteran Car Run.

	In Brighton specifically for the Run	In Brighton but not specifically for the Run
Residents	£44,800	£22,700
Visitors	£425,800	£294,800

Figure 7.5 Total expenditure by different spectator groups at the London to Brighton Veteran Car Run.

Motivation and opportunity to spend are key factors in explaining the large disparity in expenditures between spectators who came to Brighton specifically to watch the Run and those tourists for whom the Run was a secondary activity. The majority of the spectators were day visitors, so their time in the city was limited. These visitors were sufficiently motivated to travel to Brighton for the express purpose of viewing the arrival of the veteran vehicles in Brighton. It is therefore understandable that these spectators would want to spend as much of their limited time in the city watching the Run rather than undertaking other activities in the City.

If these figures are extrapolated to the total population of spectators at the London to Brighton Veteran Car Run, then the 5,000 Brighton residents who came specifically to view the Run would have spent £44,800 in their city. The total expenditure in Brighton by the 9,700 London to Brighton Veteran Car Run visitors from outside the City who came specifically to view the Run was *£425,800* (see Figure 7.5).

The economic benefits of the Run accruing to the Brighton and Hove include the immediate additional inward expenditure on accommodation, food, entertainment and to a lesser extent travel. The Run organisers do not provide catering for the public, so almost all of the non-participant spectator's food requirements are met by the City, although a small number brought food with them. Some minor event related souvenirs such as programs are provided by the organisers but aside from this all other retail expenditure is in the local community.

Motivation according to age group

It is apparent that age was a key variable for understanding the motivations of spectators. Those spectators in older age groups were more likely to have come to Brighton specifically to view the Run while those in younger age groups were

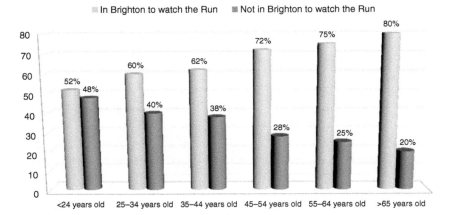

Figure 7.6 The relationship between age and motivation to watch the London to Brighton Run.

more likely to watch the Run as part of a wider range of activities in the city. The under 24-year-old age group was more or less equally divided between those who came specifically for the event (52%) and more casual observers (48%). Successive age groups are more likely to be in Brighton and Hove specifically to see the Run. Of those spectators who were over 65 years old 80% were in the city to watch the Run (see Figure 7.6).

Spectator composition

The Run attracted slightly more male (56%) than female (44%) spectators. The average group size of spectators watching the Run was 2.2 people suggesting that most people attended as a couple, predominantly without children. 17% of all spectators were members of a vehicle club.

Spectator loyalty

It is apparent that the Run engenders considerable loyalty among spectators. 65% of the respondents had seen the event previously and a staggering 92% intend to see the event again. Clearly the Run has a huge potential to convert spectators into return visitors to the City. Moreover, 27% stayed longer in Brighton because of the event. This spectator loyalty is often seen at prestigious historic vehicle events (cf. Kaminski *et al.*, 2013a: 230–231).

The participants

A postal survey was sent to participants of the Run in mid-December 2010. This elicited 138 responses (27%). Aside from the drivers there are often numerous

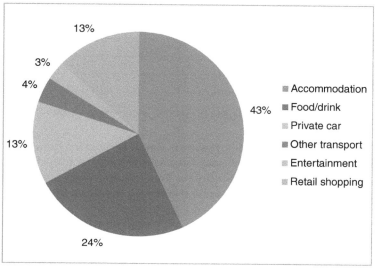

Expenditure type	Amount
Accommodation	£137,100
Food/drink	£76,000
Private car expenses	£43,200
Other transport	£13,200
Entertainment	£9,000
Retail shopping	£42,000
TOTAL	**£320,500**

Figure 7.7 Participant expenditure in Brighton relating to the Veteran Car Run.

other associated participants such as owners, friends, family and mechanics. Consequently, the average party size for participants was 5.2 compared to 2.2 for public spectators. The average spend per person of the participants was £142.00. Four hundred and thirty-four cars completed the 2010 Veteran Car Run giving a total expenditure of £320,500 based on 2,257 participants and their associates (see Figure 7.7).

The economic impact on the city

The London to Brighton Veteran Car Run results in a number of injections of capital from outside the City (see Figure 7.8). These are:

- *Spectator expenditure*: The expenditure of visitors from outside of the City who came specifically to see the Run was *£425,800*. The expenditure of the 3,000 (15%) spectators (£294,800) who were from outside of the town

Expenditure in Brighton and Hove	Amount
Spectator spend (non residents who came specifically for the Run)	£425,800
Participant spend	£320,500
Organiser spend	£84,500
Total Spend	**£830,800**

Figure 7.8 Expenditure sources used to calculate the impact of the Veteran Car Run.

and did not come specifically to see the Run was excluded from the impact assessment, even though they may have been partially motivated to come to the City on that weekend because of the Run. Residents' expenditure totalling £67,500 was also excluded because that money may have been spent in the City anyway.

- *Participant expenditure*: The participant's total expenditure was *£320,500*. Interestingly it was the participants in the Run who made the largest relative contribution to the local economy (38% of Run related expenditure). This group had an average per person spend of £142.00 compared to £43.90 for Run-specific spectators. Of this expenditure 43% was associated with accommodation and 24% with food. The disparity between the expenditure of the participants and spectators was because many participants stayed in the city overnight. This is because there are formal dinners for the participants in the evening after the Run which provides an incentive to stay. Moreover, the participants come to Brighton with larger groups (5.2 compared to 2.2 for spectators).
- *Organisers' expenditure*: The expenditure of the Royal Automobile Club in the city included the license fee, infrastructure costs, services, catering and other general events costs. The total expenditure incurred by the organisers in Brighton and Hove was *£84,500*.

The visitor and organiser expenditure is only part of the impact on the City. These external injections of capital are re-circulated in the Brighton and Hove economy. A multiplier is used to capture these secondary effects of spending on the City's economy. In the case of the London to Brighton Veteran Car Run the *£830,800* expenditure on the event by those specifically visiting the Run and on the Run itself translated to *£1,124,000* worth of benefit for the City through indirect and induced effects. Clearly this impact relates to one small part of the route of the London to Brighton Veteran Car Run, the total economic impact of the entire event will be considerable. Clearly this does not compute the social cost of the Run. These, so called negative externalities may include difficulties with parking, traffic congestion and crowding out of other activities. All of which may result in a social cost for some however, in the case of the Run, numerous factors help to mitigate these potential costs.

There are two components to the Veteran Car Run in Brighton. First the vehicles are timed in at Preston Park to the north of the city centre. This is the same park where the original Emancipation Day vehicles gathered before proceeding to the Metropole hotel on the seafront in 1896. The vehicles then proceed along a pre-scribed route through the City to the public finish at Madeira Drive on Brighton's seafront. Both locations coincidentally help minimise the negative externalities on the town.

Preston Park is Brighton's largest urban park covering 63 acres (250 hectares). The Veteran Car Run activities take only a small fraction of this space on the western side of the park next to the London Road. The event does not therefore detract from the activities of locals wishing to use the park for recreational pur-poses. Moreover, the park is to the north of the City centre and is not generally vis-ited by tourists. It does not therefore conflict with, or crowd out, tourist activities.

After Preston Park the vehicles proceed to the seafront. The differing capabilities of the vehicles, mechanical issues, and the length of the course ensure that the veterans do not arrive in Brighton in a group but they tend to come into the City individually and in small groups – something that was all too familiar to Harry Lawson on the original Emancipation Run. This however, reduces the traffic con-gestion caused by having relatively slow moving vehicles on the City's roads.

The second element is the public finish at Madeira Dive. Madeira Drive itself stretches for about 2km along the seafront to the east of Brighton Pier. It is the finishing point for many motoring events and has been the home of the Brighton National Speed Trials since 1905. Madeira Drive is for the most part a cul-de-sac, although there is the possibility of vehicular access through Duke's Rise this is usually closed to traffic with the exception of special events such as the Veteran Car Run where restricted access for participants and organisers is permitted. This means that despite its prime location the road is not essential for traffic movement in the City. It can be closed off for events like the London to Brighton Veteran Car Run with minimal disruption to the City, the most noticeable impact being the loss of approximately 350 public parking spaces. Of course the biggest factor that affects the impact of the negative externalities on the City is the short dura-tion of the event. The Run lasts for only a day with most vehicles arriving in the afternoon.

Strategic considerations

Brighton welcomed its first recorded leisure visitors in the 1730s and as such has a highly developed tourist economy (Kaminski, 2010). However, a key event such as the London to Brighton Veteran Car Run which takes place in the November shoulder season does represent an additional boost to the economy. Moreover, because the event takes place in November for historical reasons, it does not con-flict with high season events.

The event is organised by the Royal Automobile Club to preserve the tradition of the Emancipation Run and maintain the veteran vehicle heritage. The financial cost of the Run is borne by the Club which ultimately derives from the partici-pant's entry fees. Some of the economic benefit of the Run accrues to the City of Brighton. From the perspective of the City of Brighton and Hove the London to Brighton Veteran Car Run does not require large-scale infrastructure outlay compared with the inward expenditure it generates and it does not require an economic outlay beyond that which is borne by the organisers of the event. The Run is privately funded and requires no major investment at national, regional or local level. The Run's legacy is the event itself, the experience, and the preservation of motoring heritage.

The City of Brighton and Hove has the potential to enhance the economic benefit of the Run. Currently the majority of the spectators are day visitors (52%) and residents (34%), with only 14% staying overnight in the City. Clearly from the perspective of the City converting these day visitors into staying visitors would be advantageous and would greatly improve the overall economic benefit to the City. This could be achieved by making the Run part of a weekend event. A similar technique has been used in London, where the Run is now part of a three-day motoring celebration. A veteran car auction on Friday is followed by an international concours, where spectators can see the cars in London's Regent Street on Saturday, before the Run from Hyde Park, London to Brighton's Madeira Drive, on Sunday. The first Saturday concours took place in 2003 and hosted around 50 of the cars that were due to run in the following day's Run. For the first two years it was held in Waterloo Place near the Royal Automobile Club's clubhouse in Pall Mall. In 2005 it moved to Regent Street where 100 cars took part. An estimated 250,000 spectators viewed the concourse in 2010.

However, from the perspective of Brighton easy access to the capital (circa 1 hour by train), and good road links to many parts of the south east, is both beneficial and detrimental. It provides a ready source of visitors but conversely many of those visitors may be less lucrative day visitors. However, 31% of spectators do come from areas outside of the south east and so may wish to stay.

One issue that is sometimes levelled at large events is the crowding out effect, where one event monopolises resources such that it supplants rather than supplements the tourist economy. This effect is especially prevalent in already popular tourist destinations where accommodation and restaurants in the host city may already be at or near capacity (Brännäs and Nordström, 2006; Carlsen, 2004: 257). However, the Veteran Car Run does not cause such an effect. This is because the main focus of activity is limited to Madeira Drive on the seafront, and a small section of Preston Park, both are close to the city centre but sufficiently removed so as not to cause issues with congestion. Moreover, there are moderately few overnight stayers so the City's accommodation is not inundated, especially as it takes place in the shoulder season. The social cost to the city is limited to some increased congestion caused by slow moving vehicles and some parking issues.

Intangible benefits

Simply using the financial expenditure associated with the Run to provide an estimate of the economic value on the City of Brighton and Hove will underestimate the event's overall impact and benefit because it does not capture the brand value of the event to the City. The event is known globally. Consequently, participants are willing to travel vast distances with their cars to take part. Moreover, some spectators are willing to travel internationally to see the spectacle. While the route from London to Brighton has long been the venue for races, runs and other competitions few have captured the public imagination as the Veteran Car Run (Harper 1906).

Perhaps more significantly, the London to Brighton formula has become the foundation for a plethora of other motoring events. There are now 'London to Brighton' runs for Land Rovers, Minis, Citroën 2CVs, MGs, Jaguars, Triumph TRs, Smart Cars, Volkswagen vans and campers, Pioneer motorcycles, vintage motorcycles and vintage commercial vehicles. Just as with the London to Brighton Veteran Car Run many of these motoring events also finish at Madeira Drive on the seafront.

The links do not stop there. There are other London to Brighton vehicle events including Steam Heavy Haulage, cycling events such as the annual London to Brighton cycle ride for the British Heart Foundation, The Moonriders night cycling event, Capital to Coast challenge, running events such as the ultra-marathon (1951–2005) which is now a trail run and walking events such as the St. Dunstan's London to Brighton 100K Challenge. There have even been attempts to create Brighton to London events based on the same route such as the 'Brighton to London Future Car Challenge' (2010–2012). The cumulative benefit of all these events and the publicity they generate for the city is huge and can in part be attributed to the decision of Harry Lawson to take the Emancipation Day Run to Brighton in 1896.

Interestingly, the event has spawned other 'London to Brighton' runs and events globally. The appeal of the event is such that in 2005 the SotaMINIs Car Club created the 'New London to New Brighton' Mini rally in Minnesota, in the USA. The car club could take advantage of the fact that Minnesota is the only US state that has both a New London and a New Brighton. In an extraordinary quirk of fate, the distance between the two towns is 110 miles (177 km); about twice the distance from London to Brighton in the UK.

The bigger picture

The London to Brighton study gives an indication of the economic impact of a prestigious historic vehicle event on a city. How this relates to the wider consumption of historic vehicle events in the UK is only just beginning to emerge. Research conducted by the Heritage Vehicle Research Institute (HVRI) indicated that the historic vehicle movement was worth £4.3 billion to the UK economy in 2010–11. Part of that figure is made up of historic vehicle tourist activities. Segmentation analyses revealed that there are three principal groups of consumers of heritage motoring events; heritage vehicle owners, enthusiasts who do not own heritage vehicles and the general public. This research established that non-owner enthusiasts spent an average of £920 per annum on their hobby. These costs include the costs of attending events (fuel, meals, accommodation, etc.) and buying historic vehicle media, etc.

The types of historic vehicle event attended by respondents were predominantly non-competitive, but a significant minority participate in competitive motor sport. Owners use historic vehicles when attending events on 86% of occasions. They are active participants at 67% of the events they attend. It is also apparent from this research and the London to Brighton study that large numbers of the general public attend historic vehicle events (Frost *et al.*, 2011: 18). Across the UK there are thousands of these events each year ranging from similarly high profile events such as the Revival Meeting at Goodwood (Kaminski *et al.*, 2013c), the Beaulieu International Auto Jumble (Kaminski *et al.*, 2013b) or the Classic Motor Show at the National Exhibition Centre, Birmingham, to Runs, meetings (Kaminski, *et al.*, 2013a), and local historic vehicle shows that can be no larger than a village fête. In contrast to the free-to-view London to Brighton Veteran Car Run the cost for attending some of the larger historic vehicle events can often be in excess of £20 even before travel is considered (Kaminski *et al.*, 2013d).

Conclusions

In 1896 the Emancipation Run attracted competitors from Europe and America to take part and brought over half a million spectators onto the streets of London to watch the spectacle. Reports of the Run were included in newspapers across the former British Empire and beyond. More than a century later enthusiasm for the Run has not wavered. The London to Brighton Veteran Car Run is part of a global celebration of early motoring that brings together an international community of enthusiasts for one weekend every November. A veteran car auction on Friday is followed by an international concours, where the spectators can see the cars in London's Regent Street on Saturday, before the Sunday Run from Hyde Park, London to Madeira Drive, Brighton. The 2010 London to Brighton Veteran Car Run contributed £1,124,000 worth of income to the City of Brighton and Hove through indirect and induced effects. All this is funded by the participants of the Run and the Royal Automobile Club, but the overall impact of the event is far more significant than any pounds and pence analysis. The Run is a highly visible, positive element of the overall brand and image of Brighton. Moreover, the history of the Run has been a catalyst for numerous other vehicle runs choosing Brighton as a finishing point. This is the legacy of the London to Brighton Veteran Car Run; it has generated a huge benefit to the City of Brighton and Hove and will continue to do so for years to come.

Acknowledgements

The research team is indebted to the Royal Automobile Club who organise the London to Brighton Veteran Car Run, and Motion Works who have been of exceptional help. We are also grateful to the many participants and spectators of the 2010 London to Brighton Veteran Car Run who responded to the questionnaire without which this research would not have been possible. The following individuals have been of particular help; Peter Foubister of the Royal Automobile Club, Roger Etcell of MotionWorks, and Lord Montagu of Beaulieu.

References

Anon. (1896a) Liberty Day: The autocar ride to Brighton, *The Autocar*, 56.1, Saturday 21 November, 1896, 666–672.

Anon. (1896a) The trial of the motor car – London to Brighton, *Sheffield Daily Telegraph*, Monday 16 November, 6.

Anon. (1896b) New motor cars: Run from London to Brighton, *Aberdeen Journal*, Monday 16 November, 6.

Anon. (1896c) The emancipation of the motor car, *Falkirk Herald*, Wednesday 18 November, 4.

Anon. (1896d) How the first motor cars came from London to Brighton, *The Brighton Herald*, Saturday 21 November, 1896, 7.

Anon. (1896e) Motor car run to Brighton, *Kalgoorlie Western Argus*, Friday 31 December, 18.

Anon. (1897) Motor car run to Brighton, *The West Australian*, Sunday 2 January, 3.

Anon. (1899) From London to Brighton with a hundred motor cars, *The Brighton Herald*, Saturday 18 November, 5.

Brännäs, K. and Nordström, J. (2006) Tourist accommodation effects of festivals, *Tourism economics*, 12 (2), 291–302.

Burgan, B. and Mules, T. (1992) Economic impact of sporting events, *Annals of Tourism Research*, 19(4), 700–710.

Carlsen, J. (2004) The economics and evaluation of festivals and events, in I. Yeoman (ed.) *Festival and events management: An international arts and culture perspective*, Oxford: Butterworth-Heinemann, 246–259.

Davies, L., Ramchandani, G. and Coleman, R. (2010) Measuring attendance: issues and implications for estimating the impact of free-to-view sports events, *International Journal of Sports Marketing & Sponsorship*, 12 (1), 11–23.

Della Bitta, A. and Loudon, D. (1975) Assessing the economic impact of short duration tourist events, *The New England journal of business and economics: Tourist event impacts*, 7, 37–45.

Frost, P., Hart, C., Smith, G. A. and Edmunds, I. (2009) *Maintaining our transport heritage*, Stonewold: Federation of British Historic Vehicle Clubs.

Frost, P., Hart, C., Kaminski, J., Smith, G. A. and Whyman, J. (2011) *The British historic vehicle movement – A £4 billion hobby*, Stonewold: Federation of British Historic Vehicle Clubs.

Gardiner, T. (2004) *The Brighton National Speed Trials in the 1960s, 1970s and 1980s*, Poundbury: Veloce Publishing.

Harper, C. G. (1906) *The Brighton road: speed, sport, and history on the classic highway*, London: Chapman & Hall.

Hassan, D. and Connor, S. O. (2009) The socio-economic impact of the FIA World Rally Championship 2007, *Sport in society*, 12 (6), 709–724.

Kaminski, J. (2010) No lodgings to be had for love or money, *Sussex Archaeological Collections*, 148, 183–202.

Kaminski, J., Frost, P., Smith, G. and Whyman, J. (2013a) *Economic impact of the 4th European Healey Meeting, Crieff, May 2013*, Stonewold: Federation of British Historic Vehicle Clubs.

Kaminski, J., Smith, G. A., Frost, P. and Whyman, J. (2013b) *Economic impact of the Beaulieu International Autojumble on the New Forest area*, Stonewold: Federation of British Historic Vehicle Clubs.

Kaminski, J., Smith, G. A., Frost, P. and Whyman, J. (2013c) *Economic impact of the Goodwood Revival meeting on the immediate area*, Stonewold: Federation of British Historic Vehicle Clubs.

Kaminski, J. and Smith, G. (2013d) 'Mobile heritage': motor vehicle heritage tourism in the United Kingdom, in Kaminski, J., Benson, A. and Arnold, D. (eds.) *Contemporary issues in heritage tourism*, Routledge: London, 218–235.

Merkin, R. M. and Stuart-Smith, J. (2004) *The law of motor insurance*, London: Sweet & Maxwell.

Montagu, E. D. (1990) *The Brighton Run*, Princes Risborough: Shire Publications.

Mules, T. and Faulkner, B. (1996) An economic perspective on special events. *Tourism Economics*, 2 (2), 107–117.

Munro, I. C. (1964) A "Brighton" puzzle solved, *Veteran car*, October, 77–78.

Smith, G. A., Kaminski, J. and Frost, P. (2011) *Economic impact of the London to Brighton Veteran Car Run on Brighton & Hove*, Stonewold: Federation of British Historic Vehicle Clubs.

8 Heritage motoring and tourism in Barbados

Cristina Jönsson and Lee Jolliffe

Motoring related heritage tourism involves a broad range of activities, including visiting motor themed museums, attending historic car rallies, racing as well as exhibiting collectable cars in public parades and meets. On the Caribbean Island of Barbados, motoring heritage is closely related to the history and culture of the independent former British colony. This chapter will identify the motoring heritage of Barbados and profile the role of such heritage in the tourism product, highlighting opportunities for developing related niche motoring products such as historic racing.

The motor-car is the foci of motoring heritage whereby the car as artefact is presented in passive (such as antique car shows) and active (such as motoring competitions) pursuits. Motoring museums are a specialist type of museum devoted to the history of the automobile and related pursuits. They are often established, nurtured and patronized by collectors of vintage cars. Both Clark (2010) and Divall (2003) note that, for the most part, motor museums are an undeveloped museum sector, pursuing a traditional object driven interpretation of the motor car. As Clark (2010) indicates, ironically, motor cars in museums are displayed in a static position, divorced from their usual motion related stance. In contrast, heritage motoring events such as classic car parades and historic racing feature the motor-car in motion in what Kaminski and Smith (2013) refer to as 'mobile heritage', with the potential to evoke some of the nostalgia related to the operation of these vehicles.

Motoring heritage is part of history that can be preserved for the future and interpreted for the present, and as a resource for heritage tourism has become sought after around the world. Heritage related to motoring can also be an attraction for tourism and can contribute to related diversification of the tourism product. In Caribbean countries, the challenge of developing sustainable heritage tourism is how the need for a varied product portfolio of visitor attractions is merged with citizens' right to gain access to their heritage, while respecting the need for income generating activities and guaranteeing the reliability of these assets (Nurse, 2008).

Both tangible and intangible heritage have been identified as being of value to the development of heritage tourism in the Caribbean region (Nurse, 2008). In terms of motoring heritage, the region holds both tangible and intangible assets that have

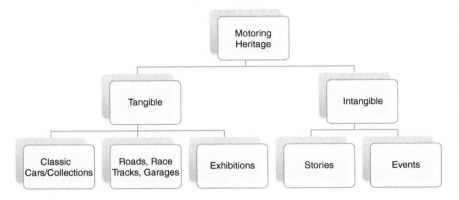

Figure 8.1 Typology of motoring heritage in the Caribbean.

the potential to be bundled into motoring heritage tourism products and experiences (Figure 8.1). These heritage resources are sometimes housed in museums, as with the Cayman Motor Museum in the Cayman Islands (Cayman Motor Museum, n.d.) showcasing the collection of local businessman Andreas Ugland. The Mallieau Motor Collection in Barbados features the collection of local realtor Bill Mallieau. In both cases the cars exhibited have a heritage relationship to the respective Islands. Intangible assets for motoring related tourism are reflected in documentation such as the history of the Barbados Rally Club (Bradford, 2007) tracing club involvement in activities in Barbados and other Caribbean territories and states.

Profiling motoring heritage related tourism in the Caribbean island of Barbados, this chapter is based on participant observation and interviews with stakeholders in the Island's motoring heritage sector as well as analysis of secondary information, such as books, websites, and newspaper and magazine articles. Case studies of motoring heritage tourism products will be presented and analysed on a comparative basis. This includes the Mallalieu Motor Collection, the Holetown Festival Car Parade, the Classic Car Revival Shows and the Barbados Historic Rally Carnival. The case study approach is suitable for investigating a phenomenon in tourism (Beeton, 2005); in this chapter, the issue being investigated is that of the use of motoring heritage in the development of heritage tourism in Barbados.

Overview of Barbados's motoring heritage

The first motor-car in Barbados (an Orient Buckland) is noted to have arrived from the United States in 1903 (The Ins and Outs of Barbados, 2011). A picture in the Mallalieu Motor Collection shows a group outing by car to scenic Cherry Tree Hill around 1907. By 1908 the number of cars on the Island numbered 25 and by 1912 there were 250 vehicles (Fraser and Hall, 2013). According to Fraser and Hall (2013) all of the later vehicles were not only for private use; tourists were able to rent motorcars for the duration of their stay or for the day with respect to cruise passengers. The introduction of the car to the Island was critical to the development of tourism, as sightseeing by motor-car became a major touristic activity. A 1913 tourist guide indicated that the Island was well served by an excellent network of 492 miles of carriage roads. Courtesy Garage, founded in the 1920's, was the local dealer for Hudson and Essex cars. The British government at that time imported the Island's first police car in 1937. In the period between the first and second world wars motor rides around the Island were noted as part of the tourism product (Fraser and Hall, 2013). The cover of a 1937–1938 Barbados tourism brochure with the tagline 'All Year Round Sunshine and Sea Bathing' features images of sea bathing, golfing, sailing and a motor-car (Ronald Watson Collection in Fraser and Hall, 2013). Visitors arriving by steamer were now able to hire a licensed guide and motor-car by the hour or hire a car. A 1943 report on tourism in Barbados indicated that Barbados was capable of accommodating 800 visitors in a pleasant climate with considerable social life, the destination was described as a place where 'living is cheap, servants are plentiful, and there are drives over an excellent system of motor roads' (Anglo American Caribbean Commission, 1945).

An interest in motor sports on the Island led to the establishment in 1957 of the Barbados Rally Club by a group of motoring enthusiasts brought together by founder Bill Mallalieu. The club held its first competitive car rally on Island roads on June 16, 1954. This laid the foundation for an interest in both car collecting and motor sport. On the tenth anniversary of the Barbados Rally Club in 1964 the then Chairman Trevor Gale commented on the connection of motor sport to tourism:

> The club is very aware that motor sport and particularly motor racing, is something which can assist the tourist industry. That it would attract the visitor to the Island there is little doubt.
>
> (Bradford, 2007: 17)

The fifty-year history of the Barbados Rally Club (Bradford, 2007) shows that it's volunteer members were instrumental in not only nurturing motor sport on the Island but in creating and supporting related motoring heritage products that will be profiled later in this chapter. There is thus little doubt that the activities of the Barbados Rally Club have encouraged an interest in both motoring sport and heritage on the Island.

In Barbados, motoring heritage also reflects the transition from British colony to an independent country and a member of the British Commonwealth. For example, the privately owned Mallalieu Motor Collection includes the car of the first Governor General who took office in 1966, at the time of the country's independence from Britain under the Barbados Independence Act declared by the British parliament. Wheeler (2011) indicates that motor sport is 'comfortably the most popular sport in the Island' and that cars have been present in Barbados since the early 1900's. However, since Barbados does not have a motor-car industry of its own, all automobiles are imported.

Merriman (2009) indicates, 'motor roads have shaped our experience of space and place'. On a small Island such as Barbados, the road systems for the most part follow the coast and allow for inland access. The existing road structure is mostly from the pre-independence colonial period, prior to 1966, with the exception of a four-lane highway system that now crosses the Island. Place-based motoring heritage is typically evidenced by the presence of motor museums that often feature private collections, and Barbados is no different in this respect. The Mallalieu Motor Collection features Bill Mallalieu's private collection reflecting his long involvement as part of a community of motoring enthusiasts on the Island, in particular with the Barbados Rally Club.

The Barbados Motoring Federation Inc. (BMF) currently represents all aspects of motoring on the Island. It is the national association of automobile clubs for motoring and motor sport recognized by the Government of Barbados and affiliated with the Federation Internationale de l'Automobile (F.I.A.). The BMF constitution includes the purpose of 'preserving and conserving all documents concerning motoring in order to trace its History within the territory' (BMF Constitution, 2011). These historical resources, in the form of vintage vehicles and documentation related to motoring in Barbados could be a resource for further developing motoring heritage related tourism on the Island. The member clubs of the BMF are: the Barbados Rally Club, The Motoring Club of Barbados Inc., the Barbados Auto Racing League, the Barbados Karting Association the Vaucluse Motorsport Raceway Club and Bushy Park, the latter having been recently redeveloped to host major motor sport events such as Top Gear Festival as part of a national strategy to develop motor sports as a niche tourism activity and economic driver.

Related tourism development in Barbados

The Barbados Tourism Authority identified the value of sport tourism as a potential lucrative area for the expansion of tourism (Delpy, 1998). It was noted that the Island is an ideal location for sporting holidays for both the participant and the spectator. Ibrahim and Gill (2005) suggested sport, including motor sport as one of the possible niche markets along with recreation, culture and eco-tourism for repositioning Barbados as a destination. This is part of a strategy to develop niche tourism products for Barbados'. There is interest in motoring as sport as Sullivan (2001) reports that car racing is popular in Barbados and fans can see top international drivers competing throughout the year. Motor sport is therefore making a significant contribution to the sport tourism product of Barbados, fulfilling the predictions that motor sport could benefit tourism made by the organizers of the Barbados Rally Club some fifty years earlier (Bradford, 2007).

In 2008 the Barbados government pledged to develop strong links between tourism and sports so as to maximize the tourism benefits that motor sport events and activities can provide. As a result, the Barbados Ministry of Tourism has identified motor sports events as a niche. In order to tap into the lucrative motor sport tourism market the marketing strategies of Barbados have been revamped. The Barbados Minister of Tourism has stated that the renovation of the Bushy Park

Circuit is the realization of a dream that has been a long time coming, which now places Barbados at the heart of Caribbean motor sport. However, more work still needs to be done for the circuit to be 'the Mecca for the region and viewed as one of the finest places to have motorsports in the world' (Barbados Today, 2014). In 2014 the Top Gear Festival (a popular media event that garners high quality exposure among motor sport supporters) was held in Barbados, for the first time in the Western Hemisphere. After this event the Barbados Tourism Authority (BTA), whose main job is to market Barbados as a tourism destination, signed a three-year contract with the producers of the Top Gear Festival for future events.

There is also the potential for those from the Diaspora (overseas visitors with a Barbadian heritage) to reconnect with home through motor sport related events and experiences (Joseph, 2011). This can potentially be part of a new kind of alternate tourism that appeals to visitors from the Diaspora as being more reflective of everyday life and as a form of tourism is less reliant on capital investment (Conway and Timms, 2010). With interest in contemporary motor sport it should be possible to cultivate, given adequate motoring heritage assets, heritage motoring as a heritage tourism product for the Island. The redevelopment of Bushy Park into the leading circuit racing track in the Caribbean is accompanied with a plan to construct a related museum (Bushy Park, n.d.) The management of Bushy Park has referred to future activities to be developed, including a car museum (Loop Barbados, 2014).

Heritage motoring products in Barbados

The heritage tourism product related to motoring can be divided along the lines suggested by Nurse (2008) in his study of heritage tourism in the region, into (1) natural attractions, (2) cultural/heritage attractions, (3) manmade attractions and (4) events. Figure 8.2 illustrates these categories with reference to the motoring heritage of Barbados.

Figure 8.2 Assets for motoring heritage tourism in Barbados.

Both locals and visitors to Barbados come into contact with, and experience the motoring heritage of the Island through four main venues: first, The Mallalieu Motor Collection, second The Holetown Festival Antique Car Parade, third, the Classic Car Revival Shows and fourth the Barbados Historic Rally Carnival. In the following section these four venues for a motoring heritage tourism experience are profiled.

Mallalieu Motor Collection

Bill Mallalieu's collection exhibited as the Mallalieu Motor Collection is a personal one. Mallalieu had many cars at home and it became a museum around 1993 (located adjacent to his own real estate office in a historic compound, former military hospital, now called Pavilion Court, Hastings, Christ Church, Barbados). According to Mr. Mallalieu 'there was simply more space here'. The cars in the collection are in working order, and some can be regularly seen at events on the Island such as the Holetown Festival. The museum is described as 'the only old car collection in Barbados' and as representing 'a history of motoring on the Island and in particular the story of the Barbados Rally Club which was founded in 1957' (The Ins and Outs of Barbados, 2011).

The collection has personal connections to the owner's life. He reports getting about 3,000 to 4,000 visitors annually, indicating he finds the guests are very interested (Interview with Bill Mallalieu, December 2013). Some visitors to the museum come to Barbados specifically to do research at the museum if they want to see a particular car. A visitor book is kept and analysed every year. For example in 2008 visitors came from England, Canada, United States, Ireland, Finland, Germany, Belgium and France. Barbados is known as a destination with a high level of repeat visitation and a few of these visitors to Barbados will visit the museum annually. When interviewed, Bill Mallalieu talked about a new type of tourist, the automobile tourist who belongs to car collector clubs and travels to meets every year (such as Mr. Mallalieu himself, who visits the UK every year for this purpose). He is typical of the motoring heritage enthusiasts referred to by Divall (2003).

The museum displays 27 cars in a garage like setting (all are operational) with more stored at home, so cars are sometimes swapped in and out. Automobile memorabilia is also displayed on the walls of the garage. This practical display is so that his mechanic can work on the vehicles. Mr. Mallalieu indicated that his favourite automobile museum; the Haynes Museum in the UK has a similar philosophy. He regularly visits other museums, in the UK and elsewhere to see how they present their cars. When interviewed he reflects that the garage like setting for the cars is something that ordinary people can relate to. The museum is privately owned and operated, and when interviewed the owner indicated (as he is post retirement age, still working in his office mornings when there is also access to the museum) his children may be planning for the future of the collection/museum.

The museum reflects upon the history of the Barbados Rally Club established in 1957 (that Bill Mallalieu participated in). The 1955 Rover that he drove in the

1957 Rally forms part of the collection of the museum. The Rally is still on-going on an annual basis. For example in 2013 over 40 cars will be temporarily imported to Barbados for this purpose.

Interviewing Bill Mallalieu, much of the discussion about the museum focused on stories related to the cars in the collection, which include the following:

- 1930 Austin Roadster, British built for the American Market.
- 1948 Wolseley Police Car.
- 1937 Chevrolet built in Oshawa, Ontario, Canada.
- 1965 Singer.
- 1953 Citroen, built in England, used in the 1979 T.V. Film, A Caribbean Mystery (Mrs. Marple).
- A Beardmore from the 1950's, the type used as a London Taxi.
- 1963 Volvo, owner's car, still uses this one occasionally as well as a few others in the collection.
- 1965 Vampire Princess, purchased in 1965 to be used as the first car for the Governor General of the newly independent (from Britain) Barbados.
- 1947 Bentley Drophead Coupe, made to order for Prince Bernard of the Netherlands.

The Mallalieu Motor Collection is thus displayed in a traditional manner in terms of exhibiting collected automobiles in a garage-like setting, accompanied by related memorabilia. This celebrates the romance of the automobile. Putting the automobile in context in motoring through the collecting of 'motoring paraphernalia' (Clark, 2010), in this case it allows the museum to augment the stories presented by the static cars on display. The adaptive use of an existing building for the museum provides some restrictions in terms of facilities, in contrast to the more recently purpose built Cayman Motor Museum (Cayman Motor Museum, n.d.).

Promotion of The Mallalieu Motor Collection is accomplished through the use of a dedicated brochure and also an advertisement in tourist publications such as *Ins & Outs of Barbados* (2011). These promotional materials feature photographs of some of the cars on exhibit at the museum. Through its membership in the Fédération Internationale de l'Automobile (FIA) the museum is also listed on the FIA website for heritage automobile collections (FIA, n.d.). This rich collection, through exhibition and participation in historic motoring events has potential for contributing to the ongoing development of heritage tourism related to motoring heritage in Barbados.

Holetown Festival Antique Car Parade, Barbados

A vintage car parade is part of the Holetown Festival that occurs every year during February. This weeklong festival celebrates the arrival of the first English settlers in Barbados who arrived in Holetown on February 17, 1627, the day Barbados became a British colony. The festival was established in 1977 (Carrington *et al.*, 1990) and is now a weeklong annual festival running from Monday through

Sunday early in February. This event attracts locals and visitors, many parts of the festival are free, some are ticketed and known as one of the highlights of the tourist season. Besides a variety of cultural events, on the Saturday of the festival a vintage car parade is organized by the Barbados Association of Classic Cars (BACC) and was in 2014 sponsored by Courtesy Garage Ltd. This parade of old vehicles offers an opportunity to showcase in motion the vintage cars that have a connection to the Island's motoring heritage. This is one of the main events for the BACC, along with the Classic Car Revival Show profiled in the next case.

In addition to cars owned by private collectors across the Island, the parade of vintage motorcars includes some of those usually on view in a static situation at the Mallalieu Motor Collection. As collectors showcase their vintage vehicles, spectators have an opportunity to view the cars in motion close up as there are no barriers to viewing. After the parade, the vintage cars are exhibited at the festival for a few hours. This free exhibit gives car enthusiasts the opportunity to talk too many of the car owners who are exhibiting their vehicles in person and to view, and in some cases touch the vintage cars up-close.

Classic Car Revival Shows

Around the world, car shows are a typical event related to the exhibition of vintage and collectable automobiles. Classic cars are usually exhibited in a static situation so that visitors can circulate and speak with the owners of the cars. This reflects an interest in vintage automobiles on the part of both the owners and the public. At present in Barbados there is an annual Classic Car Revival Show sponsored by a local business, Courtesy Garage Inc. The lead organizer for the event is the Barbados Association of Classic Cars (BACC). The criteria for participation are that classic cars must be over thirty years old and historic rally cars over twenty-five years old. Entries also include what is referred to as 'barn finds', old cars that have not been operational for a number of years and have now been brought back to life. In addition the volunteer organizers of the event welcome the entry of restored and unfinished projects.

In 2013, the day long Classic Car Revival Show was held at Content, Saint Thomas, and unlike previous shows only open to club members, it was opened up to the public (The Nation, 2013). BACC secretary-treasurer George Ullyett indicated the event was a family outing for classic car owners, whose main event was their big car show and parade at the annual Holetown Festival. 'This year we decided to invite members of the public who are interested. They are seeing nothing else but classic cars in fine condition. The cars here are 30 years old and older, which is the criteria to join the club', (The Nation, 2013).

In 2014 the Classic Car Revival Show was again held at Content, Saint Thomas. However, one media report speculated that due to the popularity of the event there is consideration of holding the event three times a year (Thorpe, 2014). This is particularly important considering the developing motor sport segment on the Island, which these historic car events could complement. For example the event is promoted as 'this Vintage Car Show is one of Barbados' many Motoring Events for 2014' (Thorpe, 2014).

> Show coordinator and secretary of the BACC, George Ullyett, told the media that interest was so high, not only from the public but from members, that some people were asking for a show to be held monthly. Where it may sound good and exciting, it would not be possible and could lose its attractiveness over time, but two shows are held annually and we may just be able to add one more", Ullyett noted.
>
> (Thorpe, 2014)

Examples of classic cars exhibited at the event, according to The Nation (Thorpe, 2014), were the recently restored MGA owned by enthusiast Dr Christopher Maynard and a Lancia restored by John 'Ding' King, both winners at the October show last year. The popularity of this event, and the suggestion by The Nation newspaper article (Thorpe, 2014) that it should be held more often reflect potential for further developing audiences interested in experiencing motoring heritage. Also, in 2014 it should be noted that a Retro and Classic Car Club of Barbados was established, as noted on their Facebook page (Retro and Classic Car Clubs Community, 2014). This new club in particular is encouraging the collection of vintage cars and the restoration of what the Classic Car Revival Show refers to as 'barn finds'.

The Barbados Historic Rally Carnival

The Barbados Rally Carnival, founded by Greg Cozier, was established in 2000 and rebranded in 2010 as the Barbados Historic Rally Carnival (BHRC). Organized by the Vaucluse Raceway Motorsport Club in 2010 the emphasis was changed to the use of historic rally cars. The web site of the BHRC indicates that the transition of the event to a 'historic' car rally reflects worldwide interest in historic rallying on the part of both spectators and competitors. The event is run under 'a set of "clubman" regulations for cars built before 1982 and host Group B cars as well for class position only' (BHRC, n.d.). The event is noted to reflect the fifty-year history of car rallying on the Island dating back to the 1957 establishment of the Barbados Rally Club.

It is also significant to note that Barbados has a dense network of paved public roads suitable for tarmac rallying, and also with diverse character. In addition the track at Vaucluse Raceway adds a new dimension to local rallyists' motorsport experience (BHRC, n.d.). According to the BHRC 'this event celebrates the History of Rallying through the social interaction of enthusiast competitors in a unique and friendly environment that preserves the spirit of the period' (BHRC, n.d.). The classes of cars include Historic (series production and special touring cars – 4 seater – marketed before 1967), Post Historic (Production and special touring cars – 4 seaters – marketed between January 1, 1968 and December 31, 1974), and Classic (Special and grand touring cars – 2 and 4 seaters) marketed between January 1st, 1975 and December 31st, 1981. Organized in late summer for two weeks, the event also includes a one-day Rally Sprint and a tarmac special stage rally at the Vaucluse Raceway. The rally on Island roads takes advantage of spectacular scenery and is widely accessible to viewers, leading to it reportedly being the sporting event with the highest number of spectators.

After the 2010 event the Barbados Tourism Authority (BTA) signed a three-year marketing agreement with the Barbados Historic Rally Carnival, demonstrating the BTA's recognition of the role of motor sport in the diversification of the Barbados tourism product (BHRC, n.d.). By 2007 the Barbados Rally Club commented that government appeared to have taken notice of events such as the Barbados Historic Rally Carnival as a potentially important part of the sports tourism product (Bradford, 2007).

This event is thus now seen as part of the sports tourism product. It also reflects a connection with the various aspects of motoring heritage in Barbados, including the rich motoring history of the Barbados Rally Club and the individual collectors of operational vintage motor vehicles, while presenting a popular spectator sport that is attractive to both locals and visitors.

Discussion

The existing motoring heritage products in Barbados can be compared using a number of criteria derived from the literature on motoring heritage tourism (Clark, 2010; Clark, 2013; Divall, 2003; Jeremiah, 2003; Kaminski and Smith, 2013), including type, duration, interaction and audience (Table 8.1). Reviewing the case studies as a group a number of common threads are evident. The first is that a variety of types of motoring heritage venues are present in Barbados, ranging

Table 8.1 Comparison of motoring heritage products in Barbados

Product	Type	Duration	Interaction	Audience
Mallalieu Motor Museum	Motor museum	Open daily, year round	Static	Limited to a few collectors and tourists
Holetown Festival Antique Car Parade	Antique Car Parade	Annually, in February on the Saturday of the Holetown Festival	Static (display), active (parade) and interactive (viewing)	Holetown Festival visitors (locals and tourists)
Classic Car Revival Shows	Classic Car Show	Day long annual event	Static (display), and interactive (viewing)	Mostly local car collectors/ spectators
Barbados Historic Rally Carnival	Historic Car Rally Event	Annually, several weeks each summer	Active (rally) and interactive (viewing)	Designed to attract locals and tourists

from a traditional motor museum, to an antique car parade, to a vintage car show and a historic rally. The second characteristic is that access to these venues is varied, from the motor collection that is accessible year round to one-time annual events ranging from part of a day to a full day to several weeks. The third factor is the level of contact between the visitor and the vintage vehicles not only varies but runs the full range of contact from the viewing of static cars to seeing some of these cars on parade and show (where interaction between owners and spectators is possible) to a historic rally situation where the vintage cars can be seen in action. The fourth point relates to audiences as the events seem to have a broad appeal, it can be noted that motor sport, and in particular the racing of historic motorcars has a broad appeal to the visiting drivers and their families as well as to other visitors to the Island and residents. The audience experiencing these motoring heritage products ranges from a few collectors and tourists (at the museum venue) to large groups of spectators (at the events). Through the FIA the historic motoring products of Barbados are linked to a dedicated global community of vintage car enthusiasts.

The Mallalieu Motor Collection has a limited appeal at present as it only seems to be visited by enthusiasts and researchers, and is open on a somewhat restricted basis, by appointment. The main audience for this attraction seems to be motoring heritage enthusiasts, who visit for the purpose of viewing specific cars in the collection. Accessibility to the collection is however increased by participation in the Holetown Festival Antique Car Parade. If other ways were found to make this private car collection more accessible, for example through mobile exhibits at historic racing events or through a renewed exhibition venue, its appeal could be broadened.

The Holetown Antique Car Parade has an even more limited appeal in terms of access, only taking place once a year as part of the Holetown Festival. Nonetheless the car parade does provide free access up close for visitors interested in motoring heritage, while exposing other visitors to classic car collectors and their cars. For spectators, even though this event only happens annually, this provides a unique opportunity to view the cars in the parade and when on display to interact with the owners. The Mallalieu Motor Collection, a participant in the event, could be using their participation to encourage increased attendance at their own exhibition venue.

The Classic Car Revival Shows have been opened up to be accessible not only to club members, but to the public. The involvement of volunteers in this event, mainly drawn from the major car clubs on the Island is notable. The integration of the contemporary motoring trade on the Island into heritage endeavours such as this event sponsored by Courtesy Garage is evident. This also provides the companies with a platform for featuring their new models, thus attracting new customers.

The Barbados Historic Rally Carnival is reportedly the sport event on the Island with the highest attendance. It is a dedicated historic event held for two weeks every summer. It provides a unique opportunity to see the historic rally cars up close and is a good product fit with the more contemporary motor sports events, such as the Top Gear Festival introduced in 2014, that are currently being pursued as a tourism development option on the Island.

Conclusion

This chapter has identified and profiled the motoring heritage resources of Barbados. Heritage motoring is just one of the many heritage aspects of the Island. Others include the slave trade and plantation history, colonial heritage, social and natural history. These themes are reflected in both heritage attractions (such as the Barbados Museum and Historical Association) and events (such as the Crop Over Festival and the Holetown Festival).

With the overall tourism development push towards motor sport in Barbados, the heritage motoring scene within Barbados could be best described as a heritage niche within tourism related to motor sport. There would seem to be some opportunity for the packaging of elements of the case studies reviewed in this chapter into a motoring heritage tour product. Such a tour could be of interest as a shore excursion for cruise ship passengers, or a stand-alone day or half-day tour targeted to tourists attracted by the Islands growing motor sport sector. Tours could also take advantage of events, for example during the period of the Holetown Antique Car Parade or the Barbados Historic Rally Carnival, a visit to the Mallieau Motor Collection could be organized prior to attending one of the latter events. Given the strong interest of the motoring enthusiasts on the Island it might even be possible for one of the car clubs to develop and conduct tours as a project, enlisting their members as guides, with the profits from the tours going back to the club or possibly being donated to local charities.

Resources for the development of motoring heritage tourism on the Island should be available through the Barbados archives, from the historical records of the Barbados Motoring Federation and through the private collections of individuals, such as Bill Mallalieu and his Mallalieu Motoring Collection. The Barbados Rally Club has produced a history, '0–50: The Barbados Rally Club, 1957–2007' (Bradford, 2007), which could provide valuable information for product development.

A limitation in the development of motoring heritage tourism on the Island is certainly the restricted resources in the sector, the main attraction is opened on a voluntary basis and the heritage motoring events are all staffed by volunteers, some of whom (for example, Bill Mallalieu) are involved in several of the motoring heritage products. Clark (2010) calls for a focus on the renewal of the motor museum, a goal that may not be achievable for small private museums, such as The Mallalieu Motor Collection in Barbados. Given the recent focus on developing motor sport as a niche tourism activity on the Island, the further development of the motoring heritage tourism sector would seem to compliment this tourism product direction. Should the Barbados Tourism Authority and or the Ministry of Tourism recognize this potential of integrating heritage motoring into the sport tourism product, resources for product development would certainly be required.

Acknowledgment

The authors would like to acknowledge the contribution to this chapter of Bill Mallalieu of the Mallalieu Motor Collection and Founder Member of the Barbados Rally Club.

References

Anglo American Caribbean Commission. (1945) *Caribbean tourist trade: a regional approach.* Washington, DC: Kaufmann Press.

Barbados Historic Rally Carnival. (n.d.) Regulations http://barbadosrallycarnival.com/sites/default/files/Vehicle_regulations_-_historic_2015_to_2017.pdf (accessed 16 October 2014).

Barbados Motoring Federation. (2011) Constitution. http://www.baddmotorsports.com/documents/BMF%20Constitution/ (accessed 15 December 2014).

Beeton, S. (2005) The Case Study in Tourism Research: A Multi-Method Case Study Approach, In: Ritchie, B.W., Burns, P., Palmer, C. (Eds.), *Tourism Research Methods: Integrating Theory with Practice.* Wallingford: CABI, 37–48.

Bradford, R. (2007) *0–50: The Barbados Rally Club, 1957–2007.* Barbados: Barbados Rally Club.

Bushy Park (n.d.) http://www.bushyparkbarbados.com/ (accessed 19 December 2014).

Carrington, S., Fraser, H., Gilmore, J. and Forde, A. (1990) *A–Z or Barbados Heritage.* Oxford: Macmillan Education Ltd.

Cayman Motor Museum. (n.d.) http://www.caymanmotormuseum.com/ (accessed 17 December 2014).

Clark, J. (2010) The "rough and tumble": displaying complexity in the motor museum. *Museum Management and Curatorship, 25* (2), 219–234.

Clark, J. (2013) Peopling the Public History of Motoring: Men, Machines, and Museums. *Curator: The Museum Journal, 56* (2), 279–287.

Conway, D., and Timms, B. F. (2010) Re-Branding Alternative Tourism in the Caribbean: The Case for "Slow Tourism." *Tourism and Hospitality Research, 10* (4), 329–344.

Delpy, L. (1998) An overview of sport tourism: Building towards a dimensional framework. *Journal of Vacation Marketing, 2,* 23–38.

Divall, C. (2003) Transport museums: another kind of historiography. *The Journal of Transport History, 24* (2), 259–265.

FIA (n.d.) Museums page. http://www.fiaheritagemuseums.com (accessed 15 October 2014).

Fraser, H. and Hall, K. (2013) *Island in the Sun: The Story of Tourism in Barbados.* Bridgetown: Miller Publishing.

Ibrahim, E. E., and Gill, J. (2005) A positioning strategy for a tourist destination, based on analysis of customers' perceptions and satisfactions. *Marketing Intelligence & Planning, 23* (2), 172–188.

Jeremiah, D. (2003) Museums and the History and Heritage of British Motoring. *International Journal of Heritage Studies, 9* (2), 169–190.

Joseph, J. (2011) A Diaspora Approach to Sport Tourism. *Journal of Sport & Social Issues, 35* (2), 146–167.

Loop Barbados (2014) Bushy Park Development Creating Jobs, December 11, 2014 http://loopnewsbarbados.com/2014/11/14/bushy-park-development-creating-jobs/ (accessed 19 December 2014.

Kaminski, J., and Smith, G. (2013) Mobile heritage, In *Contemporary Issues in Cultural Heritage Tourism,* London: Routledge, 218–235.

Merriman, P. (2009) Automobility and the Geographies of the Car. *Geography Compass*, 3 (2), 586–599.

Nurse, K. (2008) *Heritage Tourism in the Caribbean*. Bridgetown, Barbados: Caribbean Tourism Organization.

Retro and Classic Car Clubs Community (2014). https://www.facebook.com/pages/Retro-Classic-Cars-Barbados/1446790632199166 accessed 23 October 2014).

Sullivan, L. (2001) *Adventure Guide to Barbados*. Edison, NJ: Hunter Publishing Inc.

The Nation. (2013) Monday January 21, 2013, Classics on show. http://www.nationnews.com/articles/view/classics-on-show/ (accessed 20 June 2014).

Thorpe, T. (2014) Weekend of Motor Thrills, The Nation, October 17, 2014 http://www.nationnews.com/articles/view/weekend-of-motor-thrills/ (accessed 26 October 2014).

The Ins and Outs of Barbados, 2011. (2011) Barbados: Miller Publishing Ltd.

Wheeler, M. (2011) Sporting Surprises, In *Sporting Barbados Magazine*, St. George Barbados: Hilltop Publications 132.

9 Potential for heritage motoring tourism in Sri Lanka

M. S. M. Aslam

Introduction

The heritage of a country or a society is a prominent element in the contemporary world. Preserving and conserving heritage has become crucial socially, economically and politically. Often heritage has been re-conceptualized as capital in anticipation of the development needs through tourism (Garrod *et al.*, 2006). Edward (2013) observes that visitation for heritage-based attractions become a source of revenue and investment capital in addition to the contribution for preservation and conservation. Heritage motoring is a dominant cultural element from the aristocratic to common peoples in the twenty-first century (Jeremiah, 2003). Transport is an inseparable component of tourism. While it provides access to recreational activities, on the other hand it is a form of recreation in its own right (Page, 2004). As visitors' interest and love of automotive technologies leads them to choose motor museums as fascinating attractions (Clarke, 2013), heritage motoring tourism is therefore an emerging segment of tourism industry in many destinations. Due respect of establishing the very first permanent transport museum to the public goes to Norway and during 1897 in Hamar when a small railway museum was established (Divall, 2001).

Automobiles, which were preserved as antiques or extricated from human usage, are being repurposed as an arm of heritage tourism. Indifferent from the western part of the world Sri Lanka is one of the countries in the east, where history of motoring began with a chain-driven single cylinder two-seater Wolseley (de Alwis, 2002). This first car has been preserved at late Hithakami Chidhrupa Peiris's home. Her home, which is now a museum, houses vintage cars of Sri Lanka to provide opportunities for the present and future generation to admire and marvel over the creations of those distant days. The enthusiastic vintage car lovers with their personal interest have preserved and restored the old automobile, which were abandoned and almost scrapped. The responsibility for national heritage and strengthening the national economy through tourism challenges the state sector's role in preservation and conservation of motoring heritage while incorporating it with tourism. Admirably, individual car collectors and their associations and clubs such as Automobile Association of Ceylon (AA), Ceylon Motor Sports Club (CMSC), Vintage Car Owners Club (VCOC) and Ceylon Classic Car Club (CCCC) play the prevalent role in preservation and conservation of motoring heritage of Sri Lanka.

The tourism potential of motoring heritage has been under-observed during the tourism development programme, even though Sri Lanka tourism began to boom since 2009 after the ending of prolonged war between civil forces and Liberation Tigers of Tamil Elam. However, existential heritage tourism reinforces the importance of tangible and intangible new tourism resources (Stamboulis and Skayannis, 2003). This enables the tourism industry to re-invent a fascinating heritage tourism product to attract another cluster of special interest tourists or enrich tourists' satisfaction through heritage delights of Sri Lanka.

Although the Sri Lanka Tourism Development Authority failed to recognize this emerging heritage motoring tourism in Sri Lanka, ad hoc and informal participation of tourists during the rallies and event of CCCC and other occasions reveal increasing interest of tourists in heritage motoring tourism in Sri Lanka. Lack of literature and previous research in the relevant area alert the state and private sectors to learn and understand, in particular how to incorporate heritage motoring as a segment of tourism to ensure the sustainability while enhancing the revenue of tourism and satisfaction of tourists.

Methodology

A suitable road-map to accomplish this study of heritage motoring tourism in Sri Lanka has been derived through a qualitative case study approach. Lack of previous research and reports leads to explorative and in-depth investigations to elucidate interpretations of the socially constructed world (Merriam, 2009). Participative observation (Tjora, 2006) and semi-structured interviews (Yin, 2009) were employed to extract the data from settings of preservation and conservation of heritage motoring in Sri Lanka. As recommended by many authors, such as Creswell (1998), Marshall (1996), Merriam (2009) and Wilmot (2012) purposive sampling technique was used to select a sample of individual car collectors, members and office bearers of associations and clubs and relevant authorities. This was followed by in-depth interviews in different natural settings to bring forth the interpretations on preservation and conservation of heritage motoring and its incorporation with tourism in Sri Lanka. This also will lead to interpreting the intervention of authorities in preservation and conservation of heritage motoring and incorporation into tourism. Participant observations were carried out at the residences or private yards of individual car collectors and during the rallies or events organized by CCCC. In addition, observing and recording of informal visits and participation of international tourists related to heritage motoring at the car collectors' residences, private parking yards, old car vendors' yards, and on public roads and in public areas enrich the naturalistic interpretation of the setting. The study was accomplished with 9 interviews and 5 participant observations and several informal observations in addition to artefactual and documentary reviews. Descriptive analysis along with triangulation of data from multiple sources such as social interpretation, documentation, artefacts and field notes enabled the study to derive clear categories and themes.

Heritage motoring in global tourism

Culture and heritage is a primary motivation for a large number of travellers and is a growing market segment (UNWTO, 2011). Since motoring is part and parcel of the socio-economic development of human society, motoring is an inseparable component of human heritage. 'Motor vehicles don't exist in technological isolation. They are the products of human genius, skill, and effort; they are driven by people in order to serve human ends; and there is a dire human consequence when things go awry' (Clark, 2013: 279). Automobiles began to play a critical role in various aspects of human life. In the light of collective and personal memories along with interweaving statistic narratives motoring by car was a dominant culture of twentieth century from the aristocratic to the common people (Jeremiah, 2003). Tangible and intangible assets, artefacts, and culture are recognized as significant components of heritage tourism (Garrod and Fyall, 2000). Such tourism is the most significant and fastest growing segment of tourism since 1990s (Poria *et al.*, 2003) and recognized as a popular form of global tourism (Chen and Chen, 2010). In the contemporary world, cultural and heritage resources are introduced or repurposed to enhance economic development and to enrich the sociocultural environment (Edward, 2013).

Motoring is a moveable tangible heritage that embraces a number of tourist attractions. Often existential heritage tourism can offer a new means of understanding destinations (González, 2008). Enjoying motoring re-enactments, and the car as an antique and investment became the object for the practical motorists and the historic car lovers (Jeremiah, 2003). Automobile museums are widely found based on collector's and visitor's interest on automotive technologies (Clark, 2013). However, tourists also have desire to explore many intangible heritage aspects of motoring while visiting authentic historic automobile attractions. This enables the tourists to practice existing intangible heritage tourism, which link the tourists and authenticity with original spirit through deeper integration (González, 2008). Visiting different heritage motoring attractions provides opportunities for tourists to experience existing tangible and intangible motoring heritage and automotive technological evolution that underpinned the culture of human society.

Heritage tourism is also similar to other forms of tourism and leisure activities embodied in experiential consumption (Chen and Chen, 2010). Enormous socio-economic consequences of the dynamic relationship between technology and human experience have been signified through the great influence of motor vehicles on human mobility (Clark, 2013). The inseparable integration of automobile and human life engenders diverse socio-political and economic phenomena historically. This enables human society to bring forth many socially constructed meanings authentically with reference to motoring heritage. Cultural and heritage venues, events and products includes many things such as aboriginal peoples, archaeological sites, breweries and distilleries, castles and forts, created cultural experiences and railway (Edward, 2013) but motoring heritage has not been given any prominence. Interactive motoring heritage attractions are considered significant, since the quality visitors perceive is much more associated with their experiences during the process of visitation than services per se provided by the destination (Chen and Chen, 2010). This enables the visitors to carry the intangible heritage back to their homes without losing authenticity (González, 2008). Many of the heritage objects cannot be shown or used as they were originally, but a number of motoring heritage attractions could provide first-hand experience to the visitors. Usually, heritage interpretation needs to be offered in a form of creative art that explains the relevant social context of the past by bringing it to life in a strong thematic way (Edward, 2013). The historical roots of transport and travel are deeper and more complex than is usually thought. And they are reflected in a rich spectrum of interpretation through diverse origins (Divall, 2001). Motoring heritage embraces diverse attractions to anticipate the desires of tourists, who interpret it with different social meaning.

Traditionally people are reluctant to visit motor museums, full of unimaginative displays of over-restored vehicles reflecting at best a nostalgic view of the past (Divall, 2001). Yet the study of Hicks (2005) on the young person's experience of visiting Sydney Technological Museum reveals that young visitors are inspired and fascinated with mechanical exhibits and models, which could be operated by visitors. As noted by Keene and Stevenson (2008: 11) 'in 1998 at the general meeting, The Museums Association of the UK agreed a revised definition of museums: 'Museums enable people to explore collections for inspiration, learning and enjoyment' which strongly implies access beyond exhibiting selected objects. This confirms, even at the museums, that tourists demand interactive and experiential heritage rather than viewing stagnated and inexpressive objects. Further, automobiles are moveable objects and visitors' expectations are more from motoring heritage than just visiting static heritage monuments. Investigating and exploring a socially constructed world of motoring heritage enabled this study to elucidate multiple realities on the interactive and experiential heritage tourism beyond traditional museums.

Heritage motoring in Sri Lanka

Sri Lanka is a historically popular landmark in the global travel map and is renowned for its rich heritage and profound history and prehistory. Since the country had been invaded by the Portuguese, Dutch and English from Europe for a long period of time, it could not escape the influences of industrial revolution and developments in western parts of the world. After the automobile inventions in Europe in 1902, the first motor car imported to Sri Lanka was an 8 horsepower single cylinder steam driven Rover locomobile (Karunanayake, 2013). As a bench mark for the motoring history of the island, the Sri Lanka Automobile Association of Ceylon was found on 7th November 1904. (de Alwis, 2002). Since the early 1900's, roads in Sri Lanka were meant only for horse-carriages and bullock carts; driving cars was a little adventuresome and time consuming on rough surface roads (Karunanayake, 2013). In 1904, there were only 20 car owners and the Automobile Association of Ceylon was founded in Kandy with 100 members, one year before the Automobile Association of Great Britain was established (de Alwis, 2002; Karunanayake, 2013).

Today, some of these vintage cars are still well maintained and in running condition. For example, the Wolseley, the first car owned by Lieutenant Skelton is still in running condition. Another example, a Pipe, a hand painted car manufactured by Pipe Bros in Belgium in 1913, is in well maintained running condition (Karunanayake, 2013). In 1987, the Vintage Car Owners Club (VCOC) was found with 200 members to mark the national heritage of Sri Lanka in motoring These efforts have been further extended through the establishment of Classic Car Club of Ceylon (CCCC) in 1992. The club currently has over 250 members from different parts of the island. When explaining the objective of the CCCC, the president stated (Personal Communication, 2014) 'basically, we wanted to safeguard the remaining classic cars, which were exported over the year from Sri Lanka and to help one and other to restore and preserve the cars that were put a side without using for a long time'. An ex-president of Classic Car Club of Ceylon, a prominent vintage car lover in Sri Lanka took the author from his garage to his residence and showed more than sixty vintage cars in very good running condition housed in his home garden. The way he maintains and protects the cars elucidate his unbelievable interest and enthusiasm in preserving and conserving the cars. Another elder founder member and ex-president of the CCCC (Personal Communication, 2014) stated 'I did not start to preserve old cars for rallies or shows but for my own interest and love over the classic cars ... Still I don't allow even my sons to drive my cars'. This reveals the commendable interest and desires of Sri Lankans who love heritage motoring. Moreover, observation during the gathering of more than hundred CCCC members and their lovely presentation of old cars along the street in Colombo on October 11, 2014 for the memorial rally of late Mana Jayawardena, a founder member and ex-president of CCCC brought forth their broad and deep social meanings of their commitment to preservation and conservation of heritage motoring.

These observations brought out many interpretations, such as the prolonged traditions of classic car lovers, strong social-networking among car lovers, stimulating awards for members on maintaining and preserving cars, and motivation and opportunities for locals and non-locals to experience heritage motoring in Sri Lanka. To mark the tourists' interest, the author could observe many local and international tourists, who were waiting for the starting of the rally without prior invitation or notice. In an interview a vintage car seller beside Colombo – Kandy Road stated (Personal Communication, 2014) 'Here, these cars are meant to sell to people, who search for very old cars with authentic condition, without any alteration or modification'.

When I asked him, does anybody ask for a trial drive or experience driving? He said 'yes really, people like to explore and experience these cars but we are unable to provide them that opportunity (yet, they are allowed to take pictures and look around the cars'. He stated that unaffordable maintenance and unavailability of spares at reasonable price curtail the provision of experiential visits. He also confirmed that the prolonged heritage value is the underpinning reason for locals or non-locals to buy the old cars. Both the president and immediate past president stated that the many vintage cars were brought in boxes, buckets and trailers to restore them into original forms. Many of the previous owners in Sri Lanka disassembled and scattered the old cars as parts and pieces in different corners, where cars were parked. Yet, infinite interest of some people in heritage motoring has pushed to restore and preserve the cars in original conditions. Divall (2001) encapsulates that the enthusiasts who are both individuals and societies, sometimes as private companies saved some of the most significant transport artefacts of the nineteenth century and early twentieth century.

Exploration of heritage motoring in the tiny island, Sri Lanka also reveals a large number of individuals owning varieties of old cars in different brands from different countries to claim its renowned national heritage in automobiles. Nevertheless, state sectors have expressed negligible interest in cooperation and contribution for preserving and conserving motoring heritage of Sri Lanka. Individuals, associations and clubs could preserve and restore automotive artefacts and their own traditions and lifestyle in relation to motoring heritage. Before 1939 in Western Europe also the state museums were founded with private gifts and voluntary initiations of individuals (Divall, 2001). Yet, beyond related artefacts and owners' cultural stratifications motoring heritage of Sri Lanka has not been explored and restored for present and future generation. Clark (2013) points out that motoring museums should include rediscovering stories of forgotten, lost and overlooked groups, women and childhood interpretations on motoring, and road accidents that kills more 1.2 million people annually. Unexceptionally, Sri Lankan motoring heritage also embraces many historically benchmarked stories, accidents, incidents and developments in addition to 19th late 18th centuries' artefacts of automobiles. This brings forth the past in dramatic ways to connect with present visitors. The more humanizing connections with artefacts will generate astonishing engagement of visitors with motoring heritage (Clark, 2013). However, a wide range of tangible and intangible motoring heritages are under-observed by the prevailing Sri Lanka tourism industry to incorporate interactive and experiential heritage tourism. Sustainability of heritage motoring of Sri Lanka requires the state's intervention to incorporate it into tourism as a distinguished segment. This helps to recognize and safeguard the priceless efforts of motoring heritage enthusiasts in Sri Lanka, to regenerate the declining motoring heritage of Sri Lanka, in order to diversify Sri Lanka heritage tourism products and enhance tourist arrivals and revenues.

State intervention in heritage motoring of Sri Lanka

Sri Lanka is a country that possesses plentiful pre-historic, historic resources and renowned tangible and intangible heritage. The country's administration also provides prominent attention to preserve and conserve pre-historic and historic resources and national heritage. In other countries, the state often bears the major responsibility for the display of heritage motoring, which consequently tends to tell celebratory stories about industrial progress and nationhood (Divall, 2001). In this vein, the state's Road Development Authority has established the Highway Museum of Sri Lanka in 1989 at Pilimathalawa on the Colombo – Kandy trunk road, which connects the capital city Colombo and the hill country capital of Sri Lanka, Kandy. The museum mainly houses artefacts and remnants of the A1 road, the first highway construction of the country. Similarly, the Sri Lanka Railway has established first Railway Museum in Colombo and opened a second one at Kadugannawa on December 27, 2014. The railway museums also accommodate a number of artefacts and machines connecting to the glorious heritage of the railway system of the country. In addition, 'The Viceroy Special Vintage Train' steam engine 75 years old private train service is still in operation for visitors to experience the national railway heritage (Sri Lanka's Railway, n.d.).

However, preservation and conservation of heritage motoring has been ignored by the state in Sri Lanka, except for holding one or two cars in the collection of the National Museum. Confirming this situation, the immediate past president of CCCC (Personal Communication, 2014) stated:

> We could see no favouritisms or supports from the government for our effort to restore or maintain these old cars, rather we have to pay license and insurance fee similar to other new vehicles. I pay Rs. 3500.00 for my new BMW, the same amount to be paid for even for the old cars. We may drive any of these cars once in a way on the road for a short distance, still I have to pay a big sum to renew license and insurance every year ... we do not make any income out of these cars, we preserve them as heritage, when generation to come no one knows about these cars or their technology [sic].

This view was reconfirmed by the present president of the CCCC. This implies the poor recognition and least contribution of the state for preservation and conservation of vintage automobiles. Yet Edward (2013) notes the need of voluntary sector funding and tax exemption for the activities of individuals in preservation and conservation of old automobiles. Another member of CCCC (personal communication, 2014) stated 'we cannot get into the road with these cars, traffic police officers run behind us to check the license and insurance to find fault with us. We never drive these cars for a long distance, we use to do trail drive only. Yet, we have to accomplish although state's requirement perfectly to avoid the hindrances of traffic police'. Poor understanding of the heritage value of the old cars engenders inferior impressions amongst the people about the vintage car owners. The President of CCCC also stated (Personal Communication, 2014) 'very difficult to restore and maintain the old cars due to unavailability and increasing cost of spares. In case, if we need to import any spare part, same importation taxes to be paid like other modern vehicles'. Conversations with the President and members of CCCC also brought forth that they have made approaches to the political hierarchy up to His Excellency President of Sri Lanka to get the concessions and supports for licensing and importation of spare parts for old cars, but still they have not received any positive response. These interpretations reveal that the government does not have any concern over the preservation and conservation of old automobiles as national heritage of the country. Yet Edward (2013) notes cultural or heritage based attractions are the major source of income and likely to become more significant in the future. The State of Sri Lanka has failed to explore and restore the potentials and values of motoring heritage, even though artefacts and monuments of highway and railway heritage have been housed in museums to exhibits remarkable heritage. As for the rich motoring heritage of Sri Lanka till today a large number of vintage old automobiles have been preserved and conserved by individuals and groups as their hobby.

Sustainability of heritage hotoring in Sri Lanka

Although individuals' through their interest in old automobiles have been shouldering the survival of motoring heritage, its sustainability becomes a prevalent issue. An elderly old car collector stated (Personal Communication, 2014) 'my interest pushed me to collect and preserve old cars and motor bicycles, I took my children to school in the same old cars, my son [lawyer] has gone to the court also in the same cars. But, now I am going to sell them out. Since I am interested my son takes care of my cars, they are going to be further burden together with me'. These heritage artefacts been survived by chance or through the efforts of far-sighted individuals (Divall, 2001). Yet, in the present generation there are no many people, who are very keen to collect and preserve old cars with their busy schedules with occupation. According to the President of CCCC (Personal Communication, 2014) CCCC was founded with members counting in fingers but with networking and interactive and interesting activities has led to an increase in membership to more than two hundred and fifty).

Cooperative and integrative effort to preserve and conserve vintage automobiles as clubs and associations bring forth possible avenues to sustain motoring heritage. Developing collaborative relationships has been intensified through increasing numbers of organizations (Edward, 2013). One of the major functions of VCOC and CCCC is to share the information and provide assistance among the members to find spare parts and restore the old vehicles into their original status (president of CCCC, personal communication, 2014). Collective efforts of heritage motoring enthusiasts enabled survival of the national heritage related to motoring, without the intervention of state sector, as the nationally responsible body.

However, the future of motoring heritage is threatened by many factors such as increasing cost for maintenance and spare parts, increasing price and value of lands, and complex and busy life style. The immediate past president of CCCC spelled out the challenges (Personal Communication, 2014) 'you see, we thought of a museum, then our problem is the land and the facilities, that we need for the museum, personally not that I don't want to display the cars. I use all my cars, for all the cars licenses are done'. Suitable surfaces and facilities become barriers for individuals to maintain the collections of all cars due to increasing value and price for the land. In Sri Lanka, as a tiny island, it is very difficult to find space in the capital city and its suburbs, where the majority of old car lovers live. In general, motoring heritage museums have usually grown up around the private car collections of individuals (Clark, 2013). As per the opinion of a number of classic car rally observers who were Sri Lankans, they are reluctant to collect and preserve old cars due to unavailability of parking space, increasing cost of living, increasing cost of maintenance of old cars and complex and busy life. In addition, the majority of present motoring heritage enthusiasts in Sri Lanka are from social elites living in high residential areas. Many young members of those social elites migrated and live in other countries. This will lead to ignoring the hobby of present motoring heritage enthusiasts, since voluntarism is the primary factor pushing people to restore, preserve and exhibit transport artefacts (Divall, 2001). Average Sri Lankan family members will not voluntarily adapt and continue this exclusive hobby with their other survival challenges. Hence, it is inevitable to establish state intervened and cooperative strategies to preserve and conserve heritage motoring as a national heritage. This also will facilitate to expand into motoring heritage tourism as a new segment of Sri Lanka tourism.

Emerging trend of heritage motoring tourism in Sri Lanka

As Sri Lanka is a very popular destination for pre-history, history, culture and heritage traditionally, the addition of motoring heritage tourism has the ability to bridge the colonial history of the country for the present and future tourists. One of the old collectors (Personal Communication, 2014) pointed out 'many of the European tourists visit old car collections in our country not just to enjoy the artefacts but to recognize and admire our efforts in preserving and conserving their historical innovations and inventions of old automobiles'. Visiting old car collections of Sri Lanka is more than visiting a motoring museum since our motoring heritage is underpinned with political history of the country. Adding to this, the immediate past President of CCCC (Personal Communication, 2014) stated 'we did British Car Day, which is a new thing we have started and it was a big success, we wanted to do it in small way, there was a big enthusiasm, we had to strict only to British cars, and we had to wear British suits, hats of that era and British High Commissioner also got involve. They were so thrilled and we are going to have it again on January 11, 2015'.

Motoring heritage tourism therefore enables Sri Lanka to bring forth the value of colonial history in addition to technological and artefactual values of motoring history. One or two colonial architectural hotels, namely Galle Face Hotel in Colombo and the Mahaweli Reach Hotel in Kandy have kept vintage cars on display to contribute to guests' experience. Observation by the author could record a few occasions that in-house guests of the hotels were enjoying the city tour and trial of classic cars in Kandy and Colombo. Participation and interest of tourists in old automobiles of Sri Lanka without any invitation, notice and publicity show a significant trend in potential growth of heritage motoring tourism. This could be witnessed by the author, when a classic car collector opened the gate of his residence to enter, a foreign tourist ran towards the gate and got his permission to enter and view the car collection. He went around many cars and took a number of pictures and very happily left the place after thanking to the owner. When pointing out the interest of people on old cars, President of CCCC

(Personal Communication, 2014) stated 'if I use it [an old car] and park it in front of a supermarket on a Sunday, everybody goes in, looks at the car first'. He also mentioned about the increasing interest of foreign tourists and unavailability of museums and places to exhibits old cars. According to the President of CCCC they have been requested by a travel company to involve in tourism, but have yet not has a response to the query (Personal Communication, 2014). Further, conversation and interaction of tourists with the members of CCCC on the day of the car rally confirms their interest and curiosity about motoring heritage of Sri Lanka.

A vintage car sale owner also stated (personal communication, 2014) 'we have not kept any car for exhibition, but every day some tourists on the way to Kandy or Colombo visit this place to witness these old cars'. In addition, increasing visitation to National Railway Museums and National Highway Museum intensify the interest of tourists on motoring heritage. However, the potential of motoring heritage tourism is still not recognized as specified segment of Sri Lanka tourism. Confirming this the Deputy Director of Sri Lanka Tourism Promotion Bureau (SLTPB) stated that they have not classified or segmented any component of Sri Lanka tourism as motoring heritage tourism and have not previously done any study or survey concerning this potential. Edward (2013) observes that providing positive experience for visitors and increasing awareness of the visitors on the valued resource enables financial viability and contribution for preservation and conservation of resources they are responsible for. The Deputy Director of SLTPB also acknowledged motoring heritage as a significant potential of Sri Lanka tourism, even though it has not been recognized until today. A meaningful and effective interpretation and understanding of a destinations natural and cultural heritage can derive a memorable visitor experience, appreciation of the values of resources, public awareness and preservation and conservation of heritage resources (UNWTO, 2011). Recognizing and marketing motoring heritage tourism can lead to enhancing tourists' satisfaction while providing public awareness and contributing for preservation and conservation. This also encourages and supports the motoring heritage enthusiasts to continue their voluntary participation in restoring and preserving old automobiles. Diversifying tourism into heritage motoring and promoting it as new segment is an alternative socio-economic way to sustain the national heritage.

Anticipating the increasing demands of tourists in heritage motoring enables the traditional car collectors to reproduce their prolonged culture of orientation with old automobiles into a viable lifestyle entrepreneurship (Ateljevic and Doorne, 2004). However, old automobile enthusiasts in Sri Lanka are not well informed about the emerging trend for heritage motoring tourism in Sri Lanka. The immediate past President of CCCC said (Personal Communication, 2014) 'we do not have such an organized place to exhibit, when my gate is open, if someone come and ask to see the collection, I give permission. They take pictures and go'. He also informed [with very sad facial expression] that he was sad, when he could not take his car to participate for a Bristol motor rally from Singapore to Malaysia due to lack of funding. Individual car collectors are not very clearly understood as additional income generation through tourism that can contribute for preservation and conservation of heritage (Edward, 2013). Remarking on car collectors' volunteer contribution for tourism, the immediate past President of CCCC stated 'when Kandalama hotel [Heritance Kandalama] came and ask me one of my old French cars to exhibit for a French tour group, I gave them the 'Citroën', a very old car. They carried it on track and brought it back'. The need for commodification and enterprising of motoring heritage tourism also has been overlooked, since the majority of Sri Lankan vintage or classic car collectors are from the rich and elite class of society. Yet long term success depends on sustainable use of tourism assets that are well presented cultural heritage sites and living traditional culture (UNWTO, 2011). The emerging trend of tourism envisages the sustainability of motoring heritage in Sri Lanka.

Conclusion

Ensuring sustainability of socially, economically and politically significant heritage is an unavoidable task of the present generation. This inclines restoration, preservation and conservation of a heritage that is nationally and internationally remarkable. Tourism has been recognized as a tool to rediscover and reconceptualise culture and heritage as valuable resources for socio-economic development while ensuring preservation and conservation. Similarly, tangible and intangible heritage motoring has been rediscovered as a significant segment of tourism in many parts of the globe. This houses not only artefacts and automotive technological evolution but also embraces with traditional cultural, social, demographical, political and economic orientation. People prefer to visit interactive and experiential motoring heritage beyond the museums that house only the static objects. Live interpretation and communication of motoring heritage plays an unavoidable role in emerging heritage motoring tourism. Unexceptionally, Sri Lanka is also one of those countries possesses a prominent motoring heritage due to its colonial and travel link with Europe since the fifteenth century. Motoring history and heritage of Sri Lanka also embraces a long history beginning from 1902, soon after the invention of cars in Europe. The colonial regime of the British has contributed immensely for the heritage motoring of Sri Lanka. Today, as a national heritage of Sri Lanka, it possesses a vast tangible and intangible heritage.

However, preservation and conservation of motoring heritage has not been taken into consideration significantly beside individual vintage and classic car lovers along with their associations and clubs as their hobby. Although government has been playing a negligent and insufficient role, cooperation and networking through CCCC, VCOC, Ceylon Motor Sports Club, and AA of Ceylon enable preservation and conservation of heritage motoring in Sri Lanka. Yet, increasing cost of living, emerging complex and busy life style, migration of youths, declining land resource and increasing land prices, and increasing cost of the maintenance and spare parts of old cars discourage the continuation of preservation and conservation of motoring heritage as hobby. Ensuring sustainability may be underpinned with incorporation of tourism and motoring heritage potentials as a significant national heritage. This envisages fascinating and diverse interactive and experiential motoring heritage tourism beyond the museums with static objects, nevertheless Sri Lanka Tourism Development Authorities and private entrepreneurs are not enlightened with opportunities of segmenting and promoting motoring heritage as a specific segment of Sri Lanka tourism. Embracing motoring heritage of Sri Lanka for emerging global tourism market will bring forth global recognition for the pivotal role of individuals and associations in preserving and restoring tangible and intangible motoring heritage in addition to generating avenues to enhance the preservation and conservation of motoring heritage. Moreover, emerging motoring heritage tourism has the potential to stimulate tourist arrivals and revenue while enhancing visitor satisfaction.

References

Ateljevic, I. and Doorne, S. (2004). Cultural Circuits of Tourism: Commodities, Place and Re-consumption, in *A Companion to Tourism*, A. Lew, M. Hall and A.M. Williams, (eds), pp. 291–302, Oxford: Blackwell.

Chen, Ching-Fu, and Chen, Fu-Shian. (2010). Experience quality, perceived value, satisfaction and behavioral intentions for heritage tourists, *Tourism Management* 31 (1), 29–35.

Clark, J. (2013). Peopling the public history of motoring: men, machines, and museums, *Curator: The Museum Journal* 56 (2), 279–287.

Creswell, John W. (1998). *Qualitative Inquiry and Research Design: Choosing among five traditions*, Thousand Oaks: SAGE Publications.

de Alwis, W. (2002). The oldest car in Sri Lanka, *The Island*, 13.09.2002. http://www.island.lk/2002/09/15/featur04.html, retrieved on 14.12.2014.

Divall, C. (2001). The origins of transport museums in Western Europe, in *Making Histories in Transport Museums*, C. Divall and A. Scott, (eds), pp. 139–158, Continuum: London.

Edward, J. (2013). Managing Cultural and Heritage Tourism, in *Cultural Tourism*, R. Raj, K. Griffin and N. Morpeth, (eds), pp. 13–25, Wallingford: CABI.

Garrod, B. and Fyall A. (2000). Managing Heritage Tourism, *Annals of Tourism Research* 27 (3), 682–708.

Garrod, B., Wornell, R. and Youell, R. (2006). Re-conceptualising Rural Resources as Countryside Capital: The Case of Rural Tourism, *Journal of Rural Studies* 22 (1), 117–128.

González, M.V. (2008). Research Note: Intangible heritage tourism and identity, *Tourism Management* 29 (4), 807–810.

Hicks, M. (2005). 'A whole new world': the young person's experience of visiting Sydney Technological Museum, *Museum and Society* 3 (2), 66–80.

Jeremiah, D. (2003). Museums and the History and Heritage of British Motoring, International, *Journal of Heritage Studies* 9 (2), 169–190.

Karunanayake, H. (2013). *The Early Years of Motoring in British Ceylon*, https://thuppahi.wordpress.com/2013/01/08/the-early-years-of-motoring-in-british-ceylon/, Retrieved on 14.12.2014.

Keene, S. and Stevenson, A. (2008). Introduction: Context and Research, in *Collection for People*, S. Keene, (ed), pp. 11–12, Institute of Archaeology, University College London: London.

Marshall, M.N. (1996). Sampling in Qualitative Research, *Family Practice–an International Journal* 13 (6), 522–525.

Merriam, S.B. (2009). *Qualitative Research: A Guide to Design and Implementation,* San Francisco: Jossey-Bass.

Page, S. (2004). Transport and Tourism, in *A Companion to Tourism,* A. Lew, M. Hall and A.M. Williams, (eds), pp. 146–158, Oxford: Blackwell.

Poria, Y., Butler, R. and Airey, D. (2003). The core of heritage tourism, *Annals of Tourism Research* 30 (1), 238–254.

Stamboulis, Y. and Skayannis, P. (2003). Innovation strategies and technology for experience-based tourism, *Tourism Management* 24 (1), 35–43.

Tjora, A.H. (2006). Writing small discoveries: an exploration of fresh observers' observation, *Qualitative Research* 6 (4), 429–451.

Wilmot, A. (2012). *Designing Sampling Strategies for Qualitative Social Research: with Particular Reference to the Office for National Statistics' Qualitative Respondent Register.* http://www.ons.gov.uk/ons/guide-method/method-quality/general-methodology/data-collection-methodology/reports-and-publications/designing-sampling-strategies-.pdf. Retrieved on November 21, 2010.

Yin, R.K. (2009). *Case Study Research: Design and Methods,* 4th ed. Thousand Oaks: SAGE Publications.

Part IV

Products and automobile heritage

Part IV

Brothers and automobile
heritage

10 Racing back in time

The historic racing scene in Victoria, Australia

Matt Harvey

Historic racing is a great way to bring old cars and old circuits back to life and provide an entertaining spectacle that brings pleasure to both participants and spectators. It is that rare thing: genuine living history. Old cars are often more aesthetically appealing than newer ones, and the combination of inferior road holding and amateur drivers makes for plenty of action. Historic racing is mostly a minor spectator sport, but can generate enthusiastic crowds. It is also an additional attraction at commercial race meetings. While dominated by wealthy enthusiasts, it is also potentially one of the least expensive forms of motor sport. On the other hand, some historic racing cars are extremely valuable and their owners face the dilemma of keeping them in a museum or racing them as their maker intended. Historic racing addresses all of the ways in which Jeremiah (1995) identifies that the history of the motor-car and motoring heritage can be accessed as heritage: motoring landscape, pursuit of performance and cult of ownership.

This chapter surveys the historic racing scene in Victoria, Australia, tracing the fate of Victoria's historic racing circuits, and the complex blend of politics, economics and emotion that drives motor racing administration, including historic racing. Is it a tourist attraction, a branding exercise, a form of advertising, a sport, a dangerous hobby or all of these? This chapter will attempt to answer these questions. This review of historic racing in Victoria primarily draws upon the author's role as a participant observer and is supported by some secondary source material from the historic racing community in Victoria, as well as appropriate academic literature on historic racing.

Motor racing in Victoria

As the site of the first Australian Grand Prix in 1928, the State of Victoria, and in particular the Phillip Island circuit, can claim to be the spiritual home of Australian motor racing. The Mount Panorama circuit at Bathurst in New South Wales is more spectacular and demanding than any of the Victorian circuits, and the temporary Albert Park Grand Prix circuit in Melbourne would be better known to international motor sport followers. Phillip Island still hosts the Australian Moto GP in October, but the Australian Formula One Grand Prix is held at Albert Park, in an inner suburb of Melbourne, on a track which is mainly public roads for most of the year. Albert Park was used for the Australian Grand Prix in the 1950s, so it has some claim to heritage as well as its modern use, but it is also controversial due to its loss as a public park for a considerable period around the Grand Prix in March and the effect of the noise of racing cars in a predominantly residential area (Lowes, 2004). Melbourne does have a purpose-built racing circuit at Sandown in the outer south-east, opened in the 1960s, but this has not been deemed suitable as a Grand Prix venue in the modern era. There is also Calder Park 'Thunderdome' on the northwest fringe of Melbourne but it is not currently a venue for historic racing.

Perhaps we should pause to consider the purpose of motor racing. It has always been regarded as a way to test and improve automotive technology and as a form of advertising for cars and other products of interest to people interested in watching it. However, it also seems to speak to some deep inner 'need for speed' in mankind that can also be somewhat fulfilled vicariously, as noted by Jeremiah (1995). Ironically, with the exception of destination events like the historic overland Paris Dakar Rally, now known simply as 'The Dakar' and ironically held in South America due to security reasons, motor racing involves going somewhere to go nowhere fast. It is also a tourist attraction in several senses. Race tracks and circuits are often in provincial areas so race meetings bring a significant influx of tourists as spectators. The entrants will mostly be tourists if they do not hail from the region. Travelling to the track is an act of tourism and for many, getting there in their historic car and showing it off on arrival, whether or not they also race it, is a large part of the attraction.

One of the meetings considered in this chapter, Phillip Island in March, is located near Melbourne which is already a significant tourist destination, so it can be said to provide an added attraction to a destination that already has many. The rural city of Benalla, location of the Winton track at which two of the meetings discussed are held, does have other attractions (it markets itself as 'The Rose City'), but it is primarily a working agricultural centre, and while it certainly values the tourism brought by racing, it does not rely on it. Sandown, in the mid to outer suburbs of Melbourne, is not specifically a tourist attraction, but attracts entrants from around the State and the country as well as being accessible to the people of this large city. The Formula 1 Grand Prix at Albert Park is largely beyond the scope of this chapter as it does not always involve historic racing, but it is significant for the massive amount of money (around $A60 million) spent by the Victorian government to hold the race (Hudson, 2013). The claims of 'economic benefit' are almost entirely for tourism, yet the event relies on the patronage of locals and is more about the Victorian and Melbournian desire for self-promotion than proved economic benefit. Ironically, Albert Park has heritage claims as the site of the Australian Grand Prix in the 1950s but Phillip Island, a permanent track and the site of the first Australian Grand Prix in 1928, has even greater claims. The Mount Panorama circuit at Bathurst, New South Wales has the greatest claim as the heritage home of the great Holden versus Ford rivalry in touring car racing in Australia, but as it is not in Victoria or a significant site for historic racing, it is not covered in this chapter.

Historic racing

Historic racing, the racing of historic cars, has a long informal history in Australia based around car clubs. This begs the question of the difference between historic and non-historic racing. The classes of historic racing are set out below. The purest form involves cars that have an actual racing history, but if the formula was restricted to these, fields would be thin indeed. So an additional category is included comprising cars from the relevant period that have subsequently been converted to racers using parts from the period. There are cars of historic interest that compete in non-historic categories, but this chapter is concerned specifically with designated historic racing.

The Victorian Historic Racing Register was started in 1976 (VHRC, 2015). In 1978, the 50th anniversary of the first Australian Grand Prix was celebrated with a major meeting at Phillip Island. At that time, open wheeler racing in Australia had fallen into decline, while the junior formulae of Formula Ford and Formula Vee were reasonably healthy, along with a thriving touring car racing scene. The Light Car Club of Australia was also in its heyday and conducted a successful meeting at Sandown featuring the five time F1 world champion Juan Manuel Fangio in September 1978.

Australian motor racing received a boost from Alan Jones winning the Formula One World Championship in 1980 (following Jack Brabham's wins in 1959, 1960 and 1966) and Jones returned to contest what passed for Australian Grand Prix races in the early 1980's. Australian motor racing entered a new era when Adelaide secured a round of the Formula 1 Grand Prix World Championship in 1985. This was held partly through Adelaide streets and partly through a park, thus somewhat similar to the Albert Park setting in Victoria. Historic racing and displays became a regular feature of the Grand Prix program.

In 1996, Victoria 'stole' the Grand Prix from Adelaide and it went from being the last race on the calendar in October to the first, in March, at Albert Park. This in turn brought the focus of Australian motor racing back to Melbourne, where it has remained, but still without a real physical home (apart from the headquarters of the Confederation of Australian Motor Sport – CAMS). This is in contrast to permanent Grand Prix circuits like Spa Francorchamps in Belgium that also has a wonderful motor museum attached. As well as the controversies about noise and the loss of the use of the park (Lowes, 2004), the Grand Prix has attracted criticism for its cost to taxpayers. This raises issues of central concern to the tourism industry and academy – just what is the 'economic value' of the Grand Prix? An Auditor-General's Report of 2006 'Investment in Major Events' cast doubt on the optimistic estimates produced by consultants.

Historic racing is clearly in a different category from the Grand Prix though they have some features in common. The major difference is the order of expense and 'commerciality' involved. The economics of 'commercial' motor racing are beyond the scope of this chapter, but the economics of historic racing are of interest. Hardly any of the drivers are paid – indeed, most pay to enter and are risking their beloved, and often costly, machinery. There is commercial sponsorship, but the cars are only allowed to carry sponsorship if they are genuine historic racers. This raises the interesting issue of 'heritage advertising'. Cigarette companies used to be major sponsors of motor racing and even after television advertising of cigarettes was banned in 1974, cigarette sponsorship of televised motor sport was allowed to continue. It is now an interesting question whether cars bearing historic tobacco sponsorship are allowed, but as historic racing is generally not extensively televised, this does not seem to have been a major problem so far.

So historic racing is an interesting blend of the gentleman amateur in the unsponsored car, amateurs in formerly sponsored cars, and professional drivers, usually sponsored, though some retired from the commercial sport and returned to amateur status. There is also sponsorship and presence at the track of relevant service providers such as insurers, auto engineers, fuel, lubricant and tire companies. But the major economic beneficiaries would be local hospitality providers.

Camaraderie

Then there is a strong presence of car clubs in the historic racing scene. It is the opportunity to show one's pride and joy to fellow enthusiasts and a wider audience. There is also the camaraderie of car enthusiasts. There is a carnival atmosphere but also the focus provided by the racing. The cars and the paddock and garages between races are a further attraction. They are more accessible than at commercial meetings. The garages often have display boards outlining the history of the marque. This creates an impromptu automobile museum in the garage area. There is the added attraction of being able to talk to the proud owner and see under the bonnet or hood.

The circuits

There are four major historic meetings in Victoria each year: Phillip Island in March, the week before the Grand Prix, Winton in May (short track, organized by the Austin 7 Club), Winton in August (long track, organized by VHRR), and Sandown in November (Table 10.1). Of these, Phillip Island is the biggest, with

Table 10.1 Historic race meetings in Victoria

Circuit/Track	Location	Schedule	Description
Phillip Island	Phillip Island	March	Philip Island Historic Racing takes place annually before the Grand Prix.
Sandowne	Melbourne	November	Historic Sandowne is an annual event held the first weekend of November promoted and organized by the Victorian Historic Racing Register.
Winton	Benalla	May and October	Historic Winton is recognized by Historic Racing Australia as the country's longest running all-historic racing event.

Sources: Adapted from: http://www.phillipislandcircuit.com.au/; http://www.sandown.net.au/; http://www.wintonraceway.com.au/

nearly 50 events scheduled over two days. It attracts overseas and interstate visitors who also come for the Grand Prix. The late Sir Jack Brabham, the giant of Australian motor sport and three times World Champion, was patron of the VHRR and the Phillip Island meeting.

The Phillip Island circuit is some two hours' drive from Melbourne and Phillip Island has plenty of other tourist attractions including the penguin parade, seals and even whales as well as beaches and hospitality. The circuit has a spectacular backdrop of sea. It is a good circuit with many sweeping corners. A trip to Phillip Island can thus combine racing and more relaxed forms of fun. It would also be fair to say that Phillip Island does not need the circuit in order to be a tourist attraction.

Winton is located in north-eastern Victoria near the town of Benalla. It has significant wetlands nearby and the Benalla region has other attractions including wineries. It too is more than a two hour drive from Melbourne. It has short and long forms of its track. It is the long form which is used for historic racing in August. The short form is used for a meeting in May run by the Austin 7 Club but with the VHRR involved. As the first Australian Grand Prix in 1928 at Phillip Island was won by Captain Arthur Waite in a supercharged Austin 7, it is most appropriate for the club to host the meeting that includes the Arthur Waite Trophy (though it would be even more appropriate to hold the event at Phillip Island!).

Sandown is in the outer suburbs of Melbourne and thus the easiest to reach. It is not the most interesting circuit, but being owned by a horseracing club, combines grass and tarmac tracks. While the tarmac track is used much more frequently than the grass horseracing track, ownership by the Melbourne (horse) Racing Club has perhaps impeded a deeper auto presence.

Apart from Phillip Island, Albert Park is the most historic track in use, but the main arguments in its favour are its closeness to Melbourne, the quality of the circuit, and the beauty of the setting around a lake, close to the Bay, and with the Melbourne skyline as a spectacular backdrop. To those who object to a public park being put out of action for three months of the year for a race meeting that only lasts four days, it is pointed out that there was Grand Prix racing there in the 1950s and prodigious economic claims are made for the value of the event as outlined above. After eighteen years of the race at Albert Park, public support for the event seems to be on the wane, but it seems to be a brave politician who would let it go despite the soaring licence fee. Indeed, Victoria has just signed on for another five years to 2020.

It is unfortunate that Melbourne does not have a permanent circuit within easy reach that could host the Grand Prix. Calder might fit the bill, but it is in private hands and would need extensive modification. Sandown would also do and it is not clear why it does not, except that Albert Park is made available. It is unfortunate that there is no major motor museum attached to a permanent racing circuit. This suggests that motor racing has no spiritual home in Melbourne. However, the Victorian Historic Racing Register, a club based in suburban Melbourne, is the keeper of the flame for historic racing, along with car clubs of individual marques.

Motor racing politics

In Australia, motor racing has gone from being at the cutting edge of technological development to an exciting and dangerous circus. The Grand Prix and the
'V8 Supercars' (the leading Australian formula – heavily modified V8 sedans for
many years limited to Holden and Ford (see Chapter 11 by Leanne White) are
sold to the public as tourist attractions. Indeed the V8 Supercars now race in every
State and Territory and are a major contributor to regional economies. Indeed the
'CLIPSAL' event in Adelaide on the old Grand Prix circuit has proved just as
popular as the Grand Prix while being a lot cheaper.

In Victoria, motor racing seems to have fallen between the stools of massive
taxpayer support for the four-day Grand Prix circus and almost complete lack of
support for amateur racing, of which historic racing forms a part. This is not necessarily a problem. As long as there are tracks to use, the amateurs will happily
supply cars, drivers and officials. Crowds and sponsorship are sufficient to cover
staging costs and the amateurs happily bear the cost of the sport/hobby they love.

Nevertheless, the dilemma remains in this commercial age, whether there
should be an attempt to turn historic racing to commercial profit. V8 Supercars are
an instructive comparison, having been taken over by a corporation which then
franchises the racing teams. Television rights are the main source of income and
the sponsors of the teams can be assured of exposure. Historic racing has taken a
very different approach with advertising generally banned but historic advertising permitted. One senses that sensitively handled, there is a lot of commercial
potential. Historic racing could make an attractive televised package. However, it
would want to be sure not to sell its soul in the process.

It is not widely noted that motor racing involves an activity which, when conducted on the streets, is illegal. On the one hand, it provides a safe outlet for
those who wish to drive fast and to compete, but there is also the danger that it
encourages ordinary drivers to speed and race on public roads. There is also the
element that the rich can buy racing cars and circuit time whereas the poor have
no alternative but the streets. There was controversy several years ago when the
English Grand Prix driver Lewis Hamilton did some 'burn-outs' on a public road
near the Grand Prix circuit in Melbourne and criticized the 'nanny state' when
reprimanded. It should also be noted that public roads have been closed to enable
the Grand Prix cars to do publicity demonstrations. The authorities are certainly
sending mixed messages to the public!

Historic racing presents a nuanced picture. It cannot be sold as a major tourist
attraction, though it is definitely a minor one. It is a participation sport for volunteers, run by volunteers. It involves speed and is thus both an outlet for 'the
need for speed' and a possible encouragement to speed. Some very expensive
machinery is involved, but it can also be one of the cheapest forms of motorsport. Sponsorship of individual cars is generally prohibited. But there is extensive sponsorship of events. Insurers, motoring product purveyors and car dealers
are among the sponsors. But the sponsors feel like parasites. The great ethos in
historic racing is love, coupled with pride, nostalgia and fun.

Racing hearts

It is clear that owners really love their cars and so do many spectators. Apart from the drivers, there are many other volunteers: officials, scrutineers and others who make possible an activity that would otherwise not be financially viable. It is a sport with a significantly elderly demographic. This is a combination of the involvement of those who raced the cars when they were current, those who retain their interest from that time, and those who only later in life have accumulated or inherited the funds necessary to take part. There is also involvement from younger generations. It does seem to be a male-dominated activity.

Historic motor sport also offers the possibility of regularity trials and demonstrations which give the opportunity to get a car onto the track without the same stress and danger as full-on racing. As historic racing in Victoria is undertaken under the supervision of the Confederation of Australian Motor Sport (CAMS), which in turn is affiliated with the Federation Internationale de l'Automobile (FIA), it is conducted with scrupulous safety standards including the licensing of drivers. This means that all drivers regardless of age have passed health and safety examinations. It is possible to make a case for historic racing as a socially positive activity, a combination of maintaining old and beautiful cars, old and perhaps not so beautiful drivers, friendly competition, camaraderie, a lively spectacle and a good family outing. It may be seen as an encouragement to better driving, but may also be an encouragement to speed which some may take to the public roads.

Heritage

Now that much of the golden age of motor racing is beyond the living memory of most of us (1920s to the coming of the rear-engine Grand Prix car in the author's opinion!), a new concept of heritage arises. Some are fortunate to inherit historic cars from their parents, others buy them for investment or love, but acquisition is only the beginning of expense in historic racing. Maintenance, preparation and repair entail considerable time and expense. Parts are hard to get and may need to be custom-made.

Motor racing has always been a combination of amateur passion and advertising. There was a time when it was also at the cutting edge of technological development, but historic racing cannot make that claim. Conversely, it can claim to tap into a long Australian tradition of *garagisme* – home-made engineering. This was how the great Jack Brabham started in motor racing, casting his own parts at home. Although Australia has had an automobile manufacturing industry since the 1940s (now about to end with the announcements by Ford, General Motors, and others that they will cease manufacturing operations by the end of the decade) it has always had much importing and an extensive local component and repair industry. This found its expression in motor racing in the development of 'Specials', cobbled together with parts from a variety of sources. These competed with imported racers only affordable by the very wealthy. The manufacturers have concentrated on touring car racing and there has been a historic rivalry between

Holden and Ford explored elsewhere in this book. The rivalry lives on in historic racing, with the particular addition of the Mini Cooper from the 1960s.

As has been mentioned, historic racing in Australia has suffered from cars being bought by overseas buyers and taken away from these shores. There does not seem to have been any consideration given to imposing heritage protection orders on these cars to keep them in the country as part of a heritage every bit as worth preserving as historic buildings. Happily, the historic racing scene in Victoria is sufficiently vibrant to attract some overseas entrants as well as many from interstate.

France has led the way in protection of motoring heritage with the Schlumpf collection in Mulhouse being nationalized rather than being sold off and scattered. Australia has a National Motor Museum at Birdwood in South Australia, but the closest thing in Victoria is the Fox Classic Car Collection exhibiting fifty cars, still in the hands of its founder, the trucking magnate Lindsay Fox (Fox Collection, n.d).

It is tempting to adopt the idea that these historic racers are held on trust for posterity, but as valuable saleable items, this would seem hard to sustain. Conversely, any racers sourced overseas and brought to Australia may grace our tracks but are not a genuine part of our heritage. It would be great to see more cars brought out to Australia for special events like the ERA that was brought out for the Grand Prix 50th Anniversary in 1978 (which it won!), but this would have to be at the owner's expense as it is unlikely that a sponsor would find individual cars sufficiently significant to pay for.

Class struggle

Historic racing is divided into a number of classes listed below. These categories will continue to expand as more cars are 'historicized'.

J (pre-1931) now alas very rare. This is divided into Ja for cars with a competition history and Jb for cars assembled from period components.

K (1931–1940) now also rare also has the a-b distinction as above

L (1941–1960) is divided into Sports and Racing

M (1961–1965)

N Production touring cars 1961–1972

O (1966–1969)

Q (1970–1977)

R (1978–mid 80s)

S applies to production sports cars pre 1977

Groups A and C are categories used for touring cars 1973–1992.

Looking at the 2013 program for Historic Sandown, it is notable that many events involved multiple classes. This is necessary to ensure fields of reasonable sizes, but leads to anachronism and widely differing times. It may however also lead to close racing between cars of different types and eras, but of similar speeds, pleasing the racing enthusiast, if not the historical purist.

Chequered flag ... or the race that never ends?

Perhaps, like the Grand Prix, it is difficult to do a cost-benefit analysis on the historic racing events. What is certain is that historic racing is an activity that brings pleasure to many at a much more moderate cost, conducted by amateurs and volunteers. That suggests a social value that is real but hard to quantify.

Historic racing looks like an activity that can continue for the foreseeable future, and indeed, one that can grow as new eras of cars become historic. However, the older and rarer the cars become, the harder it will be to assemble a decent racing field. It may take a collector of the calibre of Lindsay Fox of the Fox Collection to assemble a stable of racers from particular eras which can then be raced regularly. It is perhaps more in the Australian spirit for proud owners to keep patching up the old classics and racing them when they can, bringing the past roaring back to life!

References

Fox Collection (n.d). http://foxcollection.org.au Accessed January 31, 2015.

Historic Commission of Confederation of Australian Motor Sport (CAMS). (n.d) A Guide to Historic Motor Racing in Australia. http://docs.cams.com.au/Motorsport/Historic/ FORMS/Guide.pdf. Accessed January 27, 2015

Hudson, F. (2013, January 23). Victorians pay millions for the right to host the F1 Grand Prix. Melbourne Herald Sun. Retrieved from http://www.heraldsun.com.au/ news/victoria/victorians-pay-millions-for-the-right-to-host-the-f1-grand-prix/story-e6frf7kx-1226559617047. Accessed August 24, 2015.

Jeremiah, D., (1995). The motor car from road to museum. *International Journal of Heritage Studies* 1, 171–179.

Lowes, M. (2004). Neoliberal Power Politics and the Controversial Siting of the Australian Grand Prix Motorsport Event in an Urban Park. *Loisir Et Société. Society and Leisure* 27 (1), 69–88.

Victorian Historic Racing Register. http://vhrr.com/

11 The motor museum of popular culture

Exhibiting the patriotic heritage of 'Australia's Own Car'

Leanne White

Introduction

This chapter examines the ways in which the history of the Holden car in Australia is presented to visitors of the National Holden Motor Museum (MHMM) in the regional town of Echuca in Victoria. The chapter also explores the museum within the broader context of the Holden car and the role it has played in Australian popular culture and the national story.

While there are a number of car museums around Australia that display vintage cars, this particular museum, which has been operating since 1992, was selected for closer analysis because the Holden has historically been the most popular car preference for Australians. Like the idea of owning your own home on a quarter acre block, purchasing your first Holden was once considered something of a rite of passage and an integral part of the great Australian dream.

The first Holden rolled off the production line in Victoria in 1948 – just three years after the end of the Second World War. To the delight of Holden executives and the assembled media, the Prime Minister Ben Chifley proudly claimed, 'She's a Beauty!' Despite having their head office located in Detroit in the United States, General Motors marketed their Australian cars with strident claims of vociferous nationalism declaring that they were 'Australian's Own Car'. More than 65 years later, Holden continues to advertise their car as an integral part of Australia's national identity. However, in 2013 the company announced that it was no longer financially viable to manufacture cars in Australia.

The chapter explores this automotive museum through the theoretical lenses of official, popular and commercial nationalism. In addition, the chapter aims to address a number of the overarching themes of this book including: the history, impact and future of museums; automobile heritage and tourism by locality, region or country; and the role of automobile heritage museums in preservation, education and tourism.

Heritage and interpretation

It has been argued that heritage has the ability to 'guide and cement national identities' (Gammon, 2007: 1). Graham, Ashworth and Turnbridge point out that the relationship between heritage and nationalism is undeniably complicated as representations of heritage cannot avoid the questions of 'whose' heritage and 'which' heritage (Graham *et al.*, 2000). When exploring our past, we are delving deeper into our own heritage and also that of the nation. Underlying this suggestion is the proposition that heritage is a 'cultural and social process' that is 'ultimately intangible' (Smith, 2006: 307). This chapter aims to shed light on the ways in which the often intangible concept of heritage is imagined, and will examine one particular car museum in Australia set in the wider context of the country's culture, to make that case. By examining the NHMM and the way in which the various exhibits are presented to the visitor, we can rethink our understanding and awareness of Holden's heritage and tradition 'in our everyday lives' (Waterton, 2010: 206).

Interpretation is the activity that provides visitors with information about the place they are visiting and often focuses on sites or artefacts described as high culture, nature's monuments, or the 'picturesque' (McArthur and Hall, 1996: 88). Since interpretation is the process of explaining to people the significance of the place or culture they are visiting, it is often the key process that influences the perceptions visitors hold and negotiate with others as they experience a site (Pearce, 2005). For interpretation to be effective, it should be interesting, engaging, enjoyable, informative and occasionally entertaining. Effective interpretation is also critical for the successful management and conservation of built heritage sites and for sustainable tourism (Moscardo, 1996).

Interpretation is now a well-integrated management practice in both public and commercial settings and warrants detailed research attention (Pearce, 2005). Tilden (1977) has argued that through guided tours, exhibits, and signs, visitors receive a special kind of education through their understanding of informative materials. Effective interpretation allows site visitors to be educated about the nature of the host region and culture (Carr, 2004), and they can 'learn informally about, and appreciate, the place they are visiting' (Light, 1995: 145). Furthermore, astute interpretation can enhance the emotional experience as the interests of visitors can be served by the presentation of a variety of narrative structures.

Official, commercial and popular nationalism

Through an examination of the NHMM we can explore the Holden car and its evolution in Australian culture and society since the 1940s. A number of significant developments in Australian motoring (and more broadly in popular culture) also become evident when exploring this museum. Since their beginnings in Australia, General Motors Holden have been in the business of selling nationalism and patriotism – effectively adopting commercial nationalism. Much of this was achieved through the relationship with their long-standing advertising agency George Patterson. While the Holden name was chosen (after James Alexander Holden who had established a saddlery business in South Australia in 1856), other names under consideration included: GMH, GeM, Lion, Austral and Canbra – the phonetic spelling of Australia's capital city of Canberra (Bebbington, 2009). The selected name had to be short, catchy, easily pronounced, and preferably identifiable with Australia (Loffler, 2006).

The Holden lion logo was designed by George Rayner Hoff – a leading sculptor in Australia in the 1920s. He based his design on the symbol of the Wembley Exhibition in 1924 which depicted a stylised Egyptian lion (General Motors Holden, 1992). At the time, the world was fascinated by all things Egyptian as archaeologist Howard Carter had recently discovered Tutankhamun's tomb (Loffler, 2000). A metal lion badge appeared on all Holden cars from 1928. The design was eventually modified in 1972, and revamped again in 1994 (Bedwell, 2009: 31).

From a theoretical perspective, similarities and differences exist between official nationalism, popular nationalism and commercial nationalism. It is useful to understand the complex relationships and interconnections between these discourses of nationalism and how they might be applied in the context of the Holden car.

Anderson contends that official nationalism is the 'willed merger of nation and dynastic empire' and argues that the concept came about in response to popular nationalism that emerged in Europe from the 1820s (Anderson, 1991: 86). He explains that official nationalism emanates 'from the state' and has as its primary feature a focus on 'serving the interests of the state first and foremost' (Anderson, 1991: 159).

Billig refers to the way in which symbols of the nation are reproduced on a daily basis as 'banal nationalism' (Tomlinson, 2004: 25). An example of the concept of banal nationalism can be seen in the words and logo of the masthead of the nation's daily newspaper *The Australian*. The concept of the 'homeland' or 'heartland' (as the nation is sometimes referred to in conservative political circles) is doubly reinforced in both the title of the newspaper and the image of the Australian landmass.

Commercial nationalism describes the style of nationalism that is overtly promoted by advertisers as it encompasses the suggestion that commerce and the nation are deliberately constructed entities which are linked. The term refers to patriotic overtures in advertisements but also alludes to the notion that the once clearer boundaries surrounding official and commercial nationalism have been eliminated and that the broader concept of nationalism, which deals with ideas and beliefs, has combined with the economic forces in the world of commerce. Thus, commercial nationalism is essentially a paradox – two potentially conflicting sectors combining their influences and occupying the same space. Commercial nationalism is a continuation and extension of the overall theme, style and symbols of official nationalism as generated by the nation-state and is often reflected in the popular culture of the nation.

The discourses of commercial and official nationalism are directly related. They contribute to the total discourse on nationalism in a community – be it 'imagined' (Anderson, 1991) or real. The official and commercial strands of nationalism are not binary oppositions – there is a significant degree of overlap between the areas. Commercial nationalism operates like a paradigm – it continues the pattern that has been firmly established by the official body. It is not in the interests of the private company to create conflict between these two types of nationalism; they are merely used for different purposes (White, 2004). Commercial nationalism (often a more vociferous manifestation of official nationalism) manifests itself in consumer-related uses of national symbols, images and icons. National signifiers such as the country's flag or landmass are adopted by the world of commerce for consumption in the market.

While popular nationalism and commercial nationalism generally perform a different function to official nationalism, these nationalisms often overlap. Images of the nation and types of nationalism intersect and change (depending on the use to which they are put). Official nationalism is the civic, formal and ceremonial nationalism such as the Australian Federal Government's planning of the Bicentennial celebrations in 1988 or the Centenary of Federation celebrations in 2001. National anthem, flag and official symbols are part of official nationalism. The concept of popular nationalism was introduced by Ward and can include nationalist messages and images as depicted in popular culture texts such as Australian film, television drama, popular songs and sport. Ward's text *The Australian Legend* attempted to 'trace the historical origins and development of the Australian legend or national mystique' (Ward, 1966: v).

Commercial nationalism refers to consumer-related uses of these national symbols, images and icons. It is the material, everyday nationalism represented by companies and brands such as Foster's Lager, Qantas, Vegemite and Holden. For many years, the phenomenon of commercial nationalism has been evidenced in advertising slogans that occasionally develop into popular jingles such as 'Aussie Kids are Weet-Bix Kids', 'I'm as Australian as Ampol' and 'Football, Meat Pies, Kangaroos and Holden Cars' (to be examined later in the chapter).

Motor museums in Australia

The NHMM is a member of the Australasian Motor Museums Association (AMMA) which was 'established to help promote the collection, preservation and promotion of motor vehicles and related memorabilia for public display, educational and research purposes' (AMMA, 2014). While car museums feature prominently as AMMA members, the association encompasses all forms of 'land based equipment' including cars, motorbikes, commercial vehicles, fire engines, military vehicles and tractors. Apart from promoting motor vehicles and related memorabilia, the association acts as a public voice for its members; it promotes the displays, exhibitions and events of members; it advises members on government related issues, regulations, grants and other assistance; and it seeks to develop tourism strategies in conjunction with the members. After an initial joining fee of $50, the AMMA charges an annual membership fee of $50 for an associate membership, or $100 for an individual or institution. Corporate supporters are also welcome to join the association for an annual fee of $1000.

The AMMA was formed in 2008. While the AMMA logo displays the land masses of Australia and New Zealand, all of its members are Australian. In 2014, the 57-strong membership consisted of: 20 members from Victoria, 10 from Western Australia, 9 from New South Wales, 6 from South Australia,

5 from Queensland, 4 from Tasmania, and 3 from the Australian Capital Territory. Some of the more prominent AMMA members in Australia include the National Museum of Australia (NMA) which displays an historic national motor vehicle fleet. In 2007 the NMA acquired what is considered its most significant and valuable motor vehicle in the collection – Australia's only surviving Holden prototype and the very first of the three that were built by hand in 1946. In 2014 the NMA also acquired the 1977 model yellow Torana hatchback with its controversial 'forensic evidence' in the Azaria Chamberlain legal battles in the 1980s. Both of these Holden acquisitions represent key moments in Australian popular culture. Some of the other AMMA members are: Australian War Memorial, National Transport Museum (with more than 120 vehicles), National Military Vehicle Museum, National Motor Museum (which displays around 300 vehicles), Fire Services Museum of Australia, Geelong Museum of Motoring and Industry, Tractor Museum of Western Australia, and the delightfully named 'Museum of Timeless Memories'.

The motor museum for 'true blue' Aussies

The NHMM is a permanent museum located in the town of Echuca in regional Victoria, Australia (see Figure 11.1). It is open seven days a week from 9am until 5pm. The museum proudly declares in their two-sided colour brochure, 'If you are a TRUE BLUE AUSSIE visiting Echuca you shouldn't go past visiting the NATIONAL HOLDEN MOTOR MUSEUM'. The NHMM declares that the visitor will be taken on a 'remarkable history of a company that put our nation on wheels' (NHMM, 2014). It has been argued that despite the obvious fallacy of the stereotype, museums are often considered to be places for society's elite (Conlin and Jolliffe, 2011: 4). The promotional material for this particular museum is squarely targeted at the Australian 'bloke'. The NHMM overtly portrays itself as

Figure 11.1 Proprietor Ted Furley and his 'utilitarian' advertising.

a museum for Australia's working class – colloquially referred to as the 'Aussie battlers'.

The museum is located in Warren Street, Euchua – just off the main shopping thoroughfare of the town. It is a private museum owned by husband and wife proprietors Ted and Deb Furley. Ted worked at Kodak for more than 20 years and brought his management skills to running the museum when they decided to open the popular tourist attrtaction 22 years ago. In many respects, Ted and the NHMM are one and the same thing. Being a seven day a week concern, Ted's life effectively IS the museum. In 22 years, he has had just 10 days away from his beloved Holdens.

The NHMM is located just a short walk from the Port of Echuca on the Murray River which acts as the border between Victoria and New South Wales. The twin towns of Echuca and Moama attract around 1.3 million visitors annually. The popular tourist towns are located about 250 kilometeres (or a three hour drive) from Melbourne. As a result of the popularity of the region and the museum's prominent location, the NHMM is the second most visited motor museum in Australia. The National Motor Museum in South Australia is Australia's most visited motor museum.

With 45 cars on display, the museum is the largest 'one brand' car museum in Australia. Almost all of the Holdens on display have been loaned to the museum thanks to a steady stream of devoted car restorers. Ted Furley owns just two of the cars. For 'died in the wool' Holden enthusiasts, the opposition (Ford) col-loquially stands for: 'Found on a Rubbish Dump' or 'Fixed on Race Day'. As Bedwell argues, the battle lines between Holden and Ford are more pronounced in Australia than any other country (Bedwell, 2009).

The NHMM also features cars that are quite rare and thus attracts many Holden fanatics from around the country. One such drawcard exhibit was an orange 1969 Holden Hurricane. The futuristic prototype vehicle was displayed for three months over the Summer school holidays of 2013 before being taken to the US for further exhibiting. Another rare car on loan for a limited time was a white GTR-X Torana which was returned to Melbourne's Holden plant in August, 2014. The word Torana effectively means 'to fly' in Aboriginal.

The NHMM website is a relatively straightfoward site displaying just three key pages (Home, Media and Contact Us). Some of the promotional claims on the home page include:

> The Holden cars have a unique place in the hearts of all Australians. Can there be an adult Australian who has never driven a Holden or at least ridden in one? The Holden Museum in Echuca is dedicated to preserving the models and their memories.

> Our visitors can enjoy the sheer nostalgia as they re-live the days when Holden played a central role in their childhood, dating or early married years. It has helped us work through decades of the harshest conditions. The Holden as an Aussie icon, rates right up there with the Kangaroo, Ayers Rock and Vegemite.

Echuca is fortunate to have the nation's largest collections of Holdens, making this private museum the largest one brand car museum in Australia.

The museum can have you in another time zone as you turn the ignition key of your memories.

In September 2014, the museum's Facebook page could boast 534 'likes' and a small selection of photographs. An examination of the 83 reviews for the NHMM on 'Trip Advisor' at the time, displayed the visitor ratings as follows: Excellent – 44; Very good – 26; Average – 11; Poor – 1; and Terrible – 1. Partial quotes from some of the reviewers follow:

'Brings back the memories. So much to learn too'. Berrill, Dubbo.

'This museum is worth a visit and will be remembered'. Graeme, Portland.

'Although smaller than some museums this is still a great place to visit'. Pam, Melbourne.

'Great place and well worth a visit. This chap really likes his Holdens and has a great collection on display'. Kim, Sydney.

'We are actually Ford fans but this museum is very interesting and has some beautiful cars on display'. Barb, Melbourne.

'My husband and I really thought the Holden Museum was awesome … I recommend that everyone that attends should sit and watch the video'. Annette, Tingira Heights.

'It had many old Holden cars in pristine condition. The documentary on Holden's first 25 years was a wonderful trip down memory lane'. Gary, Caulfield.

The video documentary which is on display in a small theatrette (see Figure 11.2) is mentioned by some of the Trip Advisor reviewers. Having purchased a ticket to visit the museum ($8 for an adult and $19.50 for a family at the time of writing), owner Ted Furley suggests that the best way to appreciate the museum is to firstly sit down and view the 15-minute video about the history of Holden. The short video plays 'on a loop' and can be faintly heard in the background when the visitor walks around the museum. With historical footage and advertising, the informative video provides an overview of Holden's distinctive place in Australian culture.

One particular advertisement on the video tape is designed to strike a nostalgic reaction (and also reinforce the Holden's connections with the nation). A 1970s television advertisement for General Motors Holden patriotically proclaims 'We love football, meat pies, kangaroos and Holden cars'. Fiske, Hodge and Turner have argued that Australia can be signified by 'kangaroos, the flag, Alan Bond, the map, images of landscape, the Sydney Opera House, and so on' (Fiske *et al.*, 1987: xi).

Figure 11.2 Visitors are encouraged to view the Holden story then explore the museum.

The jingle is sung by a combination of male and female voices and the authoritative voice-over is spoken by Australian radio and television personality, Ken Sparkes who promotes himself with the slogan 'the voice that gets results'. Australian advertising agency George Patterson created the successful campaign. The advertisement was adapted from a 1975 US advertising campaign for the General Motors brand Chevrolet (popularly known as Chevy) that uttered the words 'baseball, hot dogs, apple pies and Chevrolet' – appealing to American national pride.

Employing the tools of commercial nationalism, the montage-style commercial associates some of Australia's cultural icons with 'Australia's own car'. Senior General Motors staff in the US understood Holden's popularity in Australia and embraced it. In the 1960s, one Chairman claimed that 'the Holden has become almost as much a national symbol as the kangaroo' (Arrowsmith and Zangalis, 1965: 20). The car industry in Australia also symbolised industrial independence as Australia had had to rely on the manufacturing skills of its allies at the start of the Second World War.

The advertisement proposes that if you don't like football, meat pies, kangaroos and Holden cars, then you are not a true Australian. The company's association with working class Australians is emphasised by images of the FJ Holden, the Kingswood, the Torana and the Monaro. Appealing to Australia's outback myth, almost all of the vehicles shown in the advertisement are depicted being driven along dusty dirt tracks. The voice-over and lyrics (which were echoed in school yards across the nation at the time) to the 60 second commercial are as follows:

Australia what's your favourite sport?
Football!

Snack?
Pies!
Animal?
Kangaroo!
And what's your favourite car Australia?
Holden!

Let me see, that's football, meat pies, kangaroos and Holden cars, huh?
Right!

Well, you sure sound like Australia to me!
We are!
Well then, you better tell me again 'cause I might just forget!

We love football, meat pies, kangaroos and Holden cars
Football, meat pies, kangaroos and Holden cars
That's football, meat pies, kangaroos and Holden cars
Football and meat pies, kangaroos and Holden cars

I think you better tell me again!
We love football, meat pies, kangaroos and Holden cars

In case you're wondering, this film is brought to you by football, meat pies,
kangaroos and 'Australia's own car'

They go together underneath the Southern stars
Football and meat pies, kangaroos and Holden cars
Makes sense to me!

Football meat pies, kangaroos and Holden cars
Football and meat pies, kangaroos and Holden cars

Having been injected with the required dose of patriotism, the visitor gener-ally then proceeds to work their way around the museum in a clockwise direc-tion where the Holdens are displayed from most historic to most recent. At the rear of the theatrette, the visitor encounters the 48–215 Holden – the first mass-produced Australian car which was built in 1948. This particular vehi-cle has been lent to the NHMM by owner David Hughes who also made his vehicle available for Holden's 50th anniversary celebrations at the Fishermans Bend plant (formerly known as Fishermen's Bend) in Melbourne in 1998. Next to the vehicle is a description of the car with a photograph of former Prime Minister John Howard standing proudly beside this authentically restored first model Holden.

The 48–215 model was generally but inaccurately referred to as the FX (Luck, 1992). It weighed 1,000 kilograms and could travel up to 130 km per hour. It was a large six-cylinder sedan built for Australian conditions with plenty of space for pas-sengers and their luggage. Priced at 760 pounds, it was not a cheap car considering that a couple of blocks of land could have been purchased for that amount of money at the time (Luck, 1992). Advertised as 'Australia's Own Car', it was promoted as 'a car made in Australia, for Australia' (Bryden-Brown, 1981: 189).

However, it was the model that followed that was possibly Australia's most iconic – and 'darling of the Australian motoring public' – the FJ Holden (Loffler, 2002). Fry argues that the popularity of the FJ might well be due to the large number of vehicles which were produced but also states that the 'toothy FJ grin is an instantly recognisable image of the 1950s' (Fry, 1998: 7). The FJ Holden is Ted Furley's favourite car. The NHMM owner fell in love with the FJ when he first set eyes on it at the age of 10. An advertisement at the time for the FJ employed the tools of commercial nationalism. Headed 'Australia's Own Car – the Beautiful Holden' the magazine advertisement begins with the words, 'Cuddly koalas, a young, happy family, spreading gums, a beautiful car – all of them looking right for each other, and all of them Australian' (Loffler, 2008: 194).

So passionate are early model Holden owners that they established a club specifically for these car models. The group is known as the 'Early Model Holden Club of Victoria'. The decidedly welcoming message on their website reads:

> G'day, and welcome to the Early Model Holden Club of Victoria Inc. website. As you can gather from our club name, we cater only for FX and FJ Holdens – stock, modified or anything in between is perfect. The first meeting of the Early Model Holden Club of Victoria was on the 18th December 1970 and we are still going strong to this day. We welcome all owners of FXs and FJs to our club. Whether your 'Early' is registered or unregistered, finished or unfinished, driveable or undriveable, we welcome you. There are many potential members out there who believe that their Early is not good enough to be in a club. Believe us, ANY Early is ideal. We are a family-orientated club and invite you to join us at a meeting, or contact one of the Committee members for further information.

The Club keeps its website up-to-date and posts many photographs of meetings and restoration projects. The Early Model Holden Club is also supported by 18 sponsors, and members are actively encouraged to support the sponsors whenever they can. Another passionate group of Holden lovers can be found at the website 'Holden Heaven' who claim to be the 'official home of the worldwide Holden enthusiasts' community'.

The FJ model Holden has been replicated in the realms of Australian popular culture in a number of ways. In 1977, the film *The FJ Holden* documented the lives of two young men (Kevin and Bob) from the western suburbs of Sydney. The subtitle of the movie was 'Fast cars, fast girls, fast times'. The friends cruise the suburban streets in a canary yellow FJ Holden with the number plate 'BAD 781'. Accompanying the movie was a soundtrack featuring music from Ol' 55, Skyhooks and others. The theme song of the movie, *My Right of Way,* was performed by the band Ol '55 whose lead singer was appropriately named Frankie J. Holden. The catchy chorus of the song follows:

In my FJ, in my FJ Holden
Drive, drive, drive
In my FJ, in my FJ Holden
Drive, drive, drive
Drive, drive, drive

Other films that have included Holdens in their promotional trailers have been: *The Cars that Ate Paris, Spotswood, Metal Skin, The Castle* and *The Dish*. While some music videos featuring the car include: *The Wide Open Road* (The Triffords), *Weather with You* (Crowded House), *Amazing* (Alex Lloyd), *Chick Ute* (Jayne Denham), *You're not my Ute* (Kelly Hope) and *The Old HR* (The Bobkatz).

Australian popular culture artefacts such as the FJ Holden have also been used in various forms of advertising. Regular types of historic images seen in advertising include Australian soldiers at war, archival scenes of Australia's sporting heroes such as Don Bradman, or animals which have developed a significant place in the nation's sporting archives, such as the horse Phar Lap. Objects such as the FJ Holden, the Hills Hoist and Victa lawnmower have come to be popularly recognised as iconic Australian signifiers.

Apart from prominent advertising campaigns for Holden cars, Holdens have also featured in the advertising of other products. One such example is a television advertisement which aired in 1988 for the Victorian Dairy Industry Association's flavoured milk drink 'Big M'. The company had also featured Holdens when launching the brand in 1976.

In the advertisement, the Easybeats 1966 international hit song *Friday on my Mind* is heard in the background, connecting with the brand's slogan at the time – 'Are you in a Big M state of mind?' The advertisement portrays a scenario of tension and competition between an 'Australian' male named Dave and a 'European' man named Brad. Something of a mini battle is revealed in the 30 seconds of the advertisement. Brad, the rich European who drives a red Porsche, jokingly says to his friends 'Oh how quaint! An Australian car', when he notices Dave's FC Holden. Dave and friends purchase drinks from a milk bar, then return to the car to discover that one of the tyres has been deflated. Undeterred, Dave and friends cheerfully change the tyre, and drive away. The viewer discovers at the end of the commercial that Dave has indeed taken the ultimate revenge against Brad, by strategically placing his flavoured milk drink on the sun-roof of Brad's luxury car (and the commercial concludes with the milk about to fall on Brad). The binary oppositions are overt. Brad is unfriendly, European, and drives an expensive new car, while Dave is friendly, Australian, and drives a classic Holden which has been authentically restored.

Holden television advertising in the 1950s and 1960s reinforced the notion that the vehicle provided the family with the opportunity to escape to the country and enjoy simple pleasures such as a picnic (see Figure 11.3). At this time in Holden's history, the company had managed to capture more than 50% of the market (GMHA, 1992: 5). Reflecting the changes in emphasis of the company, some of the Holden advertising slogans since the car's introduction to Australia

Figure 11.3 The Holden enabled families to drive to picnic locations in the country.

have been the first and long-running 'Australia's Own Car'; 'The great way to move', 'Australia's Driving Future', 'People Trust Holden', 'Drive On', 'Holden Go', 'Go Better', 'Holden means a great deal to Australia', and most recently – 'Think Holden'.

As outlined above, when wandering through the NHMM, the visitor would normally slowly proceed from the earlier makes and models to the most recent. Along the side wall of the museum, a Holden Kingswood can be spotted (see Figure 11.4). In the 1970s, the Holden Kingswood became an extremely popular car and by default, Australia became 'Kingswood Country'. As Bedwell explains, the Kingswood survived seven model changes and five Australian Prime Ministers. He argues, 'the Kingswood epitomised suburban life – it was the safe middle ground' (Bedwell, 1992: 45). A 1969 advertisement for a Holden HT Kingswood sedan advertises the vehicle as the 'new generation Holden'. The Kingswood is featured on a country drive and in a beach setting and the target audience is urged to 'join the new generation'.

The notion that the Kingswood was an integral part of Australian culture was reinforced by the extremely popular 1980s television series *Kingswood Country*. The main character of the show was Ted Bullpitt whose passions in life are: watching television, racing his greyhounds (Repco Lad and Gay Akubra), and his Holden Kingswood. Ted and his family live in Wombat Crescent and one of the key phrases that emerged from the program and entered the Australian vernacular was 'The Kingswood? You're not taking the Kingswood!'

The NHMM exhibits a range of cars, posters, memorabilia and other Holden-related material. As one might expect, 'Rev Heads' are particularly well served with exhibits relating to the ultimate 'muscle car' – the Monaro. The Holden Monaro (HK), the Monaro GTS and the more powerful Monaro GTS

Figure 11.4 In the 1960s and 1970s, Australia was 'Kingswood Country'.

327 were released in 1968. The Monaro quickly established itself as an extremely popular vehicle. The word Monaro is Aboriginal for high plains and the car was named after the regional town of the same name. Thanks to Banjo Patterson's 'Man from Snowy River', high country myths and legends held a distinctive place in Australian popular culture.

The advertising jingle accompanying the launch of the campaign was 'Life is suddenly very Monaro'. The popular Monaro was awarded the *Wheels* magazine car of the year shortly after its release. Other Holdens that won the prestigious motoring prize include: The Torana (1969), the Gemini (1975), the Camira (1982), the Barina (2001) and the top-selling Australian car – the Commodore (1978, 1979, 1988, 1993, 1997 and 2006).

Since the late 1960s, three generations of the Holden Monaro have been produced. The first generation (HK, HT and HG) were made between 1968 and 1971; further models – HQ, HJ, HX, HZ and VH – rolled off the assembly lines between 1971 and 1977; while the latest generation of the Monaro – such as the V2 and the VZ were made between 2001 and 2005.

Racing car driver Peter Brock – known colloquially as 'Brocky' was one of Holden's great brand ambassadors. He is known as 'Peter Perfect' and the undisputed 'King of the Mountain' due to being the most successful driver of the Bathurst 1,000-kilometre touring car race which he won on nine occasions (Walker, 2009: 159). Brock was the lead driver of Holden's racing team, and was awarded a Member of the Order of Australia in 1980 for services to motor racing.

Bathurst is considered the ultimate race on the Australian motoring calendar and is held at Mount Panorama. As Hutchinson explains, the Australian car culture that revolves around Holden versus Ford 'is played out in the gladiatorial contest at the Bathurst 1,000 endurance race' (Hutchinson, 2002: 89).

The renowned sporting event celebrated 50 years in 2012. The Peter Brock Trophy was introduced at Bathurst in 2006 after Brock died in a racing accident in Western Australia. While Brock holds a special place in the hearts and minds of Holden enthusiasts, he has also entered the world of popular culture by virtue of a 2014 documentary *Peter Brock: The Legend* and in the lyrics of the 1990 Midnight Oil song *King of the Mountain*.

The Holden Utility (referred to as the Ute) has also become a key tool for rural farmers and urban tradesmen – generally known as 'tradies' in Australia. The first Holden Ute was launched in 1951 and remains a symbol of Australia's supposed egalitarianism to this day. As the ute was strong, light weight with a powerful six cylinder engine, it was considered an overnight success soon after its release (Simpson, 2004: 116).

In 2014, Holden Special Vehicles (HSV) announced that it had been working on plans to manufacture the world's fastest ute. The high performance V8 ute will be able to accelerate to 100 km per hour faster than a Porsche and will be the most powerful car that Australia has produced. The supercharged ute will be known as the 'Maloo' – the aboriginal word for thunder. The Maloo will sell for around $85,000 and just 250 vehicles are expected to be produced (Dowling, 2014).

Reinforcing the overall themes of popular nationalism and Australiana, selected Australian landscape and landmarks are also displayed at the NHMM. Commonly used landmarks would come as no surprise to even the most casual observer of popular culture – the Sydney Opera House, the Sydney Harbour Bridge, the Melbourne Cricket Ground, the Victorian Arts Centre, and Parliament House in Canberra are just some examples. Outback Australia in particular is a popular location for Australian television advertisements, television drama, music videos and films. These forms of popular culture can be specifically situated at Uluru (formerly known as Ayers Rock) or an equally isolated and barren land-scape. Through the power of television advertising, rather than actually going there, the majority of Australians have become familiar with the desolate outback, which was once rather ironically known as 'the interior'. Although it might only be visited once or twice in a lifetime (if at all), Australians are reassured in the knowledge that this desolate space is out there. The outback, and all that it stands for, plays an important part in the national psyche and the sense of space and place that many Australians feel, and has been an important Australian signifier of com-mercial nationalism.

At the NHMM, the juxtaposition of the car against the painted backdrop of Uluru is striking (see Figure 11.5). The contrasting predominant colours of red ochre and white seem to suggest that an oasis in the desert may have been uncov-ered. Imagery such as this has been employed to sell all kinds of products for many decades. The overt message is that the product is durable under the harsh Australian sun.

Nearby the Uluru mural towards the end of the visitor's exploration of the museum is a shiny red Holden displaying Olympic Torch Relay livery – one of the official vehicles of the Sydney 2000 event. As part of their integrated mar-keting communications, Holden was a major sponsor of Sydney 2000. The elite

Figure 11.5 This exhibit reinforces the notion that the Holden is built for Australia's harsh conditions.

sponsorship program for the Sydney Games was referred to as 'Team Millennium' (International Olympic Committee, 1997: 68). Team Millennium partners who held marketing rights in Australia included: Telstra, Westpac, Westfield, Ansett Australia, News Limited, Fairfax, Channel Seven and Holden. At the time of the Sydney 2000 Games, Holden found that their regular patriotic slogan 'Drive on Australia' needed to be further reinforced with the more specific slogan supporting the athletes – 'Olympians Drive to Win'.

The Sydney 2000 Torch Relay marked the longest – in both days and distance travelled – in the history of the Games. The relay was sponsored by the Australian Mutual Provident Society (AMP) at a cost of around $100 million. Games organisers made an emphatic point of supporting Aboriginal Australians at the beginning of the torch relay with the powerful signifier of Uluru in the background. Indigenous Australians played a critical role in the torch relay. Symbolically Nova Peris-Kneebone, the first Aboriginal Australian to win a medal at an Olympic Games was the first to carry the flame in Australia. Aboriginal television personality Ernie Dingo was given the honour of being the second runner in the relay, while former tennis champion Evonne Goolagong Cawley was the third runner. Cathy Freeman was the final runner in the torch relay and the athlete given the ultimate honour of lighting the Olympic flame at the Opening Ceremony.

Holden also played a key role in the other Olympic Games event that Australia hosted. At the 1956 Olympics in Melbourne, the torch runner was escorted by Victorian police in FJ Holden utilities as crowds lined the streets when the spectacle passed through central Melbourne (Loffler, 2008).

Another quintessential Australian that the NHMM displays a connection with is the actor Paul Hogan. Many older Australians are likely to be familiar with

Paul Hogan's role in the popular comedy *The Paul Hogan Show*, along with the highly successful Winfield advertising campaign in the 1970s. The campaign was targeted at working and middle class Australians who wanted a good honest offer, and the advertisements became some of the most successful in the history of Australian advertising. Hogan cleverly satirised the establishment which was represented by the opposition cigarette Benson and Hedges and its brand ambassador Stuart Wagstaff. Beer drinkers in the United Kingdom were also exposed to Paul Hogan's popular Foster's Lager commercials in the 1980s.

Paul Hogan's phenomenal movie successes with *Crocodile Dundee* (1986), *Crocodile Dundee II* (1988) and *Crocodile Dundee in Los Angeles* (2001) entrenched his global position as Australia's tourism ambassador. The Croc movie scripts were penned by Hogan and his business partner John Cornell, and essentially juxtapose the life of Mick Dundee, an outback larrikin crocodile hunter from Walkabout Creek, against that of Sue Charlton, a confident journalist from New York. Hogan's most recent movie (2009) was a road trip film where father and son get to know each other when travelling from the base of Australia to the 'top end' in a Holden Kingswood. Some of the memorabilia from the film *Charlie and Boots* is displayed in a cabinet at the museum. In a large island nation such as Australia, the road trip is both a rite of passage and a way of life.

Like many tourist attractions, the NHMM features a souvenir shop that is located in the foyer of the building. The large shop sells postcards, books, signed sporting memorabilia, badges, glasses, mugs, coasters, stubby holders, magnets, pens, model cars, caps, T-shirts, novelty number plates and other souvenirs which are essentially designed to savour the automobile heritage experience (see Figure 11.6). The purchasing of souvenirs enables the visitor to fondly remember the service experience after it has been consumed. Photographs taken by the museum visitor also capture the highlights of the occasion and constitute another way of remembering the event and sharing the heritage experience with others.

Conclusion

Particularly after the 2013 announcement that Holden would no longer manufacture cars in Australia, this specific brand of car holds a distinct place in the heritage, popular culture and identity of Australia. Holden's distinctive place in the 'culture of the everyday' is reflected at the NHMM where visitors can learn about the car's patriotic heritage. As motoring journalist David Morley argues, when people look back on the early decades of the motor car industry in Australia, 'it's the Holden badge they'll remember' (Morley, 2013: 11).

This chapter has revealed how Australia's intangible and tangible motoring heritage might be experienced by museum visitors at one of Australia's many museums dedicated to automobiles. In a nation with a vast road network where 'car is king', there are many constant reminders that the country's car heritage has become a key part of our national identity. Memories of the family car trip can bring an enormous amount of nostalgia. Automobile heritage, although recognised

Figure 11.6 Brand loyalty can be reinforced with purchases from the souvenir shop.

as part of national identity in Australia, is thus both historic and contemporary, integrated into the tourist gaze not only through heritage-related tourism opportunities like this museum but through the visitors' overall experience of memorable car journeys.

For the visitor of the NHMM, heritage becomes somehow embodied and personified by engaging with these historic cars and their related stories. If we understand heritage as a process that constructs meanings about the past, then the construction of automobile heritage at this particular museum is illustrative of this process. It is, essentially, an interpretation of Holden's heritage based on cars, photographs, images, video, reports, printed ephemera and memorabilia that have been carefully documented and packaged by the museum owners.

It has been argued that the car has created one of the dominant cultures of the 20th century – a culture which is accessible yet highly complex (Jeremiah, 2003: 169). Car museums seem to be starting to better present this complexity. Clark argues that while the motor museum has traditionally attracted car enthusiasts, they are 'beginning to enter the realms of social history' (Clark, 2010: 232).

Rouette further contends that museums indeed are 'in a powerful position to help people understand the world', and they have the capacity to 'strengthen communities' and 'create awareness of the richness of our society' (Rouette, 2007: 11).

Motor museums such as the NHMM offer a high level of visitor engagement with a compelling and appealing national narrative. As Ted Furley's business card states, 'As the world changes, precious memories live on at the National Holden Motor Museum'. When this particular museum ceases to exist, as is likely to occur over the next decade, the patriotic heritage on display will be a fond but distant memory for those whom were fortunate enough to visit this symbol of Australia and its unique story of the nation's motoring history.

References

Anderson, B. (1991) *Imagined Communities: Reflections on the origins and spread of nationalism* (revised edition). London: Verso.

Arrowsmith, J. and Zangalis, G. (1965) *The Golden Holden: The story of General Motors in Australia*. Melbourne: International Bookshop.

Australasian Motor Museums Association (2014) Welcome – Online document: http://www.australasianmotormuseums.com.au/index.php.

Bebbington, T. (2009) *60 Years of Holden: Complete encyclopedia of all models*. Padstow, NSW: Haynes Manuals.

Bedwell, S. (1992) *Suburban Icons: A celebration of the everyday*. Sydney: Australian Broadcasting Corporation Enterprises.

Bedwell, S. (2009) *Holden vs Ford: The cars, the culture, the competition*. Dulwich Hill, NSW: Rockpool publishing.

Bryden-Brown, J. (1981) *Ads that Made Australia: How advertising has shaped our history and lifestyle*. Lane Cove, NSW: Doubleday.

Carr, A. (2004) Mountain places, cultural spaces: the interpretation of culturally significant landscapes. *Journal of Sustainable Tourism* 12 (5), 432–459.

Clark, J. (2010) The 'rough and tumble': displaying complexity in the motor museum. *Museum Management and Curatorship* 25 (2), 219–234.

Conlin, M. and Jolliffe, L. (eds) (2011) *Mining Heritage and Tourism: A global synthesis*. London: Routledge.

Dowling, J. (2014) Holden to 100 more of HSV GTS Maloo ute – Online document: http://www.news.com.au/technology/design/holden-to-build-100-more-of-hsv-gts-maloo-ute/story-fnjwucvh-1227055683513

Fiske, J., Hodge, B. and Turner, G. (1987) *Myths of Oz: Reading Australian popular culture*. Sydney: Allen and Unwin.

Fry, G. (1998) *Golden Holden: Fifty years of an Australian icon*. Smithfield, NSW: Fairfield Regional Heritage Centre.

Gammon, S. (2007) Introduction: Sport, heritage and the English. An opportunity missed? In S. Gammon and G. Ramshaw (eds). *Heritage, Sport and Tourism: Sporting pasts – tourist futures* (pp. 1–8). London: Routledge.

General Motors – Holden's Automotive Ltd. (1992) *The Holden Heritage (Third Edition)*. Port Melbourne: Public Affairs Department, GMHA.

Graham, B., Ashworth, G. and Turnbridge, J. (2000) *A Geography of Heritage: Power, culture and economy*. London: Arnold.

Hutchinson, G. (2002) *True Blue*. Camberwell, Vic: Viking.

International Olympic Committee (1997) *Olympic Marketing Fact File.* Lausanne: IOC.

Jeremiah, D. (2003) Museums and the history of heritage in British motoring. *International Journal of Heritage Studies* 9 (2), 169–190.

Light, D. (1995) Visitors' use of interpretive media at heritage sites. *Leisure Studies* 14 (2), 132–149.

Loffler, D. (2000) *Still Holden Together: Stories of the first Holden models.* Kent Town: Wakefield Press.

Loffler, D. (2002) *The FJ Holden: A favourite Australian Icon.* Kent Town: Wakefield Press.

Loffler, D. (2006) *She's a Beauty! The story of the first Holdens.* Kent Town: Wakefield Press.

Loffler, D. (2008) *Me and my Holden: A nostalgia trip with the early Holdens.* Kent Town: Wakefield Press.

Luck, P. (1992) *Australian Icons: Things that make us what we are.* Port Melbourne: William Heinemann.

McArthur, S. and Hall, C.M. (1996) Interpretation: principles and practice. In C.M. Hall and S. McArthur (eds). *Heritage management in Australia and New Zealand: The human dimension* (pp. 88–106). Melbourne: Oxford University Press.

Morley, D. (2013) Six and Out, *The Age* (Drive supplement). 26 January, pp. 8–11.

Moscardo, G. (1996) Mindful visitors: heritage and tourism. *Annals of Tourism Research* 23 (2), 376–397.

National Holden Motor Museum (2013) Promotional brochure.

Pearce, P. L. (2005) *Tourism behaviour: themes and conceptual schemes.* Clevedon: Channel View.

Rouette, G. (2007) *Exhibitions: A practical guide for small museums and galleries.* Carlton South: Museums Australia (Victoria).

Simpson, M. (2004) *On the Move: A history of transport in Australia.* Sydney: Powerhouse Publishing.

Smith, L. (2006) *The Uses of Heritage.* London: Routledge.

Tilden, F. (1977) *Interpreting our Heritage.* Chapel Hill: University of North Carolina Press.

Tomlinson, J. (2004) Globalisation and National Identity. In J. Sinclair and G. Turner, (eds). *Contemporary World Television* (pp. 24–28). London: British Film Institute.

Walker, C. (2009) *Golden Miles: Sex, speed and the Australian muscle car.* Kent Town: Wakefield Press.

Ward, R. (1966) *The Australian Legend.* Melbourne: Oxford University Press.

Waterton, E. (2010) *Politics, Policy and the Discourses of Heritage in Britain.* Hampshire: Palgrave Macmillan.

White, L. (2004) The Bicentenary of Australia: Celebration of a Nation. In L. K. Fuller (ed). *National Days / National Ways: Historical, political and religious celebrations around the world* (pp. 25–39). Westport: Praeger.

12 Significance of Amelia Island Concours d'Elegance, Florida, USA

Asli D. A. Tasci and Jerry L. Epperly II

Transportation and tourism have been the two intricately interrelated industries, mutually affecting each other. Advancements in the transportation industry, especially the advent of automobiles, have made access to remote areas possible. Therefore, attractions and activities available for tourism consumption have been diversified tremendously. Besides the attractions and activities, aspects of automobile production have also generated tourism. More specifically, car factory destinations such as Detroit and events related to cars such as auto shows have become tourist attractions. Nowadays, there are many different auto shows and events around the world. One type of event, Concours d'Elegance, which originated in France in the seventeenth century, is a prestigious show usually attended by wealthy individuals and celebrities. However, despite their potential economic and image impact on the destination, there is a lack of academic attention to these events. The Amelia Island Concours d'Elegance is one of these events held on the east coast of Florida and is the subject of this chapter to serve the long overdue need to pay academic attention to this event.

A literature search through online and library sources revealed only minimal information sources not only about Concours d'Elegance shows in general but also and more so about the Amelia Island Concours d'Elegance. To this date, there is no empirical study shedding light on neither the demand nor the supply side of these shows. Thus a mini study using Facebook resources was conducted to gather consumer-related information regarding auto shows in general and the Amelia Island Concours d'Elegance specifically. Due to the small size of the respondents, the study is reported here only to provide a starting point for the much needed future attention on this subject matter.

The automotive industry and tourism

It is no secret that there is a special mutual love affair between transportation and tourism; they feed off of each other and nourish each other. Transportation took travel to the next level by lifting the wayfarers off of their feet. Since it provided the physical mobility for tourism to take place, it has always been the key element of the tourism phenomenon. Rodrigue (2014) dubs transportation as 'the cause and the effect of the growth of tourism … (since) the improved facilities have stimulated tourism, and the expansion of tourism has stimulated transport'. With advancement of transportation technologies, on air, water and land, international tourism has grown dramatically in the last 2 decades as can be seen in Figure 12.1.

The expansion of both domestic and international tourism went hand in hand with that of the transportation industry around the world. International travel, especially the long haul and overseas trips are dominated by air travel; however, national, especially interstate and intercity travel is dominated by automobile travel, either personal or rented vehicles (Rodrigue, 2014; Goeldner and Ritchie, 2012). Due to the advantages displayed in Table 12.1, cars are known to be the dominant mode of travel around the world; almost 80% of travel is done by driving cars, both in the world (Rodrigue, 2014) and in the US (Goeldner and Ritchie, 2012).

The nature of the relationship between tourism and transportation industries can be seen in the similarity of the graph in Figure 12.1 showing international tourism arrivals and receipts and Figure 12.2 showing car production in the world and some major car producing countries. As can be seen from both figures, both industries have been growing steadily, with some dips mainly due to economic recessions and a major upright spike since 90s.

Travel by automobiles or cars has been especially popular in the United States because of lower gas prices that US residents have enjoyed compared to many other countries, and the well-developed Interstate Highway System that developed in 1950s (Goeldner and Ritchie, 2012; Rodrigue, 2014).

The revolutionary auto production philosophy of Henry Ford (assembly line production) hailed the new era of affordable automobile travel, with the ability of average people to travel independently. Development of automobile production in

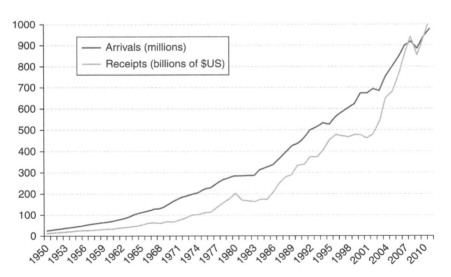

Figure 12.1 International tourism arrivals and receipts in the world.
Source: Adapted from Rodrigue, 2014.

Table 12.1 Advantages of travel by automobiles

Advantages of auto travel	Explanation of the advantage
Freedom/independence/ personal control	It is driver's decision when, where and how to travel.
Affordability/cost effectiveness	When traveling as a group, per person cost of travel is cheaper than other public modes of travel.
Convenience/comfort/ accessibility/flexibility	It does not require transfer like other modes do. The driver can travel door to door with no stopping or stopping at every scenic spot.
Enjoyment of the travel process	Due to ability to stop at scenic spots, or slowdown to be able to see the scenery and even take pictures along the way, it provides the ability to enjoy the process of getting to the destination, improving the overall travel experience.
Enjoyment of the driving experience	It provides some travellers enjoyment of the act of driving, especially when they are trying a new make or model through rental cars.

Sources: Goeldner and Ritchie (2012); Rodrigue (2014); and authors' own opinions.

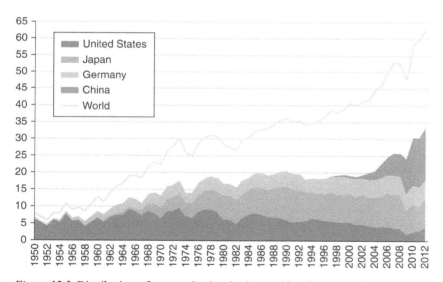

Figure 12.2 Distribution of car production in the world and some major car producing countries.
Source: Adapted from Rodrigue, 2014.

the US (see Table 12.2) lead to increasing demand and use of cars for travel, supported by the development of an effective highway system and relatively cheaper gas prices in the US, eventually leading to a dominance of cars in domestic travel in the US (Goeldner and Ritchie, 2012). It is estimated that 'the automobile accounts for about 84 percent of intercity miles travelled and is the mode of travel

Table 12.2 Landmark events in the development of automotive industry in the US

Year	Landmark events in the development of the automotive industry
19th century	Development of technology for the automobile.
1891	William Morrison constructed an electric carriage that he drove through Des Moines, Iowa.
1893	Frank Duryea exhibited a motorized truck, using an internal combustion engine in Springfield, Massachusetts
	U.S. Office of Road Inquiry was established.
1896	The first companies to produce automobiles for the public market emerged.
1898	William Metzger became the country's first automobile dealer with the establishment of his Detroit dealership.
1900	The first National Automobile Show was held in New York City at Madison Square Garden.
1908	Henry Ford introduces the famous Model T automobile.
1912	Cadillac was the first vehicle to have an effective self-starting engine.
1914	Model T sold for $490.
1920	There were over 8 million registrations.
1914–1918	World War I affected the auto industry.
1921	The Federal Highway Act.
1920s	Tremendous growth in automobile ownership.
1927	Ford's Model A was introduced.
1928	Chrysler acquired Dodge.
1929	GM, Ford, and Chrysler comprised 75% of annual auto sales in the United States.
1930	Registered drivers almost tripled to 23 million.
1936	The newly organized United Automobile Workers with the Congress of Industrial Organizations enforced a sit-down strike at GM plants in Flint, MI.
1937	GM and Chrysler recognized the UAW as the bargaining agent for its workers.
1941	Organization of the UAW and other unions at Ford.
1939–1945	World War II affected the auto industry.
1945–1950	The industry enjoyed a healthy period, with steady growth and healthy profits.
1956	President Dwight Eisenhower signed the Federal-Aid Highway Act of 1956 that created a 41,000-mile 'National System of Interstate and Defense Highways' by allocating $26 billion.
1966	The passage of the National Traffic and Motor Vehicle Safety Act, the Highway Safety Act, and the creation of the Department of Transportation.
1975	Fuel crisis, Congress passed the Corporate Average Fuel Economy (CAFE) bill which required automakers to increase the fuel efficiency of their passenger car fleet.
1980s	Production of smaller cars for sale in the U.S. The growth of the import market, from Germany and Japan.

Sources: Bentley Historical Library (2009); Goeldner and Ritchie (2012); History (2014); Rodrigue (2014); USHistory.org (2014).

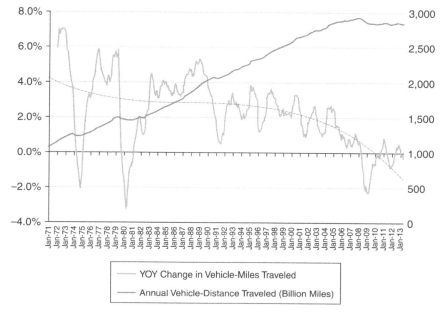

Figure 12.3 Vehicle miles travelled in the US.
Source: Adapted from Rodrigue, 2014.

for approximately 80 percent of all trips' (Goeldner and Ritchie, 2012: 41). As can be seen in Figure 12.3, vehicle miles driven in the US have been increasing steadily with a little drop in 2008 potentially due to the economic recession.

The automobile industry transformed American society and culture, influencing many different aspects of American life, including tourism. 'Tourism developed as a result of the auto industry – camp sites and motor lodges, restaurants, and tourist attractions all waited to feed, clothe, and entertain the passing motorist ... Outdoor pursuits, such as camping, hunting, and fishing gained popularity as leisure activities' (Bentley Historical Library, 2009). 'Even cuisine was transformed by the automobile. The quintessential American foods – hamburgers, french fries, milk shakes, and apple pies – were hallmarks of the new roadside diner. Drivers wanted cheap, relatively fast food so they could be on their way in a hurry' (USHistory.org, 2014).

Similar significant developments took place in other car producing regions, such as Europe. For example, the famous Michelin guides and ratings by the Michelin tire company originated in France as a service originally offered to drivers free of charge because 'André and Edouard Michelin foresaw that for the automobile to be successful, motorists had to be able to find places to refuel, charge their batteries or change their tires wherever they travelled' (Michelin, 2014).

It is clear from the connection in marketing activities between tourism and transportation that the relationship has developed as intricately interrelated at many different forms and levels of businesses, strategies and tactics. 'Indeed, the notions of freedom and spontaneous holiday making in one's own, or a rented vehicle are now so popular that they have become mass marketing slogans and are inextricably linked with the images and names of cars such as the Ford Escape, Jeep Liberty and Nissan Pathfinder' (Hardy, 2014: 2).

The predominance of travel by car in some countries has led to terminologies such as 'drive tourism' and 'road tourism' (Hardy, 2014; Prideaux and Carson, 2011). 'Road tourism' is defined as: Predominantly self-drive, but also service-provided, vehicular travel by road, involving a journey between single or multiple destinations and stopover locations – and able to be undertaken on a point to point, hub and spoke, looped or side trail basis' (DevelopTourism.com, 2012). Travel by cars is postulated to be important for regional development, especially places such as 'rural and coastal destinations ... particularly those without airports, or distant from major population centers' (DevelopTourism.com, 2012). In car travel, sightseeing while driving is an essential part of the travel experience and the attractions are scenic byways, scenic drives, scenic routes, drive trails, themed trails, touring routes, which are 'identifiable routes on roads that are promoted by organizations using maps, signs, brochures or audio material, which may be linear or circular, and pass or provide access to key attributes of the area ... [which] ... vary in length, configuration, route quality and environmental context' (Hardy, 2014: 8).

The popularity of car travel contributed to the popularity of drive destinations including, 'coast highways, mountain, gorge (and) deserts, historic regions and 'natural wonders like California's giant redwood forests' (DevelopTourism. com, 2012), Route 66, established in 1926, the Alaska Highway, Tail of the Dragon (a.k.a. US 129), and the Blue Ridge Parkway. 'The Blue Ridge Parkway is a National Parkway and All-American Road ... noted for its scenic beauty. It runs for 469 miles (755 km) through twenty-nine Virginia and North Carolina counties, mostly along the Blue Ridge, a major mountain chain that is part of the Appalachian Mountains' (Wikipedia, 2014a). This popular scenic drive is driven through by more than 15 million drivers every year (National Park Service, 2014).

However, popularity was not only the gain of those places that cars can take travellers to; also places and events related to car production and cars became popular tourist appeals. Major car production cities such as Detroit, or 'Motor City', which 'built its wealth and reputation on the automotive industry' (Bentley Historical Library, 2009), car production factories such as GM and also car related events such as rallies, and car shows joined the nourishing cycle between tourism and transportation.

Auto shows and events

There are hundreds of events and shows about automobiles around the world nowadays. Some of the major auto event categories are displayed in Table 12.3. Many car clubs, sanctioning bodies, schools and race tracks are involved in organization of these events. Auto shows like Detroit or Los Angeles auto show are new

Table 12.3 Major car event and show categories

Races/performance shows	Displays	Meetings	Educational	Other
Autocross	Shows/	Club Meetings	Driving	Cruises & Tours
Drag Racing	Concours	Banquet/	Schools	Test and Tunes
Drifting		Dinner Swap		Vintage Events
Hillclimb/Time Trial		Meets		
Karting				
Open Track/HPDE				
RallyCross				
Road Racing				
Stage Rally				
TSD Rally				

Source: MyAutoEvents.com (2007).

car shows with the manufacturers showing their latest and greatest cars. Often prototype show cars are featured showing the direction manufacturers are going. Hot rod auto corrals are a combination of auto show and car and parts swap meet. All cars are welcome and often cars are grouped in various categories depending on brand, country of origin, or the type of modification.

A list of major international auto events and shows from Yahoo Directory is also provided in Appendix A. These events draw thousands of member and non-member attendants from different origins and thus generate further travel in return. These events and shows provide not only educational, networking and product experience benefits, but also a side benefit of encountering celebrities some of whom have a hobby of collecting cars (Jay Leno, David Letterman, Nicolas Cage, and Ralph Lauren). Jay Leno, the famous American talk show host, for example, is known to have more than 100 cars and attends several car shows and events including Pebble Beach Concours d'Elegance.

Auto events are beneficial for the industry participants as well since they are found to be very helpful in boosting car sales. Hosein (2014) used the data from 740 attendees of the 2010 Northwood's Auto Show to measure the influence of attending an auto show on consumers' buying decision and found positive relationship between attendance and information gathering and consumers' intention to buy. NADAFrontPage.com (2014) reports 'a survey of nearly 7,500 new-car buyers indicated that 23 percent of them shopped for a new vehicle at an auto show ... out of the 23 percent (or 1,725 new-car buyers) who shopped at an auto show, 60 percent said they decided what brand to buy upon leaving the show'.

Besides the benefits to the participants and attendants, these events and shows also have significant impact on the economy and image of the destination as well. Since mass numbers of people attend these events, significant tourist spending occurs in the destination, including transportation, food and beverage and accommodation. Furthermore, many people get to experience the festive atmosphere at the destination, thus having a major impact on their perception of the destination as well. However, neither of these impacts has received enough academic attention thus far. The economic and image impact of major sporting events have been a focus of research for a period of time (e.g. Kaplanidou and Vogt, 2007); however, motoring events have been amiss thus far.

The North American International Auto Show held annually in Detroit is one of the major auto events in the US, which received much attention and media coverage lately due to its potential to help the economy of the Motor City that entered 2014 bankrupt, with a cumulative debt of more than $18 billion (Anders, 2013; Karoub, 2014a, b, c; Sanchez, 2013; Walsh 2014). Journalists such as Karoub (2014a) dubbed Detroit's bankruptcy as 'a 21st century paradox … the largest public case in U.S. history and facing $18 billion or more in debt'. Therefore, the potential economic and image impact of this auto event were in the spotlight for a while: 'the Motor City's resurgent auto industry is strong enough to host a show that by one estimate will generate nearly $400 million for the area's economy … Downtown hotels reported Friday that occupancy is at 85% during press days and about 70% during public days. Local restaurants and bars should be packed with an estimated 5,000 journalists and 800,000 visitors expected at the show from Monday through Jan. 26. Overall, the show provides a pick-me-up for the area, illustrated by amped-up coverage from local television stations and highway billboards welcoming visitors and industry types' (Karoub, 2014a).

The North American International Auto Show was rebranded as international in 1989, which brought heightened media coverage internationally, attention from foreign automakers generating an estimated $9.7 billion to $10.1 billion in economic impact to the area (Walsh, 2014). 'Media coverage has grown from 200 regional reporters in the 1980s to an expectation of more than 5,500 from 65 countries in 2014. The increase in coverage has led to increased investment in the show from automakers, suppliers and vendors' (Walsh, 2014).

Having realized the potential impact of automobile events for the retail automotive businesses as well as other local businesses, in 2012, the Automobile Dealers Association of Greater Philadelphia, published a press release about the Philadelphia Auto Show (www.phillyautoshow.com) to inform the public about its economic impact for the city of Philadelphia and state of Pennsylvania, ($44 million, annually) and to generate interest in attending by offering affordable entry fees (The Automobile Dealers Association of Greater Philadelphia, 2012). Another automobile event that received media attention was 2012 New York International Auto Show. Its economic impact in dollars and jobs was publicized by visuals and stories to catch public attention as can be seen from the brochure that was published by Crain's (Crain's New York Business, 2012).

Concours d'Elegance

Concours d'Elegance (concourse of elegance) is known to start as a competition of elegance, more so prestige of '17th Century French aristocracy, who paraded horse-drawn carriages in the parks of Paris during summer weekends and holidays', which turned into a competition of automobile owners (Wikipedia, 2014b). Today, there are many annually organized Concourses in the world and the USA.

One of the most popular concourses in the world is not surprisingly, in Paris, France. Others include Mumbai (formerly Bombay), India; Dubai, United Arab Emirates; and Istanbul, Turkey. There are more than 50 concours events in the US. There are multiple concourses organized in the states with higher rates of the population with prestigious cars. In time, a new competition branched out as Concours d'Ignorance, which was renamed as the Concours d'LeMons, to celebrate 'the oddball, mundane and truly awful of the automotive world' (Concours d'LeMons, 2014).

The ticket prices for concourses vary between $10 and $275 depending on the popularity of the show; this fee includes the program, parking and a shuttle service (Concours d'Elegance, 2014). High prices of concourses are justified by the primary mission of concourses, which is fundraising for a charity or cause of non-profit organizations in healthcare, medical research, education, community service, and more. It is claimed that 'millions of dollars have been raised through this unique appreciation of the history and beauty of vintage automobiles' (Concours d'Elegance, 2014).

There are many other collector car shows and car clubs raising funds for worthy causes; so, Concours d'Elegance's difference is claimed to be 'the galas, parties, sponsor events, automotive art shows, auctions, and car tours that take place over several days leading up to the main event, which most of the time is on a Sunday' (Concours d'Elegance, 2014). The success of the show is attributed to many car enthusiasts and individuals who volunteer their time and expertise to generate as high a dollar amount as possible.

Besides the show quality, a major difference of concourses from other similar type shows is that the owners and their cars are personally invited to attend. To be invited, cars need to be 'fully restored to mint condition, but many times they surpass the condition of models that originally rolled off the assembly lines'; ... not surprisingly, the owners of such cars are wealthy individuals such as Rob Walton (Wal-Mart Stores), Peter S. Kalikow (New York real estate), Otis Chandler (Times Mirror) and Bruce McCaw (cellular telephones) and celebrities such as Jay Leno, David Letterman, Nicolas Cage, and Ralph Lauren who compete in concours events for automotive bragging rights' (Neiger, 2014). Contestants are chosen based on the detailed photos of their cars that they submitted, and occasionally an interesting story of the car's history. And usually, competitors cannot compete for up to 10 years unless the car had a noticeable change such as in ownership or significant restoration since the competition (Neiger, 2014). Once invited, the competitors can formally apply for invitation for the other shows as well.

Rare, valuable and prestigious cars such as Bugattis, Duesenbergs, Stutzes, Ferraris, Alfa Romeos, Maseratis, Corvettes, and Porsches are displayed at picturesque destinations such as beachfronts, golf courses, and lake fronts. About 150–250 cars of wide range, fitting a specific category, or marque, such as 'postwar, pre-war, antique and vintage, horseless carriages, convertibles, Duesenberg, Porsche, Bentley (or) classes for open cars (cars without any windows), closed cars (cars with windows) and convertibles (which usually do have windows)' compete for the top honour (Neiger, 2014). Regardless of the many classes in a concours, the same standard rules are used while judging each group to determine the winner of the group (Neiger, 2014).

The competition takes place in one day. Judges, who are specialized in each type of car, rate each car on a scale of 100 for their authenticity and restoration quality inside or out and the littlest imperfections cause point deductions (Martin, 2000). Cars compete for a best-of-class award, and winners in each class then compete for the top honour, namely the best-in-show title (Martin, 2000). The rest of the show includes other activities such as 'automotive expert discussion panels, the screening of automotive documentaries, live auto auctions and even automotive fine art galleries' over a few days which public spectators can observe as well (Neiger, 2014).

Although the basic show concept is shared, every concours is different in its invitation criteria for competition, the types of cars, the number of competitors, competition classes, and the tribute or emphasis for each year's competition (Neiger, 2014). For example, the 2011 Amelia Island Concours featured Duesenberg, Allard, and Kurtis as the chosen featured marques and emphasized a celebration of 100 years of Chevrolet and '100 years of Indy'. Besides those select few marques, other cars were able to compete as well.

John Olman, the founder and editor of Concours d'Elegance website (http://www.concoursdates.com/concours-delegance-dates-2014) realized the aging of the concours participants. Being concerned with only 25% of collector car owners being under the age of 46, he came up with strategies to induce interests from younger segments. One of his focus areas was the entry fees; he reconsidered the admission fees for younger segments. Another area that he focused on was the promotion aspect of concours; he developed online listing of concourses, developed an additional car hobby website (www.funkhana.com), another one to provide accurate and timely information (www.ConcoursDates.com); providing 'basic concours information, such as dates, location, admission fees, and links to websites, social media and articles' and the social media (Facebook) to attract the attention of younger segments. He is pleased to see responses from younger segments already (Concours d'Elegance, 2014).

Concours d'Elegance at Amelia Island

Founded and chaired by Bill Warner, the Amelia Island Concours d'Elegance has been held since 1996. Automobile (2014) contrasts Amelia Island Concours to Pebble Beach bacchanal by attributing Amelia as 'geographically and philosophically ... the polar opposite of the Pebble Beach (due to it being) more casual, more compact, more egalitarian' (p. 81). It is suggested that spectators go to Amelia Island because they want to or because of the chair, Warner; while they go to Pebble Beach because they have to (Automobile, 2014, p. 81).

Amelia Island Concours d'Elegance is typically organized in the second full weekend (Friday, Saturday and Sunday) of March, March 7–9 for 2014, for example. The event was conceptualized by the PR personnel of the Amelia Island Ritz Carlton to attract further business. When it started, it drew 2400 spectators who came to see 125 cars; which was more than 12 times in spectators and more than double in 2014. Nowadays, it is considered 'as one of the must-attend car events

Figure 12.4 The Amelia Island Concours d'Elegance site (photo taken by Jerry Epperly in 2011).

on the international circuit' (Automobile, 2014, p.81). The increasing demand in fact is concerning to the event's management team who consider demarketing tactics such as decreasing the number of tickets or increasing the prices. In fact, doing both of them at the same time may be the more viable option. However, the father of this event, Warner is not fond of either of them (Automobile, 2014).

The venue: The destination of this show is the beautiful Amelia Island, along Florida's northeast coast, 30 miles North of Jacksonville. The island itself is known to be one of the most touristic areas in Florida. It is suggested by VisitFlorida, the State's Destination Marketing Organization, as the perfect spot for a tranquil getaway, a gentle recreation, and a historical exploration. It is praised for its golden-hued sands and guided horseback rides along the shore … dolphin and osprey and maybe even a glimpse of the endangered right whale … plus luxury hotels and a wonderful selection of bed and breakfasts … In fact, the Condé Nast Readers' Choice Awards panel agrees: Amelia Island consistently ranks among its 'Top 10 U.S. Islands' (VisitFlorida, 2014). A picture of the site can be seen in Figure 12.4. The specific location of the show is The Golf Club of Amelia Island and The Ritz-Carlton.

Contestants: The Amelia Island Concours d'Elegance features a marque and a theme every year, and both the marque and theme are developed several years in advance. The 2014 event featured the American Motor Car Company's Underslung, and also celebrated the 50th anniversary of McLaren, the British car manufacturer. The Amelia Island Concours d'Elegance is one of the few concourses that designate an honouree for each year's show. Table 12.4 displays the honourees since the beginning of this show. The honouree of the 2014 edition of the Amelia Island Concours d'Elegance is Jochen Mass, a retired race car driver from Germany, who participated in 114 Formula 1 Grand Prix races between 1973 and 1982, and won the 1975 Spanish Grand Prix. He was also successful in sports car racing, winning the 24 Hours of Le Mans in 1989, one of the most prestigious endurance races of all. (ESPN F1, 2014, Wikipedia, 2014c).

Table 12.4 Honourees and winners of the Amelia Island Concours d'Elegance

Winners of the best-in-show

Year	Honouree	Concours d'Elegance	Concours de Sport
2014	Jochen Mass	1937 Horch 853 Voll Ruhrbeck Sport Cabriolet	1958 Scarab
2013	Sam Posey	1936 Duesenberg SJN	1968 Ford GT40
2012	Vic Elford	1938 Bugatti Type 57C	1962 Ferrari 330 LM/GTO
2011	Bobby Rahal	1933 Duesenberg SJN Arlington Torpedo Sedan	1935 Duesenberg SJ Speedster
2010	Richard Petty	1937 Mercedes-Benz 540K Special Roadster	1960 Maserati Tipo 61
2009	David Hobbs	1931 Voisin C20 Demi-Berline	1923 Miller Special 122 Supercharged
2008	Parnelli Jones	1935 Duesenberg J Roadster	1957 Ferrari 335 Sport
2007	Derek Bell, MBE	1957 Talbot Lago T-150 CSS	1953 Ferrari 375MM
2006	Johnny Rutherford	1931 DuPont Model H Sport Phaeton	1961 Ferrari 250 TRI/61
2005	Bobby Allison	1931 Bugatti Type51 2005 was the first year of dual Best-in-class	1953 Porsche 550 Coupe
2004	Bobby Unser	1934 Voisin C-15	
2003	Jim Hall	1958 Dual Ghia Chrysler-powered	
2002	Dan Gurney	1937 Delage D8 120SS Aerodynamic Coupe	
2001	John Surtees, OBE	1937 Hispano Suiza Dubonnet	
2000	Brian Redman	1938 Alfa Romeo 8C02900	
1999	Carroll Shelby	1938 Delage D8 120	
1998	Hurley Haywood	1932 Lincoln KB Dual Cowl Phaeton	
1997	Phil Hill	1937 Mercedes-Benz 540K Special Roadster	
1996	Sir Stirling Moss	1938 Talbot-Lago 150SS Figoni & Falaschi	

Source: Amelia Island Concours d'Elegance (2014).

Typically, the Amelia Island Concours d'Elegance draws over 250 rare vehicles from all over the world, 330 in 2014. Similar to other concourses, the Amelia Island Concours d'Elegance is also an invite only show; invited cars are rare classic restored or survivor cars which are unusual and seldom seen classic road and racing cars. Restored cars are made new again with the original and reproduction parts to be examples of new cars frozen in time. Survivor cars are unrestored cars that have not been changed from their original configuration. Some were stored away, forgotten for years. Some survivors have been used and maintained by the original owners or the family and are still usable vehicles.

Some of the cars displayed include antique cars from before World War II, classic cars from WWII until the early 70s, hotrods, which are various antique and classic cars modified extensively, muscle cars which are midsize cars with large v8 engines from the 60s and early 70s, cars used in drag and road racing. Some of the attractive pieces are early import cars, mostly from Europe, especially British sports cars, which were very popular with American soldiers returning from WWII.

Contestants are judged by expert judges who are specialists in each car class. The chief Judge of the Amelia Island Concours d'Elegance is David Schultz, who was the President of the Classic Car Club of America (CCCA). The team of judges, however, varies year to year depending on the year's featured marque and theme. Each year, about 100 judges are hand-picked by Warner from the 'crème de la crème of the collector car universe – super rich owners, champion race car drivers, celebrated car designers, high-level car-company executives, museum curators, classic-car restorers, and other assorted experts' (Auto Features, 2014: 80).

Prices: The ticket price for the main event, the concours on Sunday is $60 in advance and $80 at the door, $40 for youth 12–18 years old and children under 12 are admitted free with paying adult ticket (Amelia Island Concours d'Elegance, 2014). This pricing strategy is commensurate with the vision of John Olman, who desires to reduce the average age of concours attendants and contestants. All other functions and social events require purchase of additional tickets. If an attendee wishes to experience more of the show, then they need to purchase Club Amelia deal for $400 per person, which includes 'admission to the Concours, VIP parking, collector program, continental breakfast, lunch, snack, three drink tickets and cash bar' (Amelia Island Concours d'Elegance, 2014). There are also other price variations for different segments and different preferences. Additional functions and socials require purchase of additional tickets.

Functions and activities: Over a 3-day span, several functions and activities take place. Some of these activities are open to general attendees as part of the ticket, some are by invitation only and some require additional tickets. The list of functions and socials of the 2014 version is provided below: The Amelia Island Concours d'Elegance is the main event that takes place on Sunday and includes:

- Honouree Jochen Mass enters the show field from the Awards Tent;
- Vintage Fashion Show presented by Fashion Group International, North Florida, Inc.;
- Flyover;
- Judges Introduction;
- Awards Presentation including Best in Show, Best in Class, Amelia and Corporate Awards.

Additional activities include:

- RM auctions Amelia Island sale preview and reception;
- The Amelia Island concours silent auction;
- Guardians of Porsche Wine Maker's dinner ($295 per person);
- The Porsche driving experience ($110 per person);
- Passport transport Eight Flags Road Tour;
- Hasselblad Automotive photography exhibit;
- Test drives with various manufacturers;
- Automobilia and luxury lifestyle merchants;
- Automotive Fine Arts Society (AFAS);

- Luxury car displays;
- Book signings;
- The Great Offy (Offenhauser) Drivers seminar presented by UBS ($30 per person);
- duPont registry live airport reception ($125 per person);
- Cars and coffee at the concours presented by Heacock Classic Car Insurance;
- The merchants of speed seminar presented by Kelly Services ($30 per person);
- Breitling cocktail reception (by invitation only);
- Mercedes-Benz gala dinner honouring Jochen Mass (by invitation only);
- After party presented by McIntosh (Amelia Island Concours d'Elegance, 2014).

Photos in Figures 12.5 and 12.6 show some snapshots of this auto show in 2011. The show and its functions are continued regardless of the rain and all proceeds go to the Amelia Island Concours d'Elegance Foundation, Inc., a public charity under section 509(a)(2) of the Internal Revenue Code and also a 501(c)(3) organization, which contributes to a number of causes including:

- Community Hospice of Northeast Florida, which cares for terminally ill children and adults in North Florida regardless of their ability to pay;
- Spina Bifida of Jacksonville, which is dedicated to raising awareness about the birth defect spina bifida and its effects;
- The Navy-Marine Corps Relief Society, which, in partnership with the Navy and Marine Corps, provides financial, educational and other assistance to members of the Naval Services of the United States, eligible family members, and survivors in need;
- Shop with Cops, which is a Christmas charity run by the Nassau County Sheriff's Office and Fernandina Beach Police Departments to help underprivileged children in both areas (Amelia Island Concours d'Elegance, 2014).

Figure 12.5 A 1927 Duesenberg Model X McFarlan Boat Roadster displayed at the 2011 version of the Amelia Island Concours d'Elegance (photo taken by Jerry Epperly in 2011).

Figure 12.6 A 1960 Plymouth XNR Prototype displayed at the 2011 version of the Amelia Island Concours d'Elegance (photo taken by Jerry Epperly in 2011).

Significance: The online magazine of Sir Stirling Moss (2014), the world famous Formula 1 driver, describes the Amelisa Island Concours d'Elegance as 'one of the United States' most innovative vintage auto events featuring over 250 rare classics from seldom-seen private collections from across the US'. With all its success and accolades, the Amelia Island Concours d'Elegance is counted as one of the top automotive events in the world. Since 1996, the show's Foundation has contributed over $2.2 million to partner charities. In fact, 'the annual International Historic Motoring Awards, in association with EFG International and Octane magazine, announced this week that the Amelia Island Concours d'Elegance has been named the recipient of the 2013 Motoring Event of the Year award. The Amelia Island Concours d'Elegance is the third winner of the Motoring Event of the Year Award, which honours automotive celebrations from Australia, Germany, Italy, the United States and the United Kingdom. Finalists in the 2013 events category included the Kensington Palace Centennial Celebration of Aston Martin, the St. James Concours d'Elegance, Schloss Dyck, Pendine Sands VRHA Hot Rod, the Kop Hill Climb, The Quail, A Motorsports Gathering and the Pebble Beach Concours d'Elegance' (Amelia Island Concours d'Elegance, 2014). All these contenders are very popular and prestigious auto shows; therefore, this is a significant victory for not only the concours itself but also for the prestige of the Amelia Island as a tourism destination.

Concourses are significant sociocultural phenomena, not only because they honour history making, rare and exquisite cars that are products of intellectual and visionary car geniuses, but also because they provide one of the strongest means for male bonding. This is evident in chairman Bill Warner's statement about the 2013 edition of the Amelia Island Concours d'Elegance that 'it turned into a family day as dads and sons brought cameras and had, quite literally, a field day' (Amelia Island Concours d'Elegance, 2014). One function of the show, the Vintage Fashion Show is an interpretation of the automotive culture from different periods. This, in fact, makes concourses, including the Amelia Island Concours d'Elegance, an important agent preserving the culture and heritage, not only at the national level but also at the international level.

Concourses also have a very important function of supporting the charitable causes in their communities. The Chairman Bill Warner reports that 'thanks to the support of our sponsors, fans and our group of selfless volunteers, we exceeded the $2.2-million-dollar mark in donations in 2013' (Amelia Island Concours d'Elegance, 2014). Some concourses, including the Amelia Island Concours d'Elegance also embrace other important aspects of life such as arts. The show occasionally includes an artistic aspect; for example, in the 2013 version, they included information about the artwork of Sam Posey, the honouree of that year.

Despite the significant impact of the auto shows and events, there is a lack of academic attention on this subject. The existing information regarding auto shows and events are mainly media stories, maybe due to media personnel having ease of access to these events due to their potential promotional roles. The Amelia Island Concours d'Elegance has been covered in car magazines such as *Car Collector*, *AutoWeek*, *Octane, Men's Journal, Automobilism DEPOCA*, and *Stirling Moss* (Amelia Island Concours d'Elegance, 2014). Also several news releases have been published by the organization every year. In these news releases, the show's significant accomplishments and charitable contributions are shared with the community. However, information about its attendees' potential impact to the community, especially economically, is still amiss. The attendees and participants of the car shows and events are potential lucrative traveller segments by the nature of their expensive hobbies; however, there is a lack of research on these travellers as well.

Research on Amelia Island Concours d'Elegance

As was also realized by John Olman, the founder and editor of Concours d'Elegance website, there is a noticeable lack of information about concourses in general and more so about individual concourses, including the Amelia Island Concours d'Elegance. Although individual concourses now have their websites, the extent of information provided on these websites is very limited. Their website information needs to be improved by adding detailed information about past events, including the number of attendants, the significant contestants such as celebrities, and the revenue generated.

As was mentioned before, academic attention is needed on these auto shows to measure their significance and to study both supply side and demand side issues. Future research is needed on consumers of these shows to understand their motivations for attending these shows and events, their perceptions of the event itself as well as the destination of the event, the benefits that they seek, and the important event attributes for their satisfaction. Results of such research could actually benefit the organizers in terms of what aspects to focus on for improvement in defining their competitive advantage.

Candid informal conversations with car enthusiasts that the authors had in the past reveal some important motivations for car enthusiasts attending car shows like concourses. Some of these motivations are related to cars and some are socially charged. Also, certain event characteristics are important for attendant satisfaction. Some potential motivation factors and show characteristics are listed in Tables 12.5 and 12.6. These scales can be used in future research.

A mini study was conducted using the above scales. Although only 7 respondents recruited through Facebook participated in the study, the results provide interesting insights in terms of auto fans' interests in these events. The respondents are usually middle aged, white, educated males with 100K or more annual income. They describe themselves as 'crazy about cars' who are attending multiple car shows. Those who never attended the Amelia Island Concours provided different reasons as lack of familiarity, timing and cost. The highest rated item on

Table 12.5 The scale to measure the importance of attendant motivations (7-point Likert Scale)

Seeing cars
Being outdoors
Feeling the status
Learning about cars
Meeting other car fans
Feeling the adrenaline
Professional networking
Being with my car buddies
Feeling well-accomplished
Learning about car models
Feeling the show atmosphere
Learning about manufacturers
Helping my decision for my next car purchase
Measured as importance or agreement 7-point Likert Scale

Table 12.6 The scale to measure the importance of auto show or event characteristics

Variety of cars
Variety of brands
Charitable causes
Helpful assistants
Social opportunities
Extent of information
Number of attendants
Upscale level of car brands
Food and beverage options
Affordable cost of attending
Printed materials for information
Information and education about cars
Professional networking opportunities
Exclusiveness (by invitation only, or higher prices)
Measured as importance or agreement 7-point Likert Scale

the motivation scale (see Table 12.7) was 'seeing cars' with a mean of 6.71, minimum rating of 6 on the 7-point scale. The second highest rated item was 'learning about cars' with a mean of 6.14 and a minimum rating of 5. All other items had a mean of 5 and lower and occasional minimum ratings of 1 on the 7-point scale. The lowest rated item was 'feeling the status' with a mean of 2.86 and a maximum rating of 4 on the 7-point Likert scale. This small group revealed that the most important reason is seeing and learning about cars followed by social reasons such as being with buddies. The psychological reasons such as status and excitement were not as high on their importance ratings. The results of this mini study supports the exertion about the car shows role in male bonding as expressed above.

The ratings on important attributes of auto shows (see Table 12.8) were commensurate with those ratings on motivations. The attributes related to seeing and leaning about cars, such as information and variety on cars and brands, are rated highest on average. Parallel to status on the motivation scale, exclusives of the

Table 12.7 Mini study descriptives on the importance of attendant motivations

Attendant motivations	N	Min.	Max.	Mean	Std. Dev.
Seeing cars	7	6	7	6.71	.488
Learning about cars	7	5	7	6.14	.900
Being with my car buddies	7	1	7	5.00	2.082
Feeling the show atmosphere	7	3	5	4.57	.787
Being outdoors	7	1	6	4.29	1.604
Meeting other car fans	7	1	6	4.14	1.676
Helping my decision for my next car purchase	7	1	6	4.00	2.309
Feeling well-accomplished	7	1	6	3.57	1.902
Professional networking	7	1	5	3.43	1.718
Feeling the adrenaline	7	1	6	3.43	2.070
Feeling the status	7	1	4	2.86	1.464
Valid N (listwise)	7				

Table 12.8 The scale to measure the importance of auto show or event characteristics

Show characteristics	N	Min.	Max.	Mean	Std. Dev.
Information and education about cars	5	5	6	5.60	.548
Variety of brands	5	4	7	5.60	1.140
Variety of cars	5	4	7	5.60	1.140
Affordable cost of attending	5	4	6	5.40	.894
Food and beverage options	5	1	6	4.20	1.924
Number of attendants	5	2	6	4.20	1.483
Upscale level of car brands	5	1	6	4.00	1.871
Professional networking opportunities	5	1	5	3.40	1.517
Social opportunities	5	1	5	3.20	1.483
Charitable causes	5	1	5	3.20	1.789
Exclusiveness (by invitation only, or higher prices)	5	1	4	2.20	1.643
Valid N (listwise)	5				

show rated lowest on average (2.20). As mentioned in the introduction of this chapter, this study can be taken only as an introductory for future studies that are much needed to understand this segment of tourism and tourists.

Conclusion

Auto shows and events are significant tourist attractions; their consumers are potentially lucrative segments with a high level of economic impact for the event as well as the destination. The impacts of auto shows for the organizers, for the attendees and for the destination in general need to be studied scientifically. The scales generated for the purpose of this study can be used as a starting point for this endeavour.

References

Amelia Island Concours d'Elegance. (2014). Accessed on 3/5/2014 on the WWW: http://www.ameliaconcours.org/

Anders, M. (2013). Detroit bankruptcy shouldn't impact North American International Auto Show. Accessed on 3/5/2014 on the WWW: http://www.mlive.com/business/index.ssf/2013/07/detroit_bankruptcy_shouldnt_im.html

Automobile (2014). July 2014. Putting on the Ritz – Bill Warner is the man who brings the Amelia Island Concours to life. pp. 80–81.

Bentley Historical Library (2009), The University of Michigan. Automotive History. Accessed on 3/5/2014 on the WWW: http://bentley.umich.edu/research/guides/automotive/

Concours d'Elegance. (2014). Accessed on 3/5/2014 on the WWW: http://www.concours-dates.com/concours-delegance-dates-2014.

Concours d'LeMons. (2014). Accessed on 3/5/2014 on the WWW: http://www.concours-dlemons.com/.

Crain's New York Business. (2012). 2012 NY International Auto Show, Crain's New York Business. Accessed on 3/5/2014 on the WWW: http://www.crainsnewyork.com/gallery/20120401/ECONOMY/330009999/2#

DevelopTourism.com. Accessed on 3/5/2014 on the WWW: http://www.developtourism.com/Drive%20Tourism%20and%20Road%20Tourism%20-%20TCDS%20Services.htm

ESPN f1 (2014), Drivers/ Joshen Mass. Accessed on 3/5/2014 on the WWW: http://en.espnf1.com/arrows/motorsport/driver/962.html

Goeldner, C.R. and Ritchie, J.R.B. (2012). *Tourism – Principles, Practices, Philosophies*, (12 Ed). New York, John Wiley & Sons, Inc.

Hardy, A. (2014). Drive Tourism: A Methodological Discussion with a View to Further Understanding the Drive Tourism Market in British Columbia, Canada. Accessed on 3/5/2014 on the WWW: http://www.unbc.ca/assets/community_development_institute/publications/a_hardy_cdi_paper.pdf.

History (2014). The Interstate Highway System. Accessed on 3/5/2014 on the WWW: http://www.history.com/topics/interstate-highway-system

Hosein, N.Z. (2014). Measuring the Purchase Intention of Visitors to the Auto Show. Accessed on 3/5/2014 on the WWW: http://www.aabri.com/LV11Manuscripts/LV11061.pdf.

Kaplanidou, K., and Vogt, C. (2007). The interrelationship between sport event and destination image and sport tourists' behaviours. *Journal of Sport & Tourism*, 12, 183–206.

Karoub, J. (2014a). Detroit auto show 'super' boost for city's economy, Detroit Free Press. Accessed on 3/5/2014 on the WWW: http://www.freep.com/article/20140111/NEWS01/301110059/Detroit-auto-show-super-boost-for-ailing-city

Karoub, J. (2014b). Auto show has large impact on Detroit. Reading Eagle. Accessed on 3/5/2014 on the WWW: http://readingeagle.com/drivetime/article/auto-show-has-large-impact-on-detroit

Karoub, J. (2014c). Detroit auto show 'super' boost for ailing city. The Huffington Post. Accessed on 3/5/2014 on the WWW: http://www.huffingtonpost.com/huff-wires/20140111/us--auto-show-detroit-impact/?utm_hp_ref=business&ir=business.

Martin, K. (2000). Collecting; It's The Stars' Cars That Steal the Scene. *The New York Times*. Feb. 25, 2000. Accessed on 3/5/2014 on the WWW: http://www.nytimes.com/2000/02/25/automobiles/autos-on-friday-collecting-it-s-the-stars-cars-that-steal-the-scene.html

Michelin. (2014). Accessed on 3/5/2014 on the WWW: http://www.michelintravel.com/about/ show-387933.html.

Moss, S. (2014). Amelia Island Concours d'Elegance 12th – 14th March – UPDATE. Accessed on 3/5/2014 on the WWW: http://www.stirlingmoss.com/articles/news/amelia-island-concours-delegance-12th-14th-march-update

MyAutoEvents.com. (2007). Accessed on 3/5/2014 on the WWW: http://www.myautoevents.com/pls/mae/frmMain.Show

NADAFrontPage.com (2014). Survey: Auto Shows Have Powerful Effect on Car Sales. Accessed on 3/5/2014 on the WWW: http://www.nadafrontpage.com/autoshows_study.xml

National Park Service. (2014). 10 Most Visited Units of the National Park System (2012). Accessed on 3/5/2014 on the WWW: http://www.npca.org/exploring-our-parks/visitation.html

Neiger, C. (2014). How a Concours d'Elegance Works. Accessed on 3/5/2014 on the WWW: http://auto.howstuffworks.com/concours-d-elegance.htm.

Prideaux, B. and Carson, D. (Ed.) (2011). *Drive Tourism – Trends and emerging markets*. London: Routledge.

Rodrigue, J.P. (2014) International Tourism and Transport Systems. Accessed on 3/5/2014 on the WWW: http://people.hofstra.edu/geotrans/eng/ch7en/appl7en/ch7a3en.html

Sanchez, E. A. (2013). Detroit Bankruptcy Won't Affect Auto Show. *Motor Trend*. Accessed on 3/5/2014 on the WWW: http://wot.motortrend.com/detroit-bankruptcy-wont-affect-auto-

The Automobile Dealers Association of Greater Philadelphia. (2012). Philadelphia Auto Show Reports Largest Opening Weekend Since 2004. Accessed on 3/5/2014 on the WWW: http://www.phillyautoshow.com/wp-content/uploads/2013/05/01-30-12-Largest-Opening-Weekend.pdf.

USHistory.org. (2014). The Age of the Automobile. Accessed on 3/5/2014 on the WWW: http://www.ushistory.org/us/46a.asp.

VisitFlorida. (2014). Amelia Island. Accessed on 3/5/2014 on the WWW: http://www.visitflorida.com/en-us/cities/amelia-island.html

Walsh, D. (2014). Media exposure fueled auto show's growth, economic impact. Crain's Detroit Business. Accessed on 3/5/2014 on the WWW: http://www.crainsdetroit.com/article/20140105/NEWS/301059971/media-exposure-fueled-auto-shows-growth-economic-impact#

Wikipedia. (2014a). Blue Ridge Parkway. Accessed on 3/5/2014 on the WWW: http://en.wikipedia.org/wiki/Blue_Ridge_Parkway

Wikipedia. (2014b). Concours d'Elegance. Accessed on 3/5/2014 on the WWW: http://en.wikipedia.org/wiki/Concours_d%27Elegance

Wikipedia. (2014c). Jochen Mass. Accessed on 3/5/2014 on the WWW: http://en.wikipedia.org/wiki/Jochen_Mass

Yahoo Directory. (2014). Automotive Events and Shows. Accessed on 3/5/2014 on the WWW: http://dir.yahoo.com/recreation/automotive/events_and_shows/

Appendix A Major international auto events and shows

Internationale Automobil-Ausstellung (IAA) – International Motor Show	Official site of the International Motor Show or Internationale Automobil-Ausstellung (IAA), the world's largest auto show, alternating between Hannover and Frankfurt.	www.iaa.de
North American International Auto Show (2)	Explore sites about the North American International Auto Show, an annual show in Detroit, Michigan.	dir.yahoo.com/.../Events_and_Shows/ North_American_International_Auto_ Show
Barrett-Jackson	Classic car auction and exposition held annually in January.	www.barrett-jackson.com
New York International Auto Show (4)		dir.yahoo.com/.../Events_and_Shows/ New_York_International_Auto_Show
Greater Los Angeles Auto Show	Featuring debuts of new cars, trucks, concepts, and motoring accessories from automobile manufacturers worldwide.	www.laautoshow.com
SEMA Show	Official site for the annual event showcasing automotive performance products and accessories.	www.semashow.com
Chicago Auto Show	Includes history of the event, photos, articles, contest information, and links.	www.chicagoautoshow.com
Progressive Automotive X PRIZE (2)		dir.yahoo.com/.../Events_and_Shows/ Progressive_Automotive_X_PRIZE
Goodwood Festival of Speed@		dir.yahoo.com/.../Events_and_Shows/ Goodwood_Festival_of_Speed
Washington Auto Show	Annual event held at the Washington Convention Center.	www.washingtonautoshow.com
Brussels International Motorshow (FEBIAC)	Annual international commercial and recreational vehicles and motorcycles show.	www.febiac.be
Mondial de l'Automobile (World of the Automobile)	Official site of the Paris auto show, providing exhibitor and visitor info, tickets, and more. In French and English.	www.mondialautomobile.com
Canadian International Autoshow	Canadian International Auto Show (CIAS) promotions, show news, and exhibitor information.	www.autoshow.ca
AutoZone Super Chevy Show	Car show series and drag racing attraction.	www.superchevyshow.com
Melbourne International Motor Show	Held annually in March. Features the exhibitors, how to get there, services, news, and times.	www.motorshow.com.au

(continued)

Cruisin' The Coast	Annual event along the Mississippi Gulf Coast featuring music, swap meet, car shows, and more.	www.cruisinthecoast.com
TRAX	Annual event in Northamptonshire. Features high-speed, chauffeured rides with experienced race drivers, karts, traders, simulators, and more.	www.traxshows.co.uk
San Francisco International Auto Show	Features info on the annual event.	www.sfautoshow.com
Summernats Car Festival	Annual festival of the street machine lifestyle in Canberra.	www.summernats.com.au
OCCARSHOW.com	Import car show and youth culture event in the Mid-Atlantic area.	www.occarshow.com
Americana International	Annual event featuring live music from the United States and the U.K., as well as a display of American automobiles.	www.americana-international.co.uk
Houston Auto Show	Annual show featuring the latest domestic and import vehicles, classic cars display, van conversions, automotive accessories, and the Safety Center.	www.houstonautoshow.com
AutoMechanika	Trade show for the automobile market.	www.automechanika.com
Quartzsite Sports, Vacation & RV Show	Also offering a classic car and hobby, craft, and gem shows.	www.quartzsitervshow.com
Importfest	Features displays and promotions from a variety of vendors, as well as competitions for import enthusiasts.	www.importfest.com
Moparfest	Canada's all Chrysler/AMC show for collectors and restorers of old Mopar vehicles. Mopar vehicles show and shine from across Canada and the U.S. With vendors, live entertainment, and more.	www.moparfest.com
Performance World Custom Car Show	Features a three-day automotive extravaganza of custom cars and trucks.	www.performanceworldcarshow.com
Pacific International Auto and Light Truck Show	Offers details about the Vancouver International Auto Show for exhibitors and visitors.	www.vancouverinternationalautoshow.com
Dallas Auto Show	Features show and exhibitor information.	www.dallasautoshow.org
British International Motor Show	Features news and ticket information about the annual event.	www.motorshow.co.uk

Appendix A (Continued)

Langley Good Times Cruise-In	Annual exhibit of classic cars, antique cars, trucks, military vehicles, and vintage emergency vehicles in Langley City, BC, Canada.	www.langleycruise-in.com
Frog Follies Street Rod Show	Street rod show of pre-1949 cars in Evansville, IN.	www.frogfollies.org
Geneva International Motor Show (4)		dir.yahoo.com/.../Events_and_Shows/ Geneva_International_Motor_Show
Atlanta Journal-Constitution International Auto Show	Official site featuring an overview of new vehicles, photo slideshow, program of events, and more.	www.ajcautoshow.com
Import Revolution	Information about the show schedule, tickets, registration, award categories, models, and more.	www.importrevolution.com
Electric Drive Transportation Association Conference & Exposition 2005	Offers participants a myriad of educational opportunities including in-depth learning forums, a comprehensive exposition, Ride'n'Drive, and valuable networking events. December 6–8, 2005, in Vancouver, B.C.	www.edtaconference.com
Iowa Gas	Annual early August swap meet and auction for petroleum collectibles, auto advertising, and gas station memorabilia.	www.iowagas.com
Car Show Finder	Single source to find and promote local car shows and automotive events in your area.	www.carshowfinder.org
Corvette 50th Anniversary	Features details about a 50th anniversary celebration on June 27–28, 2003 in Nashville.	www.corvette50th.com
4 World-Wide Shows	Includes information on the Mondial de l'Automobile and the Mondial du Deux Roues in Paris, as well as the Salon International in Bucharest, and the Salon Internacional del Automovil in Mexico.	www.amcpromotion.com
Silicon Valley International Auto Show	Features schedule and ticket info for the annual event held in San Jose, California.	www.svautoshow.com
London Motor Show	Guide to the companies, products and services on offer at the show and contact information.	www.londonmotorshow.co.uk
Pioneer Park Days	Antique engine and car show in Wauchula, FL.	Old-Engine.com/zolfo.htm
Kruisin' Krome	Presenting antique, vintage, classic, and open automobiles.	www.kruisinkrome.com

Name	Description	URL
Montreal International Auto Show	Includes location, dates, admission prices, and other event details.	www.salonautomontreal.com/en/index
Dreamcars Asia Motorshow	Showcase for high performance tuning car and aftermarket parts and accessories. In Singapore.	www.dreamcarsasia.com
Cleveland Auto Show	For consumers looking to compare new cars, trucks, SUVs, CUVs, and minivans.	www.cleveland.com/autoshow
Pepsi Street Motion Tour	Hauls hot cars, customizers, drivers, and models, along with fresh beats, breakers, and MCs. Includes downloads, tour schedule, and more.	www.pepsistreetmotion.com/?or=pw
Cars.com: Auto Shows	Exclusive coverage on recent auto shows. Includes concept car information, headlines, and new vehicle profiles.	www.cars.com/go/features/autoshows/index.jsp
Australian International Motor Show@		dir.yahoo.com/.../Events_and_Shows/Australian_International_Motor_Show
The Forge Invitational	The latest news and information on the Forge invitational muscle car show.	www.forgemusclecarshow.com
High Mileage Vehicle Competition@		dir.yahoo.com/.../Fairs_and_Competitions/High_Mileage_Vehicle_Challenge

Source: Yahoo Directory (2014).

13 The role of corporate vehicle museums in consumer brand engagement

Bradford T. Hudson

Mercedes-Benz opened a new automobile museum in 2006. Since then it has attracted more than five million visitors and been called the 'the Louvre of car museums' by the *New York Times* (Daimler, 2014; Williams, 2009). This is merely one example of a global phenomenon in which numerous vehicle manufacturers have established proprietary museums for their brands. These elaborate facilities are intended to not only preserve industrial artefacts that have historical significance, but also provide opportunities to engage consumers and build brand relationships. As such, they represent hybrids of cultural institutions and commercial promotions. These museums also illustrate the practical application of the concept of brand heritage.

Vehicle museums

The display of vintage motor vehicles is a widespread phenomenon that began soon after the second generation of automobiles was introduced. An early example may be found in the personal collection of Larz Anderson, who opened his carriage house near Boston to the public on Sunday afternoons starting in 1927 (now the Larz Anderson Auto Museum in Brookline, Massachusetts). Today there are more than 1,000 museums worldwide with significant collections of vintage automobiles.

Vehicle museums can be classified along several dimensions. These include the diversity of the collection, the purpose of the vehicles, the manufacturer of the vehicles, whether the museum is open on a regular basis, whether the museum is an independent entity, and whether the museum is operated for profit.

The first dimension describes whether the museum is devoted exclusively to motor vehicles. Although specialized museums are common, motor vehicles may be found in the diverse collections held by museums of art (Museum of Modern Art in New York), history (Heritage Museum in Sandwich, Massachusetts), science (Science Museum in London, England), and transportation (Museum of Transportation in St. Louis, Missouri).

The second dimension describes whether the museum is devoted predominantly to vehicles for personal use, such as automobiles or motorcycles. In the United States, the National Association of Automobile Museums alone represents more than 100 such institutions. There are also numerous museums that display other types of motor vehicles including trucks (Hays Antique Truck Museum in Woodland, California), buses (Oxford Bus Museum in Oxfordshire, England), and construction vehicles (National Construction Equipment Museum in Bowling Green, Ohio).

The third dimension describes whether the museum is devoted exclusively to vehicles from a single manufacturer. Although most museums display vehicles from a variety of companies, some focus on a particular marque (Museum for Historical Maybach Vehicles in Neumarkt, Germany). It should be noted that some museums featuring vehicles from a single brand have no legal affiliation with the related manufacturer (Rolls-Royce Museum in Dornbirn, Austria).

The fourth dimension describes whether the museum is open to individual members of the public on a regular basis. Although public museums are the norm, several museums prohibit unannounced visits (Pininfarina Collection in Cambiano, Italy). Some of these facilities are open by appointment, for scheduled tours, or as venues that can be rented for special events.

The fifth dimension describes whether the museum is an independent entity or a subsidiary of another organization. Many motor vehicle museums are incorporated as independent organizations, but some are subsidiaries of other organizations (Motor Speedway Hall of Fame in Indianapolis, Indiana). A few are explicit subsidiaries of manufacturers (Mack Truck Museum in Allentown, Pennsylvania).

The sixth dimension describes whether the museum is operated for profit or whether it is registered legally as a non-profit organization. Most vehicle museums are owned and operated by non-profit organizations that are independent of manufacturers. In a few cases, motor vehicle museums are controlled by companies that do not manufacture vehicles. These either function as businesses in themselves or serve as attractions to generate demand for unrelated operations, such as casinos or resorts (Gateway Canyons Automobile Museum in Gateway, Colorado).

Corporate vehicle museums

Every vehicle museum worldwide can be characterized by some permutation of the dimensions described above. This chapter will mention several types of institutions, but will focus on a particular sub-category known hereafter as 'corporate vehicle museums'. These are museums that are devoted predominantly to motor vehicles, that are devoted predominantly to vehicles for personal use such as automobiles or motorcycles, that are devoted predominantly to vehicles from one manufacturer, that are open to individual members of the public on a regular basis, and that are controlled by a vehicle manufacturer regardless of the legal incorporation or profit status of the museum itself.

Corporate vehicle museums are currently operated by manufacturers including Alfa-Romeo (Arese, Italy), Audi (Ingolstadt, Germany), BMW (Munich, Germany), Ducati (Bologna, Italy), Ferrari (Modena, Italy), Harley-Davidson (Milwaukee, Wisconsin), Honda (Hiyama, Japan), Mazda (Hiroshima, Japan),

Mercedes-Benz (Stuttgart, Germany), Porsche (Stuttgart, Germany), Toyota (Nagakute, Japan), Volkswagen (Wolfsburg, Germany), Volvo (Gothenburg, Sweden), and Yamaha (Shizuoka, Japan). Often these facilities are parts of larger efforts to define and exploit corporate history. Three prominent examples of corporate vehicle museums embedded in broader heritage programs are profiled below.

Mercedes-Benz

Carl Benz and Gottlieb Daimler arguably invented the modern automobile. Benz is certainly recognized as such, having filed an application for the first *motorwagen* with the Imperial Patent Office in 1886 (UNESCO, 2014). The name 'Mercedes' derives from several early racing cars built for a Daimler customer, who named the vehicles after his daughter Mercedes. The two separate companies were merged to create Daimler-Benz in 1926, which evolved into Daimler AG by 2007 (IDCH, 2014; Mercedes-Benz, 2014a). Mercedes-Benz remains their premiere brand today.

The pioneering status of Mercedes-Benz is celebrated throughout the company, as evidenced by extensive historical sections on the websites of both the Mercedes-Benz brand and its corporate parent Daimler (Daimler, 2014; Mercedes-Benz, 2014a). These include photographs, milestone charts, and verbal descriptions of important people, products, and events over the past century. Consumers can also order free paper brochures through the Mercedes-Benz website, which celebrate classic vehicles or otherwise relate to the history of the brand. Several of these brochures were used by the author as research sources for this chapter (Mercedes-Benz, 2012a, 2012b, 2012c, 2013a, 2013b).

Perhaps more surprising is the comprehensive 'Trail of Mobility' established by the company to recognize and promote various physical sites in the vicinity of its headquarters in Stuttgart, Germany (Mercedes-Benz, 2013b). These include the birthplace of Carl Benz and the Carl Benz Car Museum, the birthplace of Gottlieb Daimler and the Gottlieb Daimler Memorial, the Mercedes-Benz Museum, the Mercedes-Benz Archives and Collection, and the Mercedes-Benz Classic Center. Many of these sites are owned or supported financially by the company, and together they constitute an explicit and significant commitment to preserving and promoting the history of the brand.

The centrepiece of the trail is the Mercedes-Benz Museum in Stuttgart, which is a wholly owned subsidiary of Daimler. A smaller museum operated within the Daimler headquarters for decades, but the current purpose-built facility was opened nearby in 2006. The award-winning structure was designed by the celebrated Amsterdam architectural firm UN Studio (formerly Van Berkel en Bos Architectenbureau). It comprises more than 175,000 square feet on nine levels, with more than 1,500 exhibits and 150 vehicles. The museum has a professional curatorial staff and an active program of special exhibits. It includes a retail store and two restaurants, and the entire facility can be reserved for special events.

Mercedes-Benz operates the separate Archives and Collection facility in Stuttgart. This contains an archive of corporate documents, a library of printed and media material related to the brand, and a product archive with more than 700 vehicles. The archives are designed primarily for internal research and product development teams, but the centre is open by appointment to external researchers, such as journalists and historians.

The company also owns and operates the Classic Center in nearby Fellbach, which conducts restoration and repair work on any Mercedes-Benz vehicle that was discontinued more than 20 years ago. Originally intended to service vehicles in the collections of the Museum and Archives, the Classic Center now also serves the public. It has an inventory of over 50,000 parts for more than 20 discontinued models, and its staff will fabricate customized parts for other vintage vehicles on request. It includes a showroom where restored vintage Mercedes-Benz vehicles are displayed and may be purchased.

Mercedes-Benz features vintage automobiles in at least three other facilities worldwide. Mercedes-Benz World at the former Brooklands race course in Surrey, England includes a museum with vintage vehicles. Visitors there can participate in a variety of driving experiences, including the opportunity to ride as passengers (with a company driver) in an antique 300SL Gullwing Coupe. The Visitor Center for the factory tour in Vance, Alabama includes a museum with several vintage vehicles. The Classic Center in Irvine, California includes a showroom where restored vintage vehicles are displayed and may be purchased.

Harley-Davidson

William Harley designed a small gasoline engine that could be fitted onto a bicycle frame in 1901. He partnered with Arthur Davidson to manufacture motorcycles starting in 1903 (Harley-Davidson, 2014a).

The history of Harley-Davidson is documented extensively on the web pages of the Harley-Davidson Museum, which is a subsidiary section of the corporate website (Harley-Davidson, 2014b). This includes photographs, milestone charts, and verbal descriptions of important people, products, and events since the company was founded.

The Harley-Davidson Museum is located near the corporate headquarters in Milwaukee, Wisconsin. A wholly owned and operated subsidiary of the manufacturer, it opened in 2008. The impressive building, which was designed by the leading architecture firm Pentagram, is located amidst 20 acres of parkland on the banks of the Menomonee River. The museum comprises 130,000 square feet, with 12 themed exhibit areas including more than 450 motorcycles and related artefacts. The museum has a professional curatorial staff and an active program of special exhibits. It includes a retail store and restaurant, and the entire facility can be reserved for special events.

Harley-Davidson also operates an archival centre within the museum, which includes several hundred additional vehicles, as well as several thousand documents and artefacts. The archives are designed primarily for internal research and product development teams, but the centre is open by appointment to external researchers, such as journalists and historians. The general public can request guided tours of portions of the archives by advance reservation.

Toyota

The Toyota Motor Company has its roots in textiles. Sakichi Toyoda was an inventor and entrepreneur, who developed several automatic loom machines in the late nineteenth century, and founded a textile manufacturing company in 1918. His son Kiichiro started experimenting with automobile technology in a portion of the textile factory in 1930, and subsequently established an automobile division in 1933. This became a separate company in 1937 (IDCH, 2014).

The history of Toyota is documented extensively on its corporate website (Toyota, 2014a). This includes photographs, milestone charts, and verbal descriptions of important people, products, and events since the company was founded.

The Toyota Automobile Museum is located near the company headquarters in Nagakute, Japan (Toyota, 2014b). A wholly owned and operated subsidiary of the manufacturer, it was conceived during the corporate 50th anniversary celebrations and opened in 1989. The museum comprises more than 200,000 square feet in two buildings, with multiple exhibits including about 150 vehicles. The Museum has a professional curatorial staff and an active program of special exhibits. It also offers two restaurants and a retail store.

The company operates an archival unit within the Nagakute museum, which contains more than 10,000 printed and video materials. The archives are designed primarily for internal research and product development teams, but the centre is open by appointment to external researchers, such as journalists and historians.

Toyota also features vintage automobiles in at least three other facilities worldwide. The Visitor Center for the factory tour in Aichi, Japan includes the Toyota Kaikan Museum, which features about 20 vintage automobiles. The Visitor Center for the factory tour in Georgetown, Kentucky includes a small historical exhibit with the first Camry built at the Kentucky facility. Toyota also owns and operates the Toyota USA Automobile Museum near its United States headquarters in Torrance, California. This facility is open by appointment only for guided tours and special events.

Germany versus America

Although corporate vehicle museums can be found throughout the world, those in Germany arguably represent the pinnacle of the phenomenon. This is due to both the grandeur of the facilities and the fact that every major manufacturer has participated.

The Mercedes-Benz Museum is discussed above. The Audi Museum in Ingolstadt comprises about 65,000 square feet including more than 75 vehicles, three restaurants, and two retail stores. The BMW Museum in Munich comprises about 50,000 square feet including more than 100 vehicles, a restaurant, and a retail store. The Porsche Museum in Stuttgart comprises about 60,000 square feet including more than 80 vehicles, two restaurants, and a retail store.

Volkswagen has two museums that it controls through separate organizations, both of which are located in Wolfsburg. The Stiftung AutoMuseum Volkswagen (Volkswagen Auto Museum Foundation) comprises about 50,000 square feet including more than 130 vehicles manufactured by Volkswagen. This is not to be confused with the separate Zeithaus (time house) Museum, which is part of the nearby Autostadt complex. The Zeithaus, which claims to be the most visited automobile museum in the world, comprises about 50,000 square feet with vehicles from more than 50 different brands, including Volkswagen.

The participation of American manufacturers in vehicle museums has been variable and somewhat ambivalent, especially in comparison to their German counterparts. With the exception of Harley-Davidson, none of the major American manufacturers operate museums that are open to the general public on a regular basis. This is ironic, given the production scale and brand power of American manufacturers, and popular wisdom about 'car culture' in the United States.

General Motors Corporation owns and operates the GM Heritage Center in Sterling Heights, Michigan. The facility measures more than 80,000 square feet. It includes a collection of more than 600 vehicles and an archive with more than 5 million documents (Chappell, 2014). The facility may be reserved in advance by external groups for guided tours and special events, but it is not open to individual members of the public (General Motors, 2014). The Chevrolet division offers a guided tour of its Corvette factory in Kentucky, but the adjacent National Corvette Museum is an independent organization that was founded by enthusiasts unconnected to the manufacturer.

The Chrysler Group controls the Walter P. Chrysler Museum in Auburn Hills, Michigan. The facility measures more than 55,000 square feet, including 65 vehicle displays and a document archive. The museum was established after the company merged with Daimler, which probably reflects the influence of its erstwhile German parent. It was open to the public from 1999 to 2012, when it closed due to low attendance (Chappell, 2014; King, 2013; Kozak, 2012). The facility and collection remain intact, but access for external groups is now restricted to guided tours and special events on a reservation basis (Chrysler Museum, 2014).

Ford Motor Company has been involved with the Henry Ford Museum in Dearborn, Michigan since it was established in 1929. The museum has a 90-acre campus with a huge collection of more than 25 million artefacts and documents on a wide range of themes. The automobile exhibit comprises 80,000 square feet and displays more than 130 vehicles from a variety of manufacturers. Over the years, the company and family have made significant gifts to the museum in the form of automobiles, corporate documents, and cash grants (Adkins, 2006). The museum also partners with the company to offer tours of the historic River Rouge factory complex. Nonetheless, the Henry Ford Museum is an independent non-profit organization, which is completely separate from the company.

American automobile manufacturers have provided limited support to exhibits within independent museums. This includes the donation of vehicle collections and archives (the liquidated assets of Studebaker provided the basis for the Studebaker National Museum in South Bend, Indiana), the donation of individual vehicles (a Turbine Car was donated by Chrysler to the National Museum of American History in Washington, DC), and vehicle loans (such as Corvettes loaned by Chevrolet to the National Corvette Museum in Bowling Green, Kentucky).

One possible reason for the differing levels of involvement between German and American manufacturers is tax laws. In the United States, corporations operated for profit can usually make contributions to non-profit organizations in exchange for deductions that offset income taxes. Therefore, manufacturers have financial incentives to support independent museums rather than operate museums themselves. However, this does not explain why American manufacturers have failed to actively support proprietary museums through subsidiary charitable foundations. It seems clear that the German and American manufacturers have different outlooks regarding the value of museums for engaging consumers.

Related species

Corporate vehicle museums are related to several broader categories of attraction. These include museums in general, corporate museums, industrial heritage tourism sites, and industrial tourism attractions without a heritage emphasis. Each of these has its own traditions in scholarly literature, which can inform our discussion about the nature and purpose of the automotive variant.

The first category is museums in general (Carbonell, 2004; Chhabra, 2008; Chan, 2009; De Gruyter, 2012; Gofman *et al.*, 2011; Herreman, 1998; Kift, 2011; Post, 2013; Young, 1997). There are more than 50,000 museums globally, which cover an immense variety of themes and regions. Many are dedicated to the visual arts, but displays of cultural and industrial artefacts are also quite common.

The second category is corporate museums (Danilov, 1992; Livingstone, 2011; Nissley and Casey, 2002; Schwaiger *et al.*, 2010; Seligson, 2010). The phenomenon is not exclusive to the automobile industry, as a wide range of companies have established branded museums. Examples include Heineken (Amsterdam, Netherlands), Intel (Santa Clara, California), Norfolk Southern Railroad (Norfolk, Virginia), Spam (Austin, Minnesota), and Wells Fargo Bank (San Francisco).

The third category is industrial heritage tourism. A variety of consumers, preservationists and academics have shown interest in tourism related to deactivated industrial sites (Conlin and Bird, 2014; Edwards and Llurdes, 1996; Jolliffe and Aslam, 2009; Kerstetter *et al.*, 1998; Ruiz and Hernández Ramírez, 2007; Xie, 2006). This may be considered part of the larger phenomenon of cultural heritage tourism, which has received significant attention, especially in Europe (Timothy, 2011; Timothy and Boyd, 2003).

Examples of industrial attractions include resource production facilities (Zollverein Coal Mine in Essen, Germany), manufacturing plants (Masson Mills in Derbyshire, England), craft sites (Anderson's Blacksmith Shop in Williamsburg, Virginia), transportation centres (Historic Dockyard in Chatham, England), planned industrial communities (Pullman, Illinois), and industrial museums

(Museum of Industry in Baltimore, Maryland). Sites related to automobiles along the European Route of Industrial Heritage include the Cite de l'Automobile Museum (Mulhouse, France) and the Fiat Lingotto Factory (Torino, Italy).

The fourth category is industrial tourism destinations for which heritage is not the dominant component (Otgaar *et al.*, 2010). Companies in a variety of industries have established branded attractions near their headquarters, adjacent to their manufacturing facilities, or in popular tourism locations. These include visitor centres (Coca-Cola), factory tours (Crayola), product sampling areas (Ben & Jerry's), flagship retail stores (L.L. Bean), and amusement parks (Lego).

Perhaps the most impressive example of industrial tourism for automobiles is the Volkswagen Autostadt (auto city), which is located adjacent to the corporate headquarters in Wolfsburg, Germany. Covering more than 60 acres, the complex of buildings and green space is part amusement park and part automotive show. Autostadt includes separate pavilions for most of the brands owned by Volkswagen – including Audi, Lamborghini, Porsche, SEAT, Skoda, and Volkswagen – and a 'premium clubhouse' for their niche luxury brands Bentley and Bugatti. Attractions include the Zeithaus automobile museum (see above), a museum of technology, a factory tour, driving tracks for all-terrain and automated vehicles, a performance driving school, a canal boat ride, ten restaurants, and a Ritz-Carlton Hotel. Autostadt includes a distribution centre where consumers can accept delivery of new vehicles, which can be considered a type of flagship retail store (Autostadt, 2014).

In addition, a variety of vehicle manufacturers offer factory tours. In the United States alone, these include BMW (Greer, South Carolina), Ford (Dearborn, Michigan), Harley-Davidson (three locations in York, Pennsylvania, Menomonee Falls, Wisconsin, and Kansas City, Missouri), Hyundai (Montgomery, Alabama), Mercedes-Benz (Vance, Alabama), Nissan, (Smyrna, Tennessee), Subaru (Lafayette, Indiana), and Toyota (Georgetown, Kentucky).

Value proposition

The value proposition for visitors to automobile museums is multidimensional. Museums of any type offer a combination of 'cognitive, affective, reflective, and recreation' benefits (Chan, 2009). Visitors can appreciate the aesthetic nature of objects, entertain themselves during sightseeing excursions, distract families during rainy weekends, or educate and enrich both children and adults. Visitors may also be interested in discovering or exploring historical or cultural narratives for which the objects serve as symbolic representations. Some of these narratives relate to economic history, industrial development, or technological development. Automobile museums in particular offer an additional dimension of involvement for visitors who are enthusiasts of particular marques, as will be discussed below.

The value equation for donors and sponsors of automobile museums is similarly complex. Museums of any type receive support from individuals who would like to share their personal collecting or aesthetic passions, find stewards for artwork or artefacts that require care, dispose of items from estates that hold no interest for heirs, obtain deductions to offset income taxes, gain public recognition for large gifts, or indulge interests in public service or education.

Museums also receive support from companies or their subsidiary non-profit foundations. In some cases, corporate motivations are purely altruistic and related to community service or corporate social responsibility efforts, with donations given anonymously. More typical is support that involves prominent mention of the brand name, as a form of public relations that promotes the company or its products.

For both visitors and supporters, there are two additional dimensions of value that help explain the phenomenon of corporate vehicle museums. These relate to consumer experiences and brand heritage.

Consumer experiences

During the past two decades, the concept of consumer experiences has been given significant attention in academic literature (Brakus *et al.*, 2009; Ferreira and Teixeira, 2013; Palmer, 2010; Pine and Gilmore, 1998, 1999; Verhoef *et al.*, 2009). Some of this analysis concerns the experiential elements that are embedded in operations for service industries such as retail and hospitality (Chang and Horng, 2010; Grewal *et al.*, 2009). These represent fundamental parts of the value proposition that cannot be separated from the primary deliverable.

Of greater interest for this chapter are consumer experiences that are offered by companies as forms of entertainment related to, but separate from, their core products or services. This includes venues related to industrial tourism or industrial heritage tourism, as discussed above. For consumer product companies, these also include retail experiences (such as flagship stores) that are peripheral to their core activities in manufacturing.

Consumer experiences offer manufacturers the opportunity to engage with consumers in settings that explicitly promote their brands, but which use approaches that are perceived as playful or selfless rather than persuasive or avaricious. They offer an additional dimension for consumer enthusiasts who want to interact with the brand, and an additional channel for corporate designers and communications specialists to define the identity of the brand. Such experiences also represent a tool that both companies and consumers can use to deepen brand relationships.

Corporate vehicle museums exemplify the consumer experience as a form of entertainment peripheral to the core product. These are destinations in themselves, which are so compelling that many manufacturers are able to charge admission fees. As an example, the Mercedes-Benz Museum in Stuttgart charges €8 per adult, but still attracts several hundred thousand visitors per year (Mercedes-Benz, 2014b).

Brand heritage

The concept of brand heritage suggests that the consumer appeal of products and services offered by older companies may be enhanced by the historical characters of their brands. Examples of marketing related to heritage include the citation of company founding dates on packaging or in advertising, or the celebration of corporate anniversaries. Such marketing may also involve references to a company in historical context or to iconic artefacts in possession of the company. It could even include the creation of updated products that incorporate visual elements from prior versions, or the design of new offerings that refer to idealized or artificial memories of historical reality (Hudson 2011; Hudson and Balmer, 2013).

The intellectual ancestry for brand heritage includes prior streams of literature about retrospection and nostalgia in marketing (Brown *et al.*, 2003; Goulding 2001; Havlena and Holak 1991; Muehling and Sprott 2004; Stern 1992) and organizational identity in monarchies (Balmer *et al.*, 2006). Scholarship about brand heritage has also been informed by prior literature on the marketing aspects of heritage tourism (Goulding 2000; Harrison 2002; Timothy and Boyd 2003; Yeoman *et al.*, 2005).

Interest in brand heritage accelerated after the publication of a conceptual article about corporate heritage brands (Urde *et al.*, 2007). This suggested that effective management for older brands involves uncovering aspects of heritage through archival and consumer research, activating that heritage through product design and marketing communications, and protecting that heritage through stewardship and attention to continuity. Brand heritage has subsequently emerged as a distinct sub-discipline in marketing with its own body of literature (Balmer, 2013; Blombäck and Brunninge, 2013; Blombäck and Scandelius, 2013; Hakala *et al.*, 2011; Hudson, 2011; Hudson and Balmer, 2013; Merchant and Rose, 2013; Wiedmann *et al.*, 2011a, 2011b).

Heritage applied

The literature related to brand heritage informs our understanding of corporate vehicle museums in several ways. First, researchers have demonstrated that brand heritage effects occur in the automobile industry specifically. One set of researchers, who conducted interviews of consumers in Britain, found positive emotional reactions when probing for associations between the original Mini vehicle manufactured by British Leyland and the current retrospective Mini vehicle manufactured by BMW (Simms and Trott, 2006). Another group of scholars, who conducted survey research of consumers in Germany, found that brand heritage has a significant positive influence on the ability to attain a price premium for new vehicles (Wiedmann *et al.*, 2011a). Corporate vehicle museums capitalize on such attitudes.

Second, it has been suggested that older brands have unique histories that cannot be duplicated or appropriated by competitors, and therefore brand heritage constitutes a point of differentiation that may contribute to competitive advantage (Urde *et al.*, 2007). This is important in the highly competitive automobile industry, especially given the appearance of new entrants from Asia. Stefan Mueller, currently executive vice president of Renault and formerly a marketing executive with BMW, has asserted that technology 'can be copied by the competition rather quickly, so what is becoming more important for car companies is the heritage of the brand'

(Mueller in Marcus, 2010). Corporate vehicle museums allow manufacturers to convey this heritage in a tangible way.

Third, it has been demonstrated that brand heritage and heritage tourism are equivalent concepts in their respective realms, with similar motivations in consumer behaviour and comparable techniques in marketing practice. It has also been argued that these phenomena occur simultaneously in branded consumer destinations with heritage dimensions, such as historic hotels (Hudson, 2013). This suggests that corporate vehicle museums benefit from a mutually reinforcing confluence of heritage effects related to both the brand and the museum.

Fourth, a conceptual model has recently been proposed to explain consumer behaviour related to heritage effects (Hudson and Balmer, 2013). Based on the work of pioneering sociologist George Herbert Mead, the model suggests that brand heritage has two dynamics relating to symbolic interactionism and the role of the past in identity formation.

In innate heritage, the historical elements of the brand serve as signals regarding the identity of the brand itself. The value proposition for consumers is leadership, authenticity, expertise, quality or reliability of the product or company associated with the brand.

Corporate vehicle museums provide a compelling and unambiguous way to demonstrate the historic role of specific manufacturers in the development of the modern automobile, and thereby validate assertions in marketing communications regarding brand leadership in the present. If Mercedes-Benz can prove through the display of tangible evidence that they invented the automobile, and can embed themes of precision engineering and racing prowess throughout their historical narratives, then consumers may be more likely to accept claims that Mercedes-Benz manufactures superior cars today.

In projected heritage, the brand becomes an instrument of existential definition upon which consumers project their own historical associations. The value proposition for consumers is personal, historical, or utopian nostalgia. This aspect is consistent with the idea that museum visitors co-create historical narratives (Chronis, 2012).

Corporate vehicle museums provide focal points for such projection. In personal nostalgia, visitors who participated in the brand experience in the past through personal or family ownership can use a vintage automobile to activate associations that recreate youth in memory. In historical nostalgia, visitors who recognize an automobile in historical context may identify with ideas, events, or people from that era. In utopian nostalgia, visitors use the object to activate fantasies or role playing related to either the automobile or its historical context.

A museum visitor

The practical outcomes of brand heritage can be illustrated through an example from the Porsche Museum in Stuttgart. Imagine a visit last month by an American tourist, who is 35 years old and owns a new Porsche Boxster. Let us begin by exploring the innate heritage effects.

As our visitor entered one of the galleries, he discovered a 1954 Porsche 550 Spyder. He immediately noticed similarities in design between the displayed car and his own. Prior to the museum visit, he had mixed feelings about the Boxster, which was the least expensive model in the product line. The delight of owning a Porsche had always been tempered by doubts about its authenticity and prowess compared to a more expensive model, such as the 911. During the visit, he realized that the Boxster is a legitimate heir of the storied Spyder, with full claim to the Porsche identity, and he gained renewed enthusiasm for the brand.

Let us next consider the projected heritage effects. As a young child during the 1970s, our visitor enjoyed holidays with his extended family, because an uncle would sometimes take children for rides in a bright red Porsche 911. Upon arrival at the Porsche museum, our visitor noticed a similar 911 displayed near the lobby, which triggered bittersweet memories of his childhood. This is personal nostalgia.

As our visitor entered the gallery where the 1954 Spyder is displayed, he immediately compared the car to his own Boxster, as discussed above. He then realized that the movie actor James Dean died in a similar Spyder, while driving along Route 466 in California toward a racing event during 1955. Such thoughts represent the collective memory of historical events that actually occurred, but which did not happen during the lifetime of our visitor. The vehicle triggered vicarious feelings of loss, which were interwoven with powerful cultural narratives about youth and rebellion. This is historical nostalgia.

Finally, the vintage Spyder activated a fantasy in which our visitor drove a Porsche along Route 66 through Nevada, racing against James Dean in the film *Rebel Without a Cause*. This reminiscence about the 'golden age' of adventure travel along the 'mother road' is entirely mythical. The experiences of highway drivers during that era were undoubtedly more utilitarian than romantic, Route 66 never went through Nevada, the James Dean accident did not occur on this road, and the rebellious teen portrayed in the film was a fictional character. The imagined narrative was an amalgamation of fiction and reality, but it produced genuine affective reactions in our visitor. This is utopian nostalgia.

Corporate vehicle museums have the potential to activate powerful cognitive and emotional reactions to historical objects and contexts, unify these with brand positions and product attributes, and permanently insert these associations into the psyche of consumers. When our Porsche museum visitor subsequently returned from Germany, he was effectively immune to marketing communications from competing manufacturers. He also became an apostle within his personal network, convincing friends they must complete a similar pilgrimage to the birthplace of the Porsche legend.

Organizational memory

Corporate vehicle museums have one additional benefit for their sponsors. They act as internal resources for preserving and activating organizational memory (Danolov, 1992; Foster *et al.*, 2011; Nissley and Casey, 2002; Walsh and Ungson, 1991).

Maintaining records of past activities is a widespread phenomenon in the business world. In the United States alone, more than 200 companies support formal archival operations with professional staffs including Aetna, Coca-Cola, Disney, Dow Chemical, Microsoft, Procter & Gamble, Phillips Petroleum, and Weyerhaeuser (Adkins, 2006; SAA, 2014). Access to corporate archives is often restricted to internal audiences, but external researchers from the media or academia are sometimes granted access for specific inquiries. Many of the automobile manufacturers globally have such archives, some of which are located within corporate museums.

Although the most common items held by corporate archives are paper documents, manufacturers of tangible objects may also include products as historical artefacts. In the automobile industry, numerous manufacturers maintain archives of vehicles from the past. Consider the example of Mercedes-Benz, which not only displays more than 150 vehicles in its museum, but also maintains a hidden inventory of more than 700 additional vehicles in its separate archival unit.

Companies in any industry have multiple reasons for preserving their history. First, it may be advantageous or necessary to retain records for legal purposes. Second, the powerful effects of brand heritage can be applied to internal audiences, as historical narratives can be used to define organizational identity and foster employee pride (Nissley and Casey, 2002).

Third, understanding precedents can be useful for strategic planning and creative work in advertising or design. Those in the present can review actions in the past to gain inspiration, ensure continuity, or avoid repeating mistakes. In the automobile industry especially, historical reference for future design projects is often cited as a motivating factor to justify the expense of preserving large fleets of vintage vehicles (Chappell, 2014). Even though corporate vehicle museums have now taken on a life of their own, many were started as ways to capitalize on these underutilized archival collections.

Conclusion

'Corporate vehicle museums' were earlier defined as museums that are open to the general public on a regular basis, which display vehicles that are intended for personal use such as automobiles and motorcycles, and which are controlled by manufacturing companies that operate for profit. These facilities represent a distinct type of attraction that combines historical preservation with commercial promotion.

For visitors, such museums satisfy a range of motivations. Antiquarians can explore industrial and technological history, business and economic history, and the social and cultural history that provides context for exhibits. Those interested in aesthetics can admire antique cars, vintage industrial and graphic design, and contemporary architecture. Racing fans can examine classic sports cars and explore narratives about racing events, locations, and drivers. Past or current owners can discover the lineage of their own vehicles, and aspiring owners can fantasize about the priceless antiques that could be parked in their driveways.

Brand enthusiasts can immerse themselves in the artefacts and imagery of the company and its products, and those interested in the social aspects of brand communities can commune with fellow pilgrims.

For manufacturers, such museums are tools for creating and deepening the engagement between consumers and brands. They are manipulative commercial attractions that showcase products and communicate brand values, but their mission and manner are perceived as subtle and vaguely benevolent. They also serve as instruments for defining internal corporate culture, by communicating values about product leadership and corporate social responsibility. As archives of past products, they preserve organizational memory that may be useful for future strategic planning or design projects.

Corporate vehicle museums also illustrate two important concepts in prior academic literature. They exemplify how the value of physical goods can be enhanced by adding meaningful consumer experiences that are peripheral to utility benefits of the core product. They also exemplify how esoteric theories about the social and psychological aspects of heritage can be applied to deliver practical business outcomes.

Manufacturers such as Mercedes-Benz have made significant capital investments to construct facilities for exhibition and preservation, allocated scarce operating resources for conservation efforts and visitor operations, and made somewhat irrevocable decisions that their brand positions should be partly historical. Corporate vehicle museums represent strategic initiatives to build consumer engagement with brands by providing experiences that activate heritage effects. These companies are focused on the road ahead, but are constantly monitoring the rear view mirror.

References

Adkins, E.W. (2006) 'A History of the Ford Motor Company Archives', working paper, Bentley Historical Library, University of Michigan.

Autostadt (2014) *A Special Place*, corporate website, AutoStadt [www.autostadt.de].

Balmer, J.M.T. (2013) 'Corporate Heritage, Corporate Heritage Marketing, and Total Corporate Heritage Communications. What are They? What of Them?' *Corporate Communications: An International Journal* 18 (3), 290–326.

Balmer, J.M.T., Greyser, S.A. and Urde, M. (2006) 'The Crown as a Corporate Brand: Insights from Monarchies'. *Journal of Brand Management* 14 (1/2), 137–161.

Blombäck, A. and Brunninge, O. (2013) 'The Dual Opening to Brand Heritage in Family Businesses'. *Corporate Communications: An International Journal* 18 (3), 327–346.

Blombäck, A. and Scandelius, C. (2013) 'Corporate Heritage in CSR Communication: A Means to Responsible Brand Image?' *Corporate Communications: An International Journal* 18 (3), 362–382.

Brakus, J.J., Schmitt, H.B. and Zarantonello, L. (2009) 'Brand Experience: What Is It? How Is Measured? Does It Affect Loyalty?' *Journal of Marketing* 73, 52–68.

Brown, S., Kozinets, R.V. and Sherry, J.R., Jr. (2003) 'Teaching Old Brands New Tricks: Retro Branding and the Revival of Brand Meaning'. *Journal of Marketing* 67 (3), 19–33.

Carbonell, B.M., (ed.) (2004) *Museum Studies: An Anthology of Contexts*. Malden, MA: Wiley-Blackwell.

Chan, J.K.L. (2009) 'The Consumption of Museum Service Experiences: Benefits and Value of Museum Experiences'. *Journal of Hospitality Marketing & Management* 18, 173–196.

Chang, T.Y. and Horng, S.C. (2010) 'Conceptualizing and Measuring Experience Quality: The Customer's Perspective'. *Service Industries Journal* 30 (14), 2401–2419.

Chappell, L. (2014) 'From Wow to Warehouse: Concepts Keep Coming, but Historic Autos are a Chore to Store'. *Automotive News*, January 25.

Chhabra, D. (2008) 'Positioning Museums on an Authenticity Continuum'. *Annals of Tourism Research* 35 (2), 427–447.

Chronis, A. (2012) 'Tourists as Story-Builders: Narrative Construction at a Heritage Museum'. *Journal of Travel & Tourism Marketing* 29 (5), 444–459.

Chrysler Museum (2014) *About the Museum*, organizational website, Walter P. Chrysler Museum [www.wpchryslermuseum.org].

Conlin, M.V. and Bird, G.R. (eds.) (2014) *Railway Heritage and Tourism: Global Perspectives*. Bristol, UK: Channel View.

Daimler (2014) *Tradition*, corporate website, Daimler AG [www.daimler.com].

Danilov, V. (1992) *A Planning Guide for Corporate Museums, Galleries, and Visitor Centers*. Westport, CT: Greenwood Press.

De Gruyter (2012) *Museums of the World*, 19th Edition. Berlin: De Gruyter.

Edwards, J.A. and Llurdes, J.C. (1996) 'Mines and Quarries: Industrial Heritage Tourism'. *Annals of Tourism Research* 23 (2), 341–363.

Ferreira, H. and Teixeira, A. (2013) 'Welcome to the Experience Economy: Assessing the Influence of Customer Experience Literature through Bibliometric Analysis'. FEP Working Papers 481, Universidade do Porto, 1–28.

Foster, W.M., Suddaby, R., Minkus, A. and Wiebe, E. (2011) 'History as Social Memory Assets: The Example of Tim Hortons'. *Management and Organizational History* 6 (1), 101–120.

General Motors (2014) *GM Heritage Center*, corporate website, General Motors Corporation [www.gmheritagecenter.com].

Gofman, A., Moskowitz, H.R. and Mets, T. (2011) 'Marketing Museums and Exhibitions: What Drives the Interest of Young People'. *Journal of Hospitality Marketing & Management* 20, 601–618.

Goulding, C. (2000) 'The Commodification of the Past, Postmodern Pastiche, and the Search for Authentic Experiences at Contemporary Heritage Attractions'. *European Journal of Marketing* 34 (7), 835–853.

Goulding, C. (2001) 'Romancing the Past: Heritage Visiting and the Nostalgic Consumer'. *Psychology & Marketing* 18 (6), 565–592.

Grewal, D., Levy, M. and Kumar, V. (2009) 'Customer Experience Management in Retailing: An Organizing Framework'. *Journal of Retailing* 85 (1), 1–14.

Hakala, U., Lätti, S. and Sandberg, B. (2011) 'Operationalising Brand Heritage and Cultural Heritage'. *Journal of Product & Brand Management* 20 (6), 447–456.

Harley-Davidson (2014a) *H-D Timeline*, corporate website, Harley-Davidson Motor Company [www.harley-davidson.com].

Harley-Davidson (2014b) *Harley-Davidson Museum*, corporate website, Harley-Davidson Motor Company [www.harley-davidson.com].

Harrison, S. (2002) 'Culture, Tourism and Local Community: The Heritage Identity of the Isle of Man'. *Journal of Brand Management* 9 (4/5), 355–371.

Havlena, W.J. and Holak, S.L. (1991) 'The Good Old Days: Observations on Nostalgia and Its Role in Consumer Behavior'. *Advances in Consumer Research* 18, 323–329.

Herreman, Y. (1998) 'Museums and Tourism: Culture and Consumption'. *Museum International* 50 (3), 4–12.

Hudson, B.T. (2011) 'Brand Heritage and the Renaissance of Cunard'. *European Journal of Marketing* 45 (9/10), 1538–1556.

Hudson, B.T. (2013) 'Brand Heritage and Heritage Tourism'. *Boston Hospitality Review* 1 (3), 12–16.

Hudson, B.T. and Balmer, J.M.T. (2013) 'Corporate Heritage Brands: Mead's Theory of the Past'. *Corporate Communications: An International Journal* 18 (3), 347–361.

IDCH (2014) *International Directory of Company Histories*. Chicago, IL and Farmington Hills, MI: St. James Press (Gale Cengage).

Jolliffe, L. and Aslam, M.S.M. (2009) 'Tea Heritage Tourism: Evidence from Sri Lanka', *Journal of Heritage Tourism* 4 (4), 331–344.

Kerstetter, D., Confer, J. and Bricker, K. (1998) 'Industrial Heritage Attractions: Types and Tourists'. *Journal of Travel & Tourism Marketing* 7 (2), 91–104.

Kift, D. (2011) 'Heritage and History: Germany's Industrial Museums and the Re-Presentation of Labour'. *International Journal of Heritage Studies* 17 (4), 380–389.

King, J. (2013) 'Low Attendance Shuts Chrysler Classic Car Museum'. *Detroit News*, January 14.

Kozak, G. (2012) 'Walter P. Chrysler Museum to Shut its Doors'. *AutoWeek*, December 20.

Livingstone, P. (2011) 'Is it a Museum Experience? Corporate Exhibitions for Cultural Tourists', *Exhibitionist* 30 (1), 16–21.

Marcus, J.S. (2010) 'Tourists, Start Your Engines: The German Car Museums'. *Wall Street Journal*, May 22.

Mercedes-Benz (2012a) *Mercedes-Benz Classic*. Stuttgart, Germany: Daimler AG.

Mercedes-Benz (2012b) *The Legendary Silver Arrows*. Stuttgart, Germany: Daimler AG.

Mercedes-Benz (2012c) *Timeless – 60 Years of the Mercedes-Benz SL*. Stuttgart, Germany: Daimler AG.

Mercedes-Benz (2013a) *Mercedes-Benz Museum*. Stuttgart, Germany: Daimler AG.

Mercedes-Benz (2013b) *Take a Drive Where Driving was Invented*. Stuttgart, Germany: Daimler AG.

Mercedes-Benz (2014a) *History*, corporate website, Daimler AG [www.mercedes-benz.com].

Mercedes-Benz (2014b) *Museum*, corporate website, Daimler AG [www.mercedes-benz-classic.com].

Merchant, A. and Rose, G.M. (2013) 'Effects of Advertising-Evoked Vicarious Nostalgia on Brand Heritage'. *Journal of Business Research* 66 (12), 2619–2625.

Muehling, D.D. and Sprott, D.E. (2004) 'The Power of Reflection: An Empirical Examination of Nostalgia Advertising Effects'. *Journal of Advertising* 33 (3), 25–35.

Nissley, N. and Casey, A. (2002) 'The Politics of the Exhibition: Viewing Corporate Museums through the Paradigmatic Lens of Organizational Memory'. *British Journal of Management* 13, S35–S45.

Otgaar, A.H.J., Van Den Berg, L., Berger, C. and Feng, R.X. (2010) *Industrial Tourism: Opportunities for City and Enterprise*. Farnham: Ashgate.

Palmer A. (2010) 'Customer Experience Management: A Critical Review of an Emerging Idea'. *Journal of Services Marketing* 24 (3), 196–208.

Pine, B.J. II and Gilmore, J.H. (1998) 'Welcome to the Experience Economy'. *Harvard Business Review* 76 (4), 97–105.

Pine, B.J. II and Gilmore, J.H. (1999) *The Experience Economy: Work is Theatre & Every Business a Stage*. Boston: Harvard Business School.

Post, R.C. (2013) *Who Owns America's Past? The Smithsonian and the Problem of History*. Baltimore: Johns Hopkins University Press.

Ruiz Ballesteros, E. and Hernández Ramírez, M. (2007) 'Identity and Community: Reflections on the Development of Mining Heritage Tourism in Southern Spain'. *Tourism Management* 28 (3), 677–687.

SAA (2014) 'Directory of Corporate Archives', organizational website, Society of American Archivists. [www.archivists.org]

Schwaiger, M., Sarstedt, M. and Taylor, C.R. (2010) 'Art for the Sake of the Corporation: Audi, BMW Group, DaimlerChrysler, Montblanc, Siemens, and Volkswagen Help Explore the Effect of Sponsorship on Corporate Reputations'. *Journal of Advertising Research* 50 (1), 77–90.

Seligson, J. (2010) 'Corporate Culture?' One Part Education, One Part Sales: This is the Corporate Museum'. *Museum* 89 (6), 34–41.

Simms, C.D. and Trott, P. (2006) 'The Perceptions of the BMW Mini Brand: The Importance of Historical Associations and the Development of a Model'. *Journal of Product and Brand Management* 15 (4), 228–238.

Stern, B. (1992) 'Historical and Personal Nostalgia in Advertising Text: The Fin de Siècle Effect'. *Journal of Advertising* 21 (4), 11–22.

Timothy, D.J. (2011) *Cultural Heritage and Tourism: An Introduction.* Bristol, UK: Channel View Publications.

Timothy, D.J. and Boyd, S.W. (2003) *Heritage Tourism.* Harlow, UK: Pearson Prentice Hall.

Toyota (2014a) *History of Toyota*, corporate website, Toyota Motor Corporation [www.toyota-global.com].

Toyota (2014b) *Toyota Automobile Museum*, corporate website, Toyota Motor Corporation [www.toyota.co.jp/Museum].

UNESCO (2014) Patent DRP 37435. *Memory of the World Register.* Paris: United Nations Educational Scientific & Cultural Organization [www.unesco.org].

Urde, M., Greyser, S.A. and Balmer, J.M.T (2007) 'Corporate Brands with a Heritage'. *Journal of Brand Management* 15 (1), 4–19.

Verhoef, C.P., Lemon, K.N., Parasuraman, A., Roggeveen, A., Tsiros, M. and Schlesinger, A.L. (2009) 'Customer Experience Creation: Determinants, Dynamics and Management Strategies'. *Journal of Retailing* 85 (1), 31–34.

Walsh, J.P. and Ungson, G.R. (1991) 'Organizational Memory'. *Academy of Management Review* 16 (1), 57–91.

Wiedmann, K.P., Hennigs, N., Schmidt, S. and Wuestefeld, T. (2011a) 'Drivers and Outcomes of Brand Heritage: Consumers' Perception of Heritage Brands in the Automotive Industry'. *Journal of Marketing Theory & Practice* 19 (2), 205–220.

Wiedmann, K.P., Hennigs, N., Schmidt, S. and Wuestefeld, T. (2011b) 'The Importance of Brand Heritage as a Key Performance Driver in Marketing Management'. *Journal of Brand Management* 19 (3), 182–194.

Williams, S. (2009) 'Touring the Temples of German Automaking'. *New York Times*, December 31.

Xie, P.F. (2006) 'Developing Industrial Heritage Tourism: A Case Study of the Proposed Jeep Museum in Toledo, Ohio'. *Tourism Management* 27, 1321–1330.

Yeoman, I., Durie, A., McMahon-Beattie, U. and Palmer, A. (2005) 'Capturing the Essence of a Brand from Its History: The Case of Scottish Tourism Marketing'. *Brand Management* 13 (2), 134–147.

Young, L. (1997) 'Museums, Heritage, and Things that Fall in Between'. *International Journal of Heritage Studies* 1 (3), 7–16.

14 Product innovation for repositioning and destination development marketing strategies

The Museo Nazionale dell'Automobile in Turin, Italy

Antonella Capriello and Irene Mastretta

Introduction

Automobiles have been the driving force and catalyst of Turin's economy and consequently Piedmont's industrialization since the beginning of the 20th century: charismatic and innovative entrepreneurs have created an economic system linked to the world of automobiles that became a cultural and social phenomenon. With increasing work opportunities, Turin has subsequently played a key role in Italy's development and generated significant migration flows first from rural areas in Piedmont and thereafter Southern Italy.

With the growing importance of the automotive industry, the *Museo Nazionale dell'Automobile* (National Automobile Museum), the brainchild of two pioneers of the Italian world of motors, Cesare Goria Gatti and Roberto Biscaretti di Ruffia, was established in Torino in 1933. The name Carlo Biscaretti di Ruffia (Roberto's son) is inextricably linked to the Automobile Museum: he originally had the idea of starting the first collection, worked hard for its creation and incessantly sought the right location for its premises (Museo Nazionale dell'Automobile, 2011a). In 1956, ANFIA (*Associazione Nazionale fra Industrie Automobilistiche ed Affini –* National Association for Automobile and Related Industries) alongside the Agnelli Family (the owners of FIAT) and in accordance with the Municipality of Turin, supported the construction of its permanent headquarters in Turin (Museo Nazionale dell'Automobile, 2011a). By official deed, the Automobile Museum was founded on 22 February 1957. Its historical headquarters, on the left bank of the river Po, not very far from FIAT's Lingotto plant, were designed by the architect Amedeo Albertini. Construction of the building that epitomized a rare example of modern architecture began in April 1958 and was completed in the autumn of 1960. The Museum was officially opened on 3 November 1960 and was named after its first President, Carlo Biscaretti di Ruffia (Museo Nazionale dell'Automobile, 2011a).

A four-year restoration and extension project began in 2007 and the Museum reopened in 2011. This was not merely an architectural renovation, but was intended to re-launch this institution in the international cultural landscape in a dynamic and sensational way. This visitor attraction is now a point of reference of the city's cultural life rather than simply a place to visit. The concept is also coherent with the urban regeneration of Turin as the city has become a tourist destination with its historically renowned intellectual activity as a key component of its modern image. In 2014 the Museum's importance was recognized by the British newspaper The Times ranking it 35th among the world's top 50 best museums (Museo Nazionale dell'Automobile, 2014a).

This chapter aims to analyse and evaluate the product innovation and repositioning of Turin's Automobile Museum in relation to destination marketing strategies. The case study is accordingly structured as follows: first, critical issues concerning product innovation in the automobile museum are discussed in connection with the attractiveness of the collection for a wider audience; second, following an archival document analysis, Turin's history is presented to illustrate the historical link with the automobile industry. The Museum's history is instrumental to understanding the current strategic decisions to innovate the building and renew the cultural and recreational offer; third, the new product concept is investigated in terms of the collection and the new exhibition plans, while the innovative communication strategies are discussed in relation to the objectives of reaching a greater catchment area. For this last phase, different sources of data collections were combined: online data, personal observations during meetings and interviews with museum staff, which were instrumental to building an overview of the strategic orientation of the innovative recreational provision.

Developing attractive offerings in automobile museums

Traditional approaches in exhibitions

The automobile museum has traditionally focused on a visitor market of enthusiasts since the collection was largely predicated on the visitor's love of, and interest in, automotive technology (Clark, 2010: 223). Motor museums are also conservative in style with an influential and overwhelmingly male dominated collector and visitor base, and with collection traditions anchored in modernism and industrialization values (Divall and Scott, 2001; Clark 2010: 212).

The interpretation of motoring derives from the idea of admiring restored vehicles since a motor museum's collection is based on the interpretation of the vehicle as an aesthetic object to be revered (Clark, 2013). In this motoring museum context, the emphasis has always been on the cars themselves and not on the companies that produced them or those interacting with them.

New challenges in displaying collections

As the interest of a wider clientele develops, museums are beginning to enter the realms of social history including motor exhibits. The primary purpose is to display the material culture of motoring in a more contextualized way. The motor vehicle is recognized in transport museums as a momentous agent of change across a raft of social and economic indicators (Jeremiah, 2010: 180). However, one of the most difficult aspects of the motoring story is the element of human experience partly due to the strong traditional focus of the museum as a home for static material residue of past cultures (Clark, 2010). A storytelling approach in its interpretation can be instrumental to creating a link, for example, between individuals, car producers and related brands (Clark, 2013). Museums also commonly display cars as status symbols, where automobiles are the emblem of engineering arts (Jeremiah, 2010: 187).

Mc Shane (1991: 110) pointed out that the key advances in automotive technology in the last twenty years have been safety, fuel economy and pollution control. In this new perspective, curators must employ a historical interpretation to give meaning to the collections to inform the display and engage visitors in difficult issues such as environmental damage, fatal accidents and traffic congestion (Clark, 2010).

With a focus on Turin's destination marketing, the case study is instrumental to analysing how the museum sections can represent social history in relation to specific critical issues and create an emotional atmosphere to challenge visitors to reflect more deeply and critically on relevant matters.

The city of Turin

Urban development and automobile world

The National Automobile Museum's history can be analysed in light of the urban development of the city of Turin where a series of economic, social and cultural events changed its identity and vocation over the last centuries.

From the second half of the 16th century, the Savoy family assigned Turin a key role: the city was first the capital of the Dukedom, later of the Kingdom of Sardinia, and, from 1861, the Kingdom of Italy. For nearly three centuries, the Court and State bodies (legislative, executive and juridical) were the driving force of the city's economy. When the capital was transferred to Florence (1864) and later to Rome (1870), the city lost this prosperous status and faced a severe crisis. The turning point came with investments in a new emerging sector: the automotive industry (Museo Nazionale dell'Automobile, 2011b).

The first people in Italy to invest in this challenging business were a few representatives of Piedmont's bourgeoisie, passionate lovers of speed.

In 1898, Roberto Biscaretti di Ruffia founded the Automobile Club of Turin, then the Automobile Club of Italy. In 1899, in the Burello Coffee Shop, Emanuele Cacherano di Bricherasio, Roberto Biscaretti di Ruffia, Michele Lanza, Cesare Goria Gatti and Giovanni Agnelli established the 'Società italiana per la costruzione e il commercio delle automobili', which then became FIAT; Giovanni Agnelli became its first Director and Chairman. Vincenzo Lancia, a renowned car driver, founded the Lancia car manufacturing company in 1906. In 1912, Giovanni Bertone founded the workshop that then became the benchmark of international design under his son Nuccio. Bertone produced some of the world's most renowned designers such as Giorgetto Giugiaro and Marcello Gandini. The car design and engineering firm Pininfarina established the Società Anonima Carrozzeria Pinin in 1930; Farina took its name from Battista Farina (whose nickname was *Pinin*), which was then passed to his son Sergio, a world renowned designer (Museo Nazionale dell'Automobile, 2011b).

Torino also hosted various events related to the automobile world: in 1895, following the French example, the city organized the first Italian car race from Torino to Asti. The first car exhibition, which evolved into the *Salone dell'automobile* (Automobile Exhibition), took place in the 20th century (Museo Nazionale dell'Automobile, 2011a).

The automobile industry became a key sector for local development since Turin's engineering industry employed 9,000 workers and housed over 30 companies out of 100 operating in this industry in Italy (Museo Nazionale dell'Automobile, 2011b).

Around thirty years ago the structural crisis significantly affected economic growth. The city once again witnessed the disintegration of its economic and social base and had to rethink the economic model in light of the new historical, political and economic conditions.

Strategies for destination marketing

Like many post-industrial European cities, Turin has launched tourism-related regeneration strategies for urban development. Although the industrial reputation of this Italian city makes it the antithesis of a tourism destination (Russo and van der Borg, 2002: 634), an economic recovery program for the 2000–2006 period attempted to diversify the city by creating a tourism and leisure industry (Regione Piemonte, 2005). The Torino 2006 Olympic Games provided the opportunity to build the city's identity and international reputation.

After hosting this mega-event, tourism and cultural strategies were formulated to maintain the attractiveness of this destination not only by hosting events but also through the restoration of main visitor attractions in Turin. The projects included the Cinema Museum in 2006 and the Egyptian Museum to be completed by 2015. The renewed interest in the Automobile Museum is also linked to the increasing desire to narrate the history of the car through the contribution of this city.

Today, Piedmont's capital still plays a fundamental role in education, planning and design in the automobile sector: the IAAD (Istituto d'Arte Applicata e del Design), the IED (Istituto Europeo del Design) and the Facoltà di Disegno Industriale e di Ingegneria dell'Autoveicolo (Faculty of Industrial Design and Automobile Engineering) at the Turin Polytechnic have a strong international reputation and resulted in the city being awarded 'The 2008 World Design Capital' (Museo Nazionale dell'Automobile, 2011b).

History of the museum

In view of the increasing economic role of the automobile industry, Cesare Goria Gatti (1860–1939) and Roberto Biscaretti di Ruffia (1979–1959) – two Italian car pioneers and co-founders of the Automobile Club of Turin and FIAT – launched the idea of an Automobile Museum in 1932. The original aim was to celebrate

'I Veterani dell'Automobile' (The Automobile Veterans), namely, those drivers that had owned a driving licensing for at least 25 years.

Carlo Biscaretti di Ruffia (1879–1959) and Giuseppe di Miceli (1889–1944), Director of the Automobile Club of Turin, were appointed to organize a retrospective event of the automobile industry in Milan in 1933. The idea was instrumental to collecting opinions on the potential interest in a museum. As public interest was significant, the city of Turin allocated funds for this project and appointed Biscaretti as curator of the first collection. In the same year, Benito Mussolini assigned this institution the title 'Nazionale' (National).

A main issue concerned the Museum's location: it was first based in the warehouse of what had been a factory (Fabrica Aquilana Italiana); thereafter the initial collection (100 cars, the library and archives) was transferred to some venues underneath the city stadium. Benito Mussolini inaugurated the first section in May 1939.

This location however was inappropriate not only in terms of conservation, due to the unstable temperature, but also due to several logistical and functional issues that limited the number of visitors.

After the Second Word World, Biscaretti started a twenty-year battle to obtain an appropriate location for the Museum. The Association of Automobile Producers had shared and supported this idea since July 1955. The city of Turin designated a field for the building area and financial support was obtained from several Italian automobile producers, local banks, oil and tyre companies.

Amedeo Albertini, a famous designer of headquarters, proposed an innovative project sited on the scenic route in front of the Po River. The designated location was a neighbourhood that would later take the name 'Italia 1961'. This location was selected in accordance with the urban development plan for the forthcoming celebrations of the first centenary of Italy's unification. Biscaretti passed away in 1959 before the end of the project and the Museum was dedicated to his commitment and opened on 3 November 1960. In the 1970s, two new sections were added: the Documentation Centre and the Library. In 1975, the library and the centre enlarged its own collections thanks to Canestrini's donations.

For several years, the Museum was one of the most visited sites with 100,000 visitors in 1961 and 113,500 in 1986. After the 1986 peak, the number of visitors continually declined to around 40,000–50,000 with the exception of the year 2006 when the Turin Olympics took place and the visitor numbers increased to 71,000.

The Museum was transformed into a public-private association but was outdated and obsolete, requiring urgent changes to re-launch it. In 2002 the Directors emphasised the need to reposition this cultural attraction and the city of Turin approved the proposal to restructure the site the following year.

An international competition was launched that included fifty world-level architectural firms and was won in the summer of 2005 by a group composed of the architect Cino Zucchi, Recchi Engineering Srl and Proger SpA. The winning design, which complied with the tender requirements, included the reorganisation of the existing building and the creation of new spaces. In common with many contemporary European examples, the exhibition functions were enhanced with complementary activities. The new Automobile Museum was considered an interesting attraction leading the way of the urban renewal of the city's southern area. Francois Confino's experience acquired in other similar projects (he designed the interiors of the Turin Cinema Museum) and Rodolfo Gaffino Rossi's expertise (he was Director of the Innovative Product Division of FIAT) were crucial in devising a new museum concept.

The overall investment amounted to 33 million euro, of which 22 million were allocated to the building's restoration and 11 million to the internal exhibition design. In 2011 the Museum reopened after the four-year restoration and extension period and was dedicated to the memory of Giovanni Agnelli, the charismatic FIAT leader from 1966 until 2000.

The new museum

With the restoration and renovation of the setting, the exhibition design and the creation of new areas, the Museum had three fundamental goals: (a) to reposition its offer to become a point of reference on an international level; (b) to present new issues and content through the collection and the spectacular and stimulating setting; (c) to promote an education-scientific mission.

In coherence with these objectives, the collection is dedicated to specialists as well as a wider audience. The institution markets itself as a place of culture and knowledge sharing; the premises have been transformed to allow visitors to become involved and spend their free time there.

This strategic decision has had implications on visitors that now number around 250,000 annually in comparison with the average number of 40,000–50,000 before the restructuring operation. The Museum's repositioning has also generated the expected change of target audience: whilst before the reopening, the visitors were mostly men with a passion for cars and local schoolchildren, now the market segments also include foreign tourists, families and women. Important to note is that 70% of visitors are foreigners including business travellers who visit the Museum in their leisure time.

Collection

The unique collection houses treasures of the last two centuries representing the manufacturing history of over eighty companies from eight different countries. The collection consists of around 200 cars from 85 manufacturers from different countries including Italy, France, Great Britain, Germany, The Netherlands, Spain, Poland and the United States (Museo Nazionale dell'Automobile, 2011c). This exhibition is one of the rarest and most precious collections in this sector. The importance of this immense collection is not only due to the value of extremely old items, but the outstanding setting depicts the history of societies, nations and cultures across two centuries (Castella, 2011). Table 14.1 lists some of the important items in the collection.

Figure 14.1 shows the Cisitalia, which is the symbol of the Italian automobile revolution.

Table 14.1 Collection masterpieces

Item
The "steam car" designed by Virginio Bordino in 1854
The first Benz model dating back to 1893 with gear box motor belt
The first Peugeot model introduced in Italy dated 1892
The 3.5 HP Bernardi dating back to 1896, the first three-wheeled car built in Italy
The 1899 Fiat 4 HP, the first to be produced by Torino's car manufacturing company
The Fiat 12/16 HP, the first car of this company to be exported
The 1903 Florentia, the only existing example of this brand
The 1904 Oldsmobile Curved Dash, the first economy car
The 1909 Itala owned by Queen Regina Margherita and called by her majesty "Palombella"
The 1910 Renault Fiacre, the taxi that took French soldiers to the front on the Marna to rescue Paris from the German invasion
The 8A Isotta Fraschini, an extra luxurious car bought by Rodolfo Valentino and used in the 1950's 'Sunset Boulevard' movie
The 1948 202 Cisitalia, the "self-moving sculpture" that marked history
The 500 F2 Ferrari with which Alberto Ascari won his world title in 1952
The 1987 601 Trabant, a symbolic car of East Berlin

Source: MAUTO's website.

Figure 14.1 Cisitalia: a car from the collection.

Exhibition

Contents and displays

The lasting link between the history of automobiles, and that of societies and cultures is represented by 30 exhibit sections covering over 9,000 square metres. These are divided into areas that precisely define different topics and specific historical periods, providing visitors a clear narrative itinerary through titles and settings, from their origin to today. The items in the 30 new sections are perfectly positioned in the social context in which they originated and as part of our daily life: cars can mirror our tastes, habits and ideas.

The exhibition underlines the role of the car as the symbol of a world that never stops: its development and transformations are translated into changes and experiments in industry to science and art to literature. Visitors can reflect on the items in relation to the technological evolution and applications in other fields, the importance of teamwork, the factors influencing the achievement of specific technological advancements in precise historical periods. With a focus on the scarcity of resources, the exhibitions reflect the future evolution of human mobility and sustainable development. An additional objective is to share the passion that animated the entrepreneurs who became legends in the automobile world. The exhibition covers three floors and begins on the second floor.

Second floor

Twenty-one rooms in an area of 3,600 square metres explain the invention of the car and its evolving development and popularity in the 20th century. The itinerary is circular and moves from the Library in the first room called 'Genesis' – where information on the origin of locomotion is given and homage is paid to the many ingenious precursors of the mechanical engine – to the 'Destiny' room, the last on this floor. The nineteen other rooms in between tell the history of the twentieth century including Futurism, the First World War, the advent of the utilitarian car, the Italian school of bodywork, the discovery of aerodynamics, female emancipation, the race towards mass production, the fall of the Berlin Wall, American advertising slogans, consumerism and ecology.

First floor

The first floor is divided into eight rooms with an exhibition area of 3,800 square metres. Visitors are guided by the desire to examine some individual aspects of the relationship that the modern-day world has with the car and to understand what actually constitutes a motor car and how it is built. 'Autorino' evokes what the car, in terms of industries, work and progress, meant during most of the last century for the city of Turin. 'Mechanical Symphony' features car components: the engine, frame, wheels, all the parts in a single orchestra. 'Metamorphosis' shows the complex system of industrial production based on the assembly line, while 'Advertising' presents the persuasive marketing techniques from its innocent beginnings in the early twentieth century up to today's sophisticated approaches. In 'Madness', the car is represented as a dominant and obsessive human interest; this section will be hosted in a temporary exhibition at MOMA in New York. 'Jungle' presents the infinite bans and the necessary rules in driving by transmuting paradoxically into an obstacle to free circulation. The exciting world of racing, pure speed and challenge is shown on the circuit ('Formula') and illustrated in the 'Automobilissimo' showcases. In the 'Design' section, the most astonishing products of contemporary design are displayed by developing the functional, structural and aesthetic relationships identifying the industry products. This space is open to collaboration with Design Centres and a recent collaboration included Officine 83, the Fiat Design Centre.

Ground floor

The ground floor is entirely dedicated to design, showing the creative paths that precede the production of a car. 1,200 square metres and a single large room display the great design interpretations and experiences in relation to the themes of individual mobility, safety, speed, comfort and style. Laboratories on 'Driving Safety' are organized using a simulator and videos with striking images of car crashes; the purpose is to teach the importance of following the basic driving rules to avoid fatal accidents and to respect human lives.

The open garage

The Open Garage is a further area in the basement of the building including seventy cars arranged in chronological order that will find space in future visitor itineraries to innovate the exhibition sections. The area will be designated for maintenance and restoration, including the mechanic workshop and the school of restoration. Restoration operations require core competencies; in accordance with a future innovative project, professionals, artisans and experts in the historical automobile industry team up with young students to promote sharing knowledge and skills between generations. Collaborations with the Turin Polytechnic develop effective synergies for training activities and enhance the key competencies of students. This initiative not only protects the heritage and the transfer of core competencies, but also promotes Italian talent and creativity at the national and international levels. A further collaboration has been developed with the Centro Ricerche e Restauro Venaria Reale to cooperate in restoration and maintenance projects and a first project concerns 'La carrozza di Bordino', a steam-powered landau.

Communication strategies and technology innovation

New brand identity

The creation of Torino's new Museo dell'Automobile resulted in the launch of a new brand identity. This ambitious project was assigned to the 'In Testa' agency, a graphic design company of the Armando Testa Group. This choice was in honour of Armando Testa, the advertising executive from Torino whose brainchild was the Museum's historical brand in the 1990s.

The brand is not only homage to its original logo and a tribute to the history of the Museum but is also the symbol of a modern revival.

The first new element of the restyling project is the name: MAUTO, an acronym aimed at modernizing the notion of Museum. The novelty of this acronym is combined with its traditional logo and although resized remains consistent with the graphics and the vision of its creator Armando Testa.

The new logo (Figure 14.2) consists of the acronym MAUTO and the symbol of the sketched wheel that for over twenty years has accompanied the Museo dell'Automobile's name.

Figure 14.2 The new logo.

Following the same trend and vertical orientation of the original logo, the new MAUTO acronym is vertical in shape, with the M, AU and TO partitions accentuating the acronym. The three-level logotype refers to the three floors of the building that house over 200 years of car history. The AU diphthong, representing cars, is the symbol of the heart of the Museum, the liveliest part of the facility depicting continuous evolution. For this very reason, its central location and inclined position give movement and energy to the image. In contrast to the dominant black colour, AU is red: the colour that is the symbol of the language of motors. Red traditionally represents Italy in the motor sport domain. Finally, the TO syllable for Torino ideally flows into the historical logo, while O becomes the link between the city and its historical Museo dell'Automobile in a circle indicating entirety, perfection and graphic synthesis.

Events

The MAUTO reopened on 19 March 2011. This year was particularly significant for the history of Italy as 150 years previously Turin was designated as the first capital of the newly born Italian State and remained such until 1865.

The President of the Italian Republic, Giorgio Napolitano, opened the ceremony together with 150 representatives of Italian excellence in the world from car manufacturing to sports. With three press conferences, the communication strategies involved the press and opinion leaders including 2,000 Italian and 3,000 foreign journalists. The content of the communication activities focused on presenting Italian history through the Museum collection. Automobiles were not only presented as a production phenomenon, but also as a cultural and social mark, enhanced and expressed by the new Museum. By integrating media and public relations with the ceremonial activities, the impact was significant: over 1,100 articles in the national and international press and 250,000 visitors in the year of reopening (Museo Nazionale dell'Automobile, 2011d).

The communication quality was of such high standard that the communications agency that was in charge of organizing the event received the '2011 Best Event Award for Celebrity and Impact on Press Media' and the '2011 Special Award for event location' (Museo Nazionale dell'Automobile, 2011d).

The motto was 'MAUTO is not a Museum to visit, but to frequent' to highlight the importance of visitor loyalty. With temporary exhibitions, the event policy aims to attract and retain audiences: since the reopening in 2011, masterpieces of the collection, new acquisitions and the iconic pieces of car designers have been displayed. The idea is not to host mega-events in a limited time but to continuously provide cultural initiatives. Innovative proposals include celebrating anniversaries related to the automotive world: the 'Auto dell'Avvocato' (The Attorney's Cars) event was dedicated to commemorate the 10th anniversary of Giovanni Agnelli's death (whose nickname was the Attorney) by exhibiting his favourite cars; the centenary of the Bertone workshop celebration highlighted the importance of this workshop, cooperating with the most prestigious automobile companies in Europe.

Strategic alliances and partnerships

To highlight the link with the territory, strategic territorial alliances have been created to organize gastronomic activities including Master Chef charity events. The Museum is considered an innovative location to celebrate Piedmont's excellence in the wine and food industry and artisan productions in cooperation with the Chamber of Commerce of Turin and Confederazione Nazionale dell'Artigianato e della Piccola e Media Impresa (National Confederation of Crafts and Small and Medium Enterprises).

The institution hosts art exhibitions (Ettore Ghinato's hyperrealism paintings in 2012 and Stefano Bressani's Sculptures Dressed in 2013) not only to maximize the use of the venue and to increase visibility of the car collections to a wider audience, but also to emphasise the link between arts, fashion and design.

International collaborations and partnerships are also created with the scope of continuously renewing and revamping the cultural and recreational offer. The Institution has co-operated with the Shanghai Museum, the Mosca Polytechnic, the Canberra Embassy and the Mulhouse Museum and great collectors (for example, Jim Glickenhaus, Nicola Bulgari). Future collaborations will involve the Museum of Science and Technology in Milan, the Museum of Transportation in Lucerne, *Universcience Partnaires* of Paris and *Deutsches Museum* in Munich with the purpose of organizing a unique collaboration for collection exchanges and knowledge sharing. An event-marketing plan is thus instrumental to establishing the basis for exchanging material and to find new sponsors in Europe, America and the Far East.

With a focus on the importance of Turin in the contemporary arts, collaborations have been developed with a network of local galleries (GAM, Castello di Rivoli,

Agnelli Pinacoteca) and, for example, the Oldsmobile ninety-eight model will be included in the Lichtenstein exhibitions at the GAM (Museo Nazionale dell'Automobile, 2014b).

Online marketing strategies

The marketing communication activities are based on the principle of integrated online marketing strategies to cultivate customer relationships. First, a new website has been designed and developed to contribute to the creation of this new product. This website, with graphic elements recalling the Museum's plan and logo, has been designed as a multimedia content package to communicate with the audience. Its modular and flexible structure is instrumental to keeping up to date with the multifaceted activities and events of the Museum. The Museum has adopted the most popular social networks (Facebook, Twitter and YouTube) while the newsletters help connect with online visitors. The Facebook fan page is constantly updated: posts are on themes regarding the automobile world and/or simple quizzes focused on the Museum exhibition. In 2011, a photographic contest was also launched to collect photos of visitor interpretations of their own experiences. The institution also has a twitter profile to promote event programme activities while YouTube is used to load audio and video contributions to engage with the audience and generate viral marketing effects.

The Museum is also included among the visitor attractions listed in TripAdvisor and ranked as the 4th place to visit in Turin. The idea is to monitor online reputation via this popular travel portal; following the positive evaluations of tourists, the attraction has received the Travellers' Choice Award in the last three years.

Using street view technology, a virtual tour of the Museum is also offered with the aim of expanding the attraction's visibility and to remedy the misconception of inaccessibility for international audiences. The tour is structured around the Museum's three floors using the advanced 'multifloor' function that enables viewing the interior of three automobiles.

The significant potential for viral marketing via Google platforms (Google maps and G+ local) has been exploited through high-quality photos (offering panoramic views, surprise and special effects). As the online material concerns only a part of the Museum, the tool is effective in engaging online visitors and thus instrumental in promoting a real visit. This technology adopts a new language together with direct communication as visitors' comments and contributions help improve the quality of the experience on offer.

Digital technologies and museum itineraries

New digital technologies are a key element of advancing the Museum's offer and are based on developing the WI-FI network. This enhances the interaction opportunities with visitors and enables multimedia communication in the Museum itineraries. The App is a complementary tool to the exhibition panels: it allows accessing archival documents from anecdotes to selected scientific and historical materials and images, and connects with other museums. The 'tree of knowledge' is the concept on which the interactive system is based. The tree has a trunk that is composed of the thirty sections of the Museum, the branches represent the history of each car included in the exhibition and the leaves are the in-depth analysis of single pieces of the collection.

The tree grows thanks to visitor engagement and participation as the system is 'in progress' capturing preferences and thus enabling enhancing the product offer. The Museum also collects customer likes and dislikes to evaluate the strengths and weaknesses of the itineraries and information system. To emphasise the investment in technology innovation, the downloaded App can be used via touch screens at the start of each section and via tablets booked at the ticket office.

Conclusions

With a focus on urban regeneration and tourist destination development, the case study is instrumental to rethinking strategic marketing for automobile museums. The repositioning of the Museum is based on attracting new market segments to reach a wider audience. In the past decades, like similar automobile museums around the world, the main target segment was car lovers in coherence with the Museum's conservative function, which was to collect and preserve objects. The new shift relates to a mission where the focus is on visitor experience and is consistent with Turin's new identity. By targeting larger and different audiences, the product portfolio strategies are intended to fulfil the education, entertainment and research objectives. To accomplish these goals, visitor experiences are deliberatively developed to engage the sensibilities of those who come with different needs and expectations of the visit.

Competitive pressures on tourist destinations and visitor attractions are additional factors behind the development of the novel offerings and innovative products. In the case study analysed, product innovation mainly focused on a new exhibition setting linking the history of the car with the evolution of societies and emerging challenges related to a sustainable development approach. In relation to destination marketing, the new product concept also emphasises the connections of the automotive world with that of fashion, arts and design as an emblem of Turin's identity.

Museums today design exhibitions and programs that are interactive and immersive, and can be organized through narrative, theme and chronology. Technology applications also allow cultivating customer relations by sharing museum life and are instrumental to the co-creation processes through visitor online comments and contributions. Event programs enable the institution to attract a continuous stream of visitors. Marketers work to encourage repeat visits and ultimately to forge strong relationships between these visitors and the Museum.

While cyberspace can compete with museum site visits and other forms of museum participation, in the case study analysed, innovations and digital technology applications are complementary tools and help expand the attraction's visibility at the international level.

Recognizing the multi-dimensional nature of service delivery and development, partnerships and networking processes are important for this cultural organization to innovate and flourish in relation with the principle of visitor engagement.

Acknowledgments

The authors wish to express their heartfelt gratitude to Rodolfo Gaffino Rossi, Director of the 'Museo Nazionale dell'Automobile Avv. Giovanni Agnelli' of Turin, for sharing his experience and to his staff for providing useful material for the current publication.

References

Castella, V. (2011) *Torino: Il Nuovo Museo Nazionale dell'Automobile* [Turin: The New Automobile National Museum]. Torino: Agarttha Arte.

Clark, J. (2010) The 'rough and tumble': displaying complexity in the motor museum. *Museum Management and Curatorship* 25 (2), 219–234.

Clark, J. (2013) Peopling the Public History of Motoring: Men, Machines, and Museums. *Curator: The Museum Journal* 56 (2), 279–287.

Divall, C. and Scott A. (2001) *Making Histories in Transport Museums*. London: Leicester University Press.

Jeremiah, D. (2003) Museums and the History and Heritage of British Motoring. *International Journal of Heritage Studies* 9 (2), 169–190.

McShane, C. (1991) Exhibit review of the Museo Dell'Automobile Carlo Biscaretti Di Ruffia. *Radical History Review* 51, 107–115.

Museo Nazionale dell'Automobile (2011a) *Il nuovo Museo Nazionale dell'Automobile di Torino* [The New Automobile National Museum of Turin]. Torino: Allemandi & C.

Museo Nazionale dell'Automobile (2011b) Torino the capital: first the Capital of Italy in 1861 then the Capital City for Italian automobiles, press kit, accessed 20 October 2014. http://www.museoauto.it/website/images/stories/press_release/en/6_torino_capitale_mondiale_dell_automobile.pdf.

Museo Nazionale dell'Automobile (2011c) 200 Cars from all over the world, press kit, accessed 20 October 2014. http://www.museoauto.it/website/images/stories/press_release/en/1_il_nuovo_museo_dell_automobile_di_torino.pdf.

Museo Nazionale dell'Automobile (2011d) Il lancio del Museo Nazionale dell'Automobile [The launch of the National Automobile Museum], press kit, accessed 20 October 2014. http://www.museoauto.it/website/images/stories/press_release/it/bea_%20mailander_museo_auto_28_11.pdf.

Museo Nazionale dell'Automobile (2014a) Times and MAUTO, press kit, accessed 20 October 2014. http://www.museoauto.it/website/en/news/391-nella-classifica-de-qthe-timesq-il-mauto-e-al-35d-posto.

Museo Nazionale dell'Automobile (2014b) Alla GAM in Oldsmobile [To the GAM in Oldsmobile], press kit, accessed 20 October 2014. http://www.museoauto.it/website/en/news/472-alla-gam-in-oldsmobile%20

Regione Piemonte (2005) Tourism in Piedmont: The figures, press kit, accessed 20 October 2011. http://www.regione.piemonte.it/lingue/english/pagine/cultura/approfondimenti/02_piemontur_en.pdf.

Russo, A. P. and van der Borg, J. (2002) Planning considerations for cultural tourism: a case study of four European cities. *Tourism Management* 23 (6), 631–637.

15 The role of the Royal Automobile Museum in tourism and heritage education in Jordan

Salem Harahsheh and Rafa Haddad

Introduction

Tourism is thriving in Jordan since the peace treaty was signed with Israel in 1994, whereby tourists have flocked to the country in millions (MOTA, 2000). The number of tourists has doubled and tripled many times since then especially after Petra, Jordan's foremost tourist attraction, won the second place of the World New Seven Wonders competition in 2007 (Harahsheh, 2009). The latest statistics of the World Tourism Organisation (UNWTO) shows that the number of tourist arrivals to the country was 4.16 million in 2012, increased by 5.1% from 2011 (UNWTO, 2013). Most of the tourists come from the Middle East (48.2%), followed by Jordanians residing abroad (25.4%), Europe (14.2%), America (4.8%), East Asia/ Pacific (4.2%), South Asia (1.9%) and Africa (1.3%). Jordan hosts a lot of natural and man-made attractions that are of great value for tourists to visit. Those include Petra, the new seventh wonder of the world, the Dead Sea, the world's lowest and saltiest natural spa, the Golf of Aqaba with its red corals, as well as several Greco-Roman cities (the Decapolis) such as, Amman (Philadelphia), Jerash (Gerasa) and Um Qais (Gadara) and Crusader castles such as Kerak, Showbak and Ajlun. Jordan also hosts a lot of world-class museums such as the Royal Automobile Museum, the Children Museum and the Jordan Museum.

This chapter examines the Royal Automobile Museum (RAM) in Jordan and the role of that museum in tourism and heritage education as it hosts vintage cars, motorbikes and carting cars owned by the Royal family since 1915. The chapter focuses on those heritage vehicles as they are employed in the interpretation of the history of Jordan for almost 100 years under Hashemite rule.

Literature review

Motoring museums are popular places to visit as they hold old and classical kinds of official cars and motorbikes and sport cars. In Britain, for example, at least 100 museums are holding transport collections (Jeremiah, 2003); in the USA, the size of the sector is larger (Collin and Scott, 2001). Transportation is one major pillar of the tourism industry and it has an effective role upon tourist behaviour and destination selection. Automobiles play a major role in travel and tourist mobility worldwide as the many tourists travel mainly by car (Cooper *et al.*, 2008;

Goeldner and Ritchie, 2009). Historically, automobile travel was first introduced by Henry Ford through the Model T in 1908 (Goeldner and Ritchie, 2011). The number of cars worldwide is expected to triple by 2050 to reach over 2 billion cars (Urry, 2004: 25). Old or classical cars represent one important type of industrial heritage and today they are preserved and displayed in museums as one of the major tourist attractions in cities or regions. Automobile museums serve two purposes: tourism as they are a tourist attraction and heritage as they are part of our past civilisation.

Motor museums have been getting more academic attention in the last decade (Clark, 2010). Classical cars are representing an interesting typology of transport or motor heritage (vehicles, railways, airplanes, ships, motorbikes). Clark (2010) defines the motor museum as 'a place to present motor vehicles as objects of art, speed and prestige to be admired and cherished by enthusiasts'. Heritage tourism is a kind of tourism that is concerned with aspects of history, culture, events, festivals, and anything related to people's life and traditions (Burr and Zeitlin, 2011). Jolliffe and Smith (2001) note the interdependency of tourism, heritage and museums. Heritage, whether it is tangible or intangible, is part of the tourism system and a museum is a place and an attraction that exhibits this kind of tourism in terms of heritage artefacts. Therefore, learning and heritage education that takes place in a museum is of greater importance that should be recognised by the museum's management, researchers and the public of all ages.

The idea and concept of the Royal Automobile Museum

The Royal Family of Jordan and mainly late King Hussein owned many classical official cars, sport cars, motorcycles and carting cars dating back to World War I and the Arab Revolt of 1916. After the sudden death of HM King Hussein I in 1999, his successor King Abdullah II wanted to commemorate and honour his father by creating the Royal Automobile Museum to hold the dozens of cars and motorcycles used by the Royal family and King Hussein. King Abdullah II wanted to embody the history of Jordan in terms of a historical timeline from the eruption of the Arab Revolt of 1916 until now. He wanted also to enable the public to see and enjoy the cars in a museum in order to know the history of Jordan and the rule of the Hashemite Dynasty instead of keeping them parked in the garages of the Royal Hashemite Court (Al-Ali, 2007). The museum then was built on a hill west of the capital Amman in Al-Hussein Park (RAM website, 2012).

The Museum

The Royal Automobile Museum (RAM) was established in 2002 and is located in Al-Hussein National Park in the western part of the capital Amman. However, the Royal Automobile Club was founded fifty years before the Royal Automobile Museum, in 1952 (Jordan Automobile Club website, 2014). The museum was built to host dozens of classical official cars, motorbikes, sport cars and carting cars owned and used by the royal family over nearly 100 years (RAM website, 2014).

The museum is equipped with free wheelchairs for disability visitors. Furthermore, the museum has an outside terrace area that is overlooking the capital Amman and can accommodate up to 200 sitting guests and 400 standing ones (RAM website, 2012). The museum holds a multimedia room that accommodates 100 sitting guests as well as a library that accommodates 60 guests or 25 reporters for press meetings (RAM website, 2012).

The RAM documents the history of Jordan for almost 100 years since the eruption of the Arab Revolt in 1916 and then interprets the rule of the Hashemite dynasty since 1921 until now. The museum is chaired by HRH Prince Hamzah bin al-Hussein.

The exhibition

The museum has four large halls used for exhibiting classic cars dating back to 1915. The museum gives visitors an in-depth understanding about the history of Jordan through those exhibited motor vehicles from the era of the World War I until present (JTB website, 2014). These exhibits are in line with the development of automotive advancement in the country throughout 100 years of Hashemite rule of Jordan. At the entrance of the exhibition, visitors are greeted by an old wooden radio that warbles the voice of the founder of Jordan King Abdullah I who addresses a speech at the Parliament in 1947 and then the voice of King Hussein talking to his people (BBC, 2007). Cars are exhibited in a way that resembles some major roads in Amman with its cafés and shops where the royal convoy is visiting

The museum holds different motor vehicles that were used by the Royal family since the Arab Revolt in 1916 and then the creation of Jordan by King Abdullah I in 1921, King Talal rule 1950–1952, King Hussein rule 1952–1999 and now King Abdullah II since 1999. The museum also embraces old photos and archives since the Arab Revolt of 1916, as well as electronic narrations (audio guides) in five different languages, namely, Arabic; English; Spanish; French and German (JTB website, 2012). Cars such as a replica of Benz 1886, Rolls-Royce 1915, Cadillac 1916, Cord 1936, Buick and Packard 1940, Humber 1946, Lincoln 1947, Chrysler 1949, Ford 1950, Aston Martin 1952, Mercedes Benz 1955, Bentley 1961, Amphicar 1966, Excalibur 1971, Panther 1972, Lamborghini 1976, BMW 1979, Opel 1981, Range Rover 1984, Lotus 1987, Porsche 1989, Ferrari 1989, AC 1990 are some example of the whole collection of more than eighty cars, fifty motorbikes and some carting cars that were used by late King Hussein I during his rule of Jordan for almost fifty years.

The Museum as a tourism and heritage attraction in Amman and Jordan

Heritage stems from values, traditions, emotions, symbols, meaning and ideas that are associated with people and place. Jolliffe and Smith (2001) explained the notion of heritage as it 'evolved from a focus on values, traditions and ideas to a direct association with the material cultural heritage of societies'. Heritage attractions such as museums are spaces where visitors can enjoy, learn, entertain and participate in heritage education through activities rendered to them (Jolliffe and Smith, 2001).

Motoring museums are one important kind of industrial heritage and have equal value and importance to archaeological and other heritage sites (Collin and Scott, 2001). Motoring museums and their collection help in creating and preserving country, people's history and identity as they depict the memories and feelings associated with people and history (Collin and Scott, 2001). One of the aims of creating the Royal Automobile Museum was to serve as a tourist attraction in the province of Amman and then Jordan (RAM website 2014). The location is very accessible and is close to all tourism services such as hotels, transportation and other attractions in the capital Amman, a cosmopolitan city and a business centre in Jordan. The museum is not far from Marka Airport, just 15 minutes and half an hour from Queen Alia Airport. The museum lies in the heart of King Hussein National Park that holds a giant mosque of HM King Hussein, the King Hussein Memorial, the Cultural Village (a traditional Jordanian village), the Entertainment and Sport areas, the Promenade of Jordan, the Themed Agrarian Gardens and three museums: the Royal Automobile Museum, the Children Museum and the Prophet Mohammad Museum. Another museum that is being planned to be built is the Science Museum (RAM website, 2012). The museum represents a historical, political, cultural and heritage legacy of Jordan; it combines the past and present history of Amman and Jordan for around 100 years.

The museum is now celebrating its 10th anniversary with one million visitors (RAM website, 2012, Alrai, 2012). According to the latest statistics of the museum, there are more than 125,000 visitors flocking to the museum every year, which puts the museum in the third place for visitation to attractions in Jordan after Petra and Jerash (Bader, 2012; BBC, 2007). In order to promote the museum and encourage more visitors, the management decided to lower the entrance fees for the Arab tourists during the summer season from JOD 3 to JOD 1 as it is for their Jordanian counterparts (Addustour, 2011). The museum is being promoted through the following channels: online; social media; PR agencies; tour operators, through the Jordan Tourism Board (JTB) and through FAM trips for TV channel presenters and journalists.

The role of the Museum in heritage education

Heritage is what we inherited from the past in all aspects of life. In order for the following generation to enjoy their heritage, it should be preserved and protected. One of the roles of the Royal Automobile Museum is to preserve and interpret Jordan's heritage, history and the legacy of the Hashemite dynasty and mainly HM King Hussein I.

Informal learning is one of the major roles of a museum as a compliment to formal learning in schools (Harahsheh, 2007; Bencze and Lemelin, 2001). The museum is one of the best centres in Jordan used to boost public understanding and enhance visitors' knowledge in various aspect of national life, especially transportation, traffic safety, heritage, history and culture of Jordan. The museum is active in organising workshops and seminars through special education programmes designed for children to learn about transportation and the history of Jordan (Bader, 2012).

An interesting case in point is that starting in 2007 children were invited to the museum for a one week visit to know the museum as a whole, to understand what a museum is, transportation, classical cars, participating in a contest and getting gifts. The first day deals with a contest about the history of Jordan, then they are given a task to colour a car hand-out, and to make a car from wires and from mud. In 2007, 200 children came and participated in different activities at the museum, whereas in 2008 the number was less, where only under-privileged children were invited. In 2009 there were two groups of students from different social classes in order to allow them to integrate with each other. In 2010, the museum rented the arena of the Castle Mount (*Jebal al-Qala'a*) in Amman, where students got out of the museum milieu to an open different landscape. In 2011, King Abdullah Design & Development Bureau (KADBI) sliced a real car of late HM King Hussein in half to teach children about the mechanics and maintenance of the car. Most interestingly, children attended from different countries such as USA, UK, Saudi Arabia, Palestine and Jordan. In 2012, the museum, consistent with its commitment to social responsibility, invited 1,000 children in the month of Ramadan (four weeks) and urged able families to pay for that in order to allow poor children to participate. This type of social activism in programming is, as far as the authors are aware, unique to the RAM.

There is an education programme adapted to schools, where around forty thousand students visited the museum for that purpose in 2012 (Bader, 2012). The number of students is very modest because the visits are not obligatory and the Ministry of Education and Schools does not direct students to visit museums as extramural places for informal learning. Students learn about the history of Jordan and they get knowledge about the history of transportation and automobiles. Lectures on traffic safety are run under the supervision of the Traffic Department in Jordan. Students between six and fifteen get the chance to merge the curricula in their school with that in the museum in terms of Jordan's history, traffic safety and transportation (). There are no programmes designed for adults and no internships for undergraduate or graduate students to undertake their studies about a museum. Disabled persons, especially those who are blind, have special programmes to know about the cars by touching their parts.

The Department of Educational Programmes at Royal Automobile Museum organises on-going workshops on developing the skills of children and to revive the heritage toys. Students between 10–14 years are invited to design and manufacture models and cut-outs for motorbikes from simple small metal.

The Royal classic vehicles are also from time to time exhibited in open spaces such as archaeological sites, train stations, airports, to merge those vehicles with those archaeological and heritage sites as part of the history of Jordan (The museum is seen as an archive that documents the history of Jordan throughout

100 years in a narrative way that takes visitors and tourists on a tour through history with mixed feelings and memories and challenges to the existence of Jordan and its rule.

The history of Jordan through the collection of the Royal Automobile Museum (1914–1999)

The Royal Automobile Museum hosts more than eighty cars that were used by the Royal Family of Jordan over nearly 100 years. In order to simplify the review of the major cornerstones of the modern history of Jordan using those classic cars as a means of telling that history, the authors have divided that history of Jordan into four periods to match the cars timeline: 1914–1930; 1931–1952; 1953–1973; 1974–1999. Those particular periods witnessed major political, social, economic and infrastructure developments in Jordan. Almost every car in the museum has a story to tell reflecting mixed feelings of pleasure or tragedies, conspiracies or military coups throughout the reign of late HM King Hussein I (Hattar, 2007).

1914–1930 period

During World War I, Jordan was part of the Ottoman Empire and then the Greater Sharif Hussein bin Ali (King of Arabia) announced the outbreak of the Arab Revolt against the Turks on 10 June 1916 from Mecca. He gained support from Britain and Lawrence of Arabia took part in the revolt in Aqaba, Maan, Wadi Rum and Azrak in Jordan and Deraa in Syria. Jordan was created and named the Emirate of Transjordan on 21 March 1921 by Emir Abdullah bin al-Hussein under the mandate of Britain. Transjordan remained under British control until 1928, when both countries signed a treaty by which Transjordan became technically independent. The political system and the first government were established on 11 April 1921. The first Basic Law, the constitution, was initiated in 1928, where the first parliamentary elections were conducted in that year.

A replica of the 1915 Rolls Royce model which participated in the Arab Revolt is on display. This vehicle participated and led the parade in the 60th anniversary of Jordan's independence in June 2006 (RAM website, 2014). Another automobile from this period is the 1916 Cadillac Type 53 model that was used extensively in Jordan as an official car. It was used by Sharif Hussein bin Ali when he visited Amman in 1922, whereas King Abdullah I (then Prince Abdullah of Transjordan) the founder of Jordan used a 1927 Cadillac Limousine.

1931–1952 period

The second period (1931–1952) witnessed the stability of the country after security was established. Jordan became a kingdom in 25 May 1946 and Emir Abdullah was proclaimed as King Abdullah I of the Hashemite Kingdom of Jordan. During this period, Israel was also created in 1948 and the first Arab-Israeli war erupted. Then the West Bank was incorporated in the Hashemite Kingdom of Jordan in 1950 which led to the assassination of King Abdullah I on 20 July 1951 in Jerusalem. King Talal succeeded the throne and the second constitution was endorsed in 1952.

A 1936 Cord 810 Westchester was a gift to King Hussein by Sharif Hamid (father of Princess Dina, then first wife of King Hussein) at their wedding. The car was originally black and then was repainted to a cream colour. King Hussein used it occasionally for private and official visits (RAM website, 2014).

The Packard Super Eight Convertible model 1940 () was famous for being used solely by US presidents such as Roosevelt, Truman, Hoover and Eisenhower as well as rulers of other parts of the world such as King Alfonso of Spain, Czar Alexander of Russia, King Farouk of Egypt, King Saud Al Faisal of Saudi Arabia, and Chiang Kai-Shek of the Republic of China (RAM website, 2014). The car was also used by King Hussein I for both private and official visits.

The 1946 Humber model is the only car remaining from the rule of King Abdullah I. King Abdullah I used the Humber in trips around Jordan and on Fridays to Jerusalem to pray in the al-Aqsa Mosque. The car witnessed the end of the British Mandate and the independence of Jordan with Prince Abdullah I becoming King and his assassination on Friday 20 July 1951.

The Packard model 1948 was used to receive presidential and royal visitors to Jordan. Packards were amongst favourite cars to US presidents and other rulers of the world. Packard 1948 was one of King Hussein's favourite classic cars, and was used occasionally (RAM website, 2014).

The 1952 Lincoln Capri was first used by the Royal Family of Jordan in England before King Hussein became King. The car was used for the Coronation of King Hussein in May 1953. The car is considered to be one of the important cars in the history of Jordan.

A 1952 Aston Martin was the first sports car owned by King Hussein before he succeeded the throne. He used the car privately until he gifted it to his cousin, King Faisal II of Iraq. Many years later, the car was found in very bad condition in Iraq after the military coup in 1958. It was sent then to the factory and restored to its original condition (RAM website, 2014). Another sports car, a 1955 Mercedes Benz 300 SL Gullwing was used by King Hussein as a sport/rally car. He used it for the first ever Rumman Hill Climb in Jordan in 1955 and then for the Lebanese Hill Climb race in 1958 (RAM website, 2014).

1953–1973 period

The third period started when King Hussein succeeded the throne after his father King Talal was ill and then the parliament disqualified him to reign Jordan in 1952. During this period, the kingdom was in turmoil due to political and military interventions from the Baath and Nasser ideologists who stamped Jordan as pro-western or pro-British/pro-American country, in addition to military coups as well as the war with Israel in 1967 (Harahsheh, 2009).

The 1956 Cadillac was gifted to HM King Hussein from General Eisenhower, president of the U.S.A. (1953–1961), and it was the first bullet-proof car used in Jordan. This car was used by King Hussein in the 1950s and also occasionally in

the 1970s. The 1960 Mercedes Benz 300 d Cabriolet D was the first official function car used by King Hussein for many occasions including weddings, military
functions and dignitary visits. The Lincoln Continental Convertible model
1961was famous for royal weddings and coronation parades such as the wedding
of HM King Abdullah II and Queen Rania in 1993 and his coronation in 1999 and
the opening of Parliament by His Majesty the late King Hussein in 1986. This
car was used on state visits such as those by President Habib Burgiba of Tunisia,
President Hafez Al Assad of Syria, President Anwar Sadat of Egypt, Chancellor
Kurt Waldheim of Austria, the Shah of Iran and King of Nepal.

The Rolls-Royce Phantom V model 1961 was used mostly for official visits and
in some Royal Family Marriages. It was also used during visits of heads of states
such as: The Shah of Iran and Empress Farah Deeba, King Faisal of Saudi Arabia,
Habib Bourgiba of Tunis, Anwar Sadat of Egypt, Prince Philip of Great Britain
(RAM website, 2014). The Amphicar model 1966 was used by King Hussein
for relaxation on the Gulf of Aqaba in 1960s. It was made to suit the waters of
the Red Sea. The 1968 Mercedes Benz 300 SEL reflects stories of life and death
with late King Hussein; it saved his life twice in 1970. King Hussein dubbed this
car as 'al-Mabrookah', the Blessing. In this car, he was subjected to two separate
attempts on his life, both of which he survived unharmed. This car remains as a
symbol of that period of unrest in Jordan and the region. The car was one of King
Hussein favourite cars. It was restored by the manufacturer, Mercedes Benz in
Germany and then joined the collection of the Royal Automobile Museum.

The 1973 Lincoln Continental Town Car is an armoured car and was used in
official visit to Jordan. President Nixon of the United State presented this car as a
gift to King Hussein and was used for his visit to Jordan in June 1974. The car was
also used by heads of states and dignitaries during their visits to Jordan, including President Gerald Ford of U.S.A, Sultan Qabus of Oman, President Hafez Al
Assad of Syria and the Palestinian President Yasser Arafat (RAM website, 2014).

1974–1999 period

The fourth and last period witnessed a lot of developments in the country, including the economic, social and educational booms in 1970s and 1980s. Jordan
became more stable after a series of wars and unrest throughout the 1950s, 1960s
and the beginning of 1970s. This period witnessed the return of parliamentary
rule in 1989 since ceasing in 1967 due to the war with Israel. On January 25 1999,
King Hussein issued a royal decree to make a shift in the Mandate of the Covenant,
where he appointed his eldest son prince Abdullah (now King Abdullah II) as a
crown prince and exempted his brother prince Hassan bib Talal as a crown prince
after 35 years in service.

The 1975 Mercedes-Benz 600 Long Wheelbase Pullman was used mainly for
important occasions and visits made to Jordan by world leaders. Those included
King Abdullah of Saudi Arabia (then crown prince), Sultan Qabus of Oman, King
Hassan II of Morocco, President Hafez Al Assad of Syria, President Abdullah
Ali Saleh of Yemen, and Sheikh Hamad Issa Al Khalifah of Bahrain (now King).

It was used also for the Opening of Parliament. This car was the last King Hussein ever rode, upon his return to Jordan from the Mayo Clinic on 19 January1999 before he died on 7 February that year.

The BMW M1 model 1979 was gifted to King Hussein from Sheikh Zayed Bin Sultan of UAE. Its original colour was dark red and repainted blue and then white. It was used regularly by King Hussein on trips to Aqaba with King Abdullah II (then prince). Opel Ascona 400 Rally model 1980 was used at the Middle East Rally Championship. King Abdullah II (then prince) began his rallying activities in the mid-eighties and then he acquired this car to perform his hobbies in rallies. The Aston Martin Lagonda model 1984 was gifted to King Hussein from HRH Prince Zaid Bin Shaker in 1984, on the occasion of His Majesty's birthday. The 1984 Range Rover Wood & Picket 'Sheer Rover' model was used official occasions and formal visits. It was used during the visit of Queen Elisabeth II of Great Britain and her husband Prince Phillip to Petra in 1984.

Conclusion

This chapter shed a light on an important segment of tourism attractions, i.e. the motoring museum in general and the case of the Royal Automobile Museum in Jordan, in particular. The museum and its artefacts (collectable cars of the Jordanian Royal family) document the history of Jordan by means of those cars, throughout almost 100 years since World I until now. The museum collection consists of more than eighty cars and a lot of motorbikes of the Royal Family. King Abdullah II wanted to tribute and honour his father the late King Hussein I by establishing this museum in the park that holds the name of King Hussein in a spectacular place overlooking Amman. The history of Jordan is highlighted through four periods that go in the timeline of the cars, from World War I until King Hussein passed away in 1999. The cars represent a state of pleasure, tragedy, tranquil and unrest that King Hussein and Jordan passed through in their life. The museum is well constructed an organised as it holds magnificent heritage artefacts of Jordan, the motor vehicles of the Royal Family. It has become a learning centre for school children, university students and a wide spectrum of visitors who are interested in heritage, history and culture. The museum is becoming a tourist attraction in Amman and Jordan that is visited by many tourists and local people. In terms of exhibition and public programming the museum has demonstrated innovation both in displaying vehicles in context, both inside and outside of the museum and in increasing the accessibility of groups (disabled and underprivileged) that would not normally be able to experience such an attraction.

References

Addustour Daly, 2011. The Royal Automobile Museum reduces the entrance fees. *Addustour Daily*, 24 June 2011.

Al-Ali, N., 2007. The Royal Automobile Museum: The genuine memory of Jordan. *Alghad Daily*, 4 February 2007.

Bader, A., 2012. Personal interview by the authors.

Bencze, J. L. and Lemelin, N., 2001. Doing Science at a Science Centre: Enabling Independent Knowledge Construction in the Context of Schools' Museum Visits. *Museum Management and Curatorship* 19 (2), 141–157.

Burr, S. W. and Zeitlin, J., M., 2011. Heritage tourism overview. *Utah Recreation & Tourism Matters*, IORT (02).

Clark, J., 2010. The 'rough and tumble': displaying complexity in the motor museum. *Museum Management and Curatorship* 25 (2), 219–234.

Cooper, C., Fletcher, J., Fyall, A., Gilbert, D., and Wanhill, S., 2008. *Tourism: Principles and Practice*. Essex: Prentice Hall.

Divall, C., n.d. *The origins of transport museum in Western Europe*. Available from: http://www.artefactsconsortium.org/Publications/PDFfiles/Vol3Trans/3.06.Transport-Divall,TransportMuseumsGrWEBF.pdf.

Goeldner, C. R. and Ritchie, J. R. B., 2011. *Tourism: principles, practices, philosophies*. New York: Wiley Global Education.

Halaby, J., 2014a. Automobile Museum charts kingdom's history. *Jordan Times:* 18 February 2014.

Halaby, J., 2014b. Jordan Museum displays unique vehicles. *Associated Press:* 19 February 2014.

Harahsheh, S. S., 2007. *The Influence of the Energy Hunting Project Initiated by the Future Museum upon Pupils' Enrolment to Secondary Education in Borlänge, Sweden*. MSc Thesis. Dalarna University, Sweden.

Harahsheh, S. S., 2009. *An Evaluation of the image of the Hashemite Kingdom of Jordan in the British and Swedish markets and the implications for marketing the country as a tourism destination*. PhD Thesis (PhD). Bournemouth University, UK.

Hattar, S., 2007. The Royal Automobile Museum: A trip through time. *BBC Arabic*, 18 February 2007.

Hussein of Jordan, HM King, 1975. *Mon Metier de Roi*. Paris: R. Laffont.

Jeremiah, D., 2003. Museums and the History and Heritage of British Motoring. *International Journal of Heritage Studies* 9 (2), 169–190.

Jolliffe, L. and Smith, R., 2001. Heritage, Tourism and Museums: the case of the North Atlantic islands of Skye, Scotland and Prince Edward Island, Canada. *International Journal of Heritage Studies* 7 (2), 149–172.

Jordan Automobile Club website, 2014.

Jordan Tourism Board website (JTB), 2014.

MOTA, Ministry of Tourism & Antiquities, 2000.

The Royal Automobile Museum website, 2014.

UNWTO, Word Tourism Organisation, 2013. Factbook.

Urry, J., 2004. The 'System' of Automobility. *Theory, Culture & Society* 21 (4/5), 25–39.

Part V

Conclusion

Part I

Conclusion

16 Automobile heritage and tourism
Future research directions

Lee Jolliffe and Michael V. Conlin

Introduction

In this brief concluding chapter, we will review the progress in the understanding of the relationship between automobile heritage and tourism as evidenced by this volume. We began this work by highlighting the importance of the automobile to society in the twentieth century and noting the fascination with historic vehicles that drives the growing interest in vintage or classic cars and their heritage. Within the book contributors went on to explore this interest in automobile heritage, profiling evidence for its growth, delving further into the fascination with automobile heritage and analysing its relevance to tourism. We framed this investigation around three relevant components of automobile heritage, namely people, places and products, categories that were adopted for the organization of the book.

As work on the book progressed, it became clear that this industrial heritage tourism niche is much larger, both in terms of activity and in terms of influence, than we had originally imagined. To a large extent, this is due to the accessibility of the niche to a broad swath of individuals as opposed to mainly institutions and governments which is the case in other industrial heritage niches such as mines and railways. Also, we believe as a result of the investigations within this volume that the connection between individuals and automobiles is probably more intimate and meaningful than with other artefacts and experiences with industrial heritage, again railways and mines being noted along with airplanes and military transport equipment.

This final chapter will discuss the future of automobile heritage in the context of tourism and ask what more needs to be examined. We will revisit the relationship between the niche and tourism and in doing so, examine those aspects of motoring heritage that differentiate it from other industrial heritage niches. This enquiry, in turn, will assist in identifying the gaps and limitations present in this book, These gaps and limitations will lead to a further range of issues that are relevant to automotive heritage and future research into the niche.

The automobile heritage and tourism relationship

How has this volume progressed our understanding of the relationship between automobile heritage and tourism? Adopting a specific focus on automobile-related heritage has allowed for the exploration in detail of one aspect of the broader field of motoring heritage tourism, specifically those issues related to automobiles and their heritage in the context of tourism. In the case of this volume, this examination has been more related to collectable vintage vehicles in the context of both individual and public collections as well as the narratives related to their historic production and current use, than to the broader field of motoring heritage. The wider field would include more of a focus on roads and related infrastructure, in other words the physical context and environments in which the vehicles were operated. This broader focus would also include other forms of powered wheeled transport such as buses, trucks and lorries, recreational vehicles, and industrial equipment as well as motorcycles, all of which were considered to be beyond the field of enquiry for this introductory volume.

The following provides a brief review of the results of the three sections of the book: people, products and places, with some observations on linkages between them.

People

Chapter 1 provided foundations for viewing the involvement of people in automotive heritage in terms of the continuum of collecting involvement in automobile heritage tourism (Table 1.2) and the types of experiences sought by automobile heritage tourists (Table 1.3), relationships illustrated by the chapters discussed below.

The nostalgia involved in visits to classic auto museums in the USA was documented in Chapter 2. In Chapter 4 both the visitor perspectives and the issues of branding was introduced in the case of the BMW factory tour, also in the USA. People are thus essential to the story of automobile heritage, be they entrepreneurs who have contributed to automotive history or present day tour leaders, exhibiting car collectors or visitors engaged in the business of creating and consuming the nostalgia around the now vintage automobiles.

The history of automotive production also offers lessons for the study of entrepreneurship, as in the cases of the Bricklin (Chapter 3) and the DeLorean (Chapter 5). That these two cases also represent business failures is perhaps a key factor in the reluctance of the related destinations (New Brunswick, Canada and Northern Ireland) to capitalize on these narratives in terms of place branding, as others, such as Brescia, Italy, addressed in the next section, have done (Chapter 6).

Places

The first chapter of the book (Chapter 1) provided some insights into the relationship of places to motoring history including a typology with examples of motoring heritage destinations at the local, regional, national and international levels (Table 1.4). It was noted that some places will have a broader appeal and draw for automobile-related tourism than others, a theme reflected in the chapter contributions, briefly highlighted with observations below.

The case of the London to Brighton Veteran Car Run (Chapter 7) demonstrated both the importance of place in automobile-related event tourism as well as the considerable positive economic impact on host cities. In the cases of both Barbados (Chapter 8) and Sri Lanka (Chapter 9) the role of both vintage car collections and collecting organizations which have been for the most part previously undocumented are highlighted as being essential to the possible development of this heritage for tourism through offering of new heritage tourism products linked to colonial pasts.

Products

While there are many products related to automotive heritage, as a ready product for tourism, motor museums seem to dominate, as discussed in Chapter 1 which reviewed their varied ownership, focus and exhibition methods (Table 1.5). It was also observed that automotive heritage products represent a range of motion from the static (museum exhibits and car shows) to the slow moving (classic car parades) to the speeding (historic racing) (Figure 1.1).

This section thus mainly had a focus on the exhibition of automotive heritage through museums (Chapters 11, 12, 14 and 15) in the cases of relevant collections and museums in Australia (Chapter 11) Europe (Chapter 12), Italy (Chapter 14) and Jordan (Chapter 15). The contribution on heritage motor racing from Australia (Chapter 10) again highlighted the public fascination with motoring heritage linking back to the earlier theme of nostalgia (Chapter 2).

Links into previous work

How does this link back to our other work on areas of industrial heritage tourism, including mining heritage (Conlin and Jolliffe, 2011), sugar heritage (Jolliffe, 2012) and railway heritage (Conlin and Bird, 2014). These topics are certainly connected to that of automobile heritage in terms of the processes of industrialization and globalization. Juxtaposed with automobile heritage they provide a broader understanding of the current progress of industrialization. However, through the study of automobile heritage a number of differences can be identified with the other niche areas previously explored, especially in terms of scale, access and level of visitor interest. Each of these aspects is considered below.

Scale

As noted earlier in this chapter, the scale and scope of the motoring heritage niche is much larger than originally imagined. Museums, automobile shows, auctions, and historic vehicle races can be found around the world and not just in developed Western societies as the chapters on Jordan (Chapter 15), Barbados (Chapter 8), and Sri Lanka (Chapter 9) demonstrate. These activities are also not confined to larger metropolitan areas discussed in this volume such as Brescia, Italy (Chapter 6) and Turin, Italy (Chapter 14). One of the editors lives in the Okanagan Valley in British Columbia, Canada and not withstanding its primarily rural and agricultural economy, relatively small population, and comparatively isolated location in terms of large metropolitan destinations, the Valley hosts four major car shows annually which attract large numbers of enthusiasts, both from the local area and from further afield. This includes the Peachland World of Wheels, discussed in some detail in Chapter 1. Readers will find that this level of historic vehicle activity is duplicated throughout most of the world where automobiles have a presence.

Access

Again as has already been noted, access to this niche for individuals is greatly enhanced in comparison to other industrial heritage niches. Indeed, it may well be this element that sets motoring heritage well and truly apart from other heritage niches. The business of collecting, displaying, using, and selling heritage automobiles is huge as noted earlier in Chapter 1. It ranges from the local buying and selling of old vehicles with sentimental value and relatively low financial value through to the auctioning and private selling of major collectible automobiles in the range of many, many millions of dollars. And while most people cannot afford to purchase a vintage Ferrari 250 GTP for US$40 million plus, literally hundreds of thousands of people can and do purchase old vehicles reminiscent of their childhoods or dreams of their adolescence and rehabilitate them, drive them, show them, and eventually sell them. This is a process repeated over and over again throughout the world, a phenomenon that sets motoring heritage apart from other heritage sectors in terms of its accessibility.

Visitor interest

As one might expect when examining a tourism niche that is as large scale as automotive heritage is and one that is as accessible to a broad range of people, the level of interest in the niche is very high and anecdotally, seems to be growing as demonstrated earlier in Chapter 1. Attendance and participation in the various car shows referred to above in the Okanagan Valley has grown tremendously in the past decade. Audiences at major events such as the Barrett-Jackson Auction in Scottsdale, Arizona every January have also grown significantly. And attendance at iconic events such as the annual Pebble Beach Concours d'Elegance as described in Chapter 1 has grown almost exponentially. It would appear that interest in automobile related heritage is enjoying growth which many niches would envy. This growth in interest is a key element in the linkage between the niche and tourism: it underscores the potential for destinations in hosting and promoting motoring heritage activities as well as the need for further research.

Gaps and limitations

A limitation of the present volume is not delving in depth into the broader context of automobile heritage, noted earlier for example in the cases of the theory of automobility (Urry, 2004). A related concept proposed by Jeremiah (1995) was of the 'motoring landscape', including the automobile and the supporting systems of roads and traveller services. Rather, the focus of the book is on adding to the literature related to the fascination with automotive heritage. This builds on the previous literature on motor museums, as transport museums noted in particular to be an underdeveloped segment of the museum sector (Divall and Scott, 2001). This furthers prior work indicating the sense of motoring in situ captured or not in museum exhibits (Clark, 2010) that represent the cult of car ownership (Jeremiah, 1995) that led to collectors and enthusiasts dominating transport museums (Oddy, 2005). The volume also highlights the active use of vintage motor cars in a number of event venues including historic car racing (Chapter 10) and vintage car shows (Chapter 12), previously for the most part undocumented in the literature, addressing in part a gap in the research on motor vehicle event tourism identified by Kaminski and Smith (2013).

By expanding the focus of the volume beyond just Europe and North America (as evidenced by previous literature) we have uncovered a keen interest in collecting and sometimes racing historic vehicles in unlikely locations such as Australia (Chapter 11), Jordan (Chapter 15), Barbados (Chapter 8) and Sri Lanka (Chapter 9). Another finding is the trend towards using automotive collections for branding, by individual automotive companies in Germany (Chapter 13), by cities (Chapters 6 and 14) and even by states (Chapter 15). The commercial component of automobile heritage is also explored over a wide range of the ownership of vintage automobiles, from individuals to companies and even countries in the case of Jordan where the national car collection reflects the national identity. However, there are still many more locations in which the import of automotive heritage in relationship to tourism can be explored, as the editors were dependent on the authors who came forward as contributors to address broadening the geographical scope.

Areas for further research

While closing the gap in our knowledge of how automobile heritage tourism is manifested, delivered and experienced there is still much research to be undertaken. A number of potential areas identified when reflecting on the contents of this volume are outlined below.

- A sounder understanding of the fascination exhibited by people for motoring heritage would enhance the ability of destinations and events to appeal to the most efficient elements of motivation for the niche. More research thus needs to be undertaken to understand the characteristics and motivations of those attending automotive heritage events. This, in turn through planning for targeted audiences, could lead to a growth in participation and attendance.
- Allied closely to establishing visitor motivations, understanding the experiential aspects of automobile heritage from the visitor perspective could contribute to the development and marketing of related venues, events, and as noted above, even destinations. This could further the work of Gary Best (Chapter 2) who explored nostalgia in terms of visits to motor museums in California.

- The financial, economic, and social impact of motoring heritage is largely only known in an anecdotal sense. Research is necessary into all aspects of the niche to fully understand and measure its impact on communities and regions. Such understanding of impacts will undoubtedly spur further development of the niche. Destination management organizations in areas with a strong automotive history could take the lead in such research.
- In some cases, historic vehicle collections are a reminder of past colonization of countries and thus, may be viewed as contested collections, clearly a theme for further exploration and study.
- As mentioned earlier in this chapter, there is scope for examination of a much broader range of historic powered wheeled transportation devices such as trucks and lorries, buses, recreation vehicles, motorcycles, and the like in relation to tourism.

And finally, we would be remiss if we didn't raise the spectre that faces modern man in the context of independent automobile ownership and use. As we move well into the 22nd century, there are clear signs that the attitude of younger generations toward the automobile is changing. Far fewer younger people are acquiring driver licenses than in previous generations. Regardless of what is motivating this decrease of interest on the part of young people to participate in a motoring society, the impact is clear: individual automobile ownership and use will likely decline over the next several generations and this in turn, will likely impact on interest levels in motoring heritage. The move toward fully-autonomous vehicles will eliminate the importance of vehicle branding and loyalty as cars will be seen in much the same way as we currently view buses and other mass transportation systems. It is not clear if this will impact on automotive related heritage and its relationship with tourism but if we believe that much of the current interest is driven by our experiences with automobiles, the absence of that experience could be a significant negative factor in the future of automotive heritage.

As we look towards the past in terms of historic vehicles and our nostalgia towards them embodied in what we refer to as 'automobile heritage tourism', automotive planners and engineers are looking towards the future, addressing issues of urbanization, mobility, autonomous driving and connectivity. They are creating the vehicles that will be collectable in the future as a powerful documentation of our times.

References

Clark, J. (2010). The "rough and tumble": displaying complexity in the motor museum. *Museum Management and Curatorship* 25 (2), 219–234.

Conlin, M. V., and Bird, G. (2014). *Railway Heritage and Tourism: Global Perspectives.* Bristol: Channel View Publications.

Conlin, M. V., and Jolliffe, L. (2011). *Mining Heritage and Tourism: a global perspective.* London: Routledge.

Divall, C., and Scott, A. (2001). *Making histories in transport museums.* London: Continuum.

Jeremiah, D. (1995). The motor car from road to museum. *International Journal of Heritage Studies* 1 (3), 171–179.

Jolliffe, L. (2013). *Sugar Heritage and Tourism in Transition.* Bristol: Channel View Publications.

Kaminski, J., and Smith, G. (2013). Mobile heritage. In Kaminski, J., Benson, A. M., and Arnold, D. (eds) *Contemporary Issues in Cultural Heritage Tourism.* London: Routledge, 218–235.

Oddy, N. (2005). Tackling Transport. *Journal of Design History* 18 (3), 305–307.

Urry, J. (2004). The system of automobility. *Theory, Culture & Society* 21 (4–5), 25–39.

Index

For Product Safety Concerns and Information please contact our EU
representative GPSR@taylorandfrancis.com
Taylor & Francis Verlag GmbH, Kaufingerstraße 24, 80331 München, Germany

www.ingramcontent.com/pod-product-compliance
Ingram Content Group UK Ltd.
Pitfield, Milton Keynes, MK11 3LW, UK
UKHW021007180425
457613UK00019B/843

* 9 7 8 1 0 3 2 3 3 9 7 6 4 *